STAND IN THE FIRE

Also by William Crawford Woods
The Killing Zone

STAND IN THE FIRE
Three American Soldiers and Their Wars, 1900–1950

William Crawford Woods

UNIVERSITY PRESS OF KANSAS

Published by the University Press of Kansas (Lawrence, Kansas 66045),
which was organized by the Kansas Board of Regents and is operated and funded by
Emporia State University, Fort Hays State University, Kansas State University,
Pittsburg State University, the University of Kansas, and Wichita State University.

Library of Congress Cataloging-in-Publication Data

Names: Woods, William Crawford, author.
Title: Stand in the fire : three American soldiers and their wars,
1900–1950 / William Crawford Woods.
Other titles: Three American soldiers and their wars, 1900–1950
Description: Lawrence: University Press of Kansas, 2023
Identifiers: LCCN 2023008278 (print)
LCCN 2023008279 (ebook)
ISBN 9780700634637 (paperback)
ISBN 9780700634644 (ebook)
Subjects: LCSH: Crawford, Louis R., 1883–1921. | Crawford, William Riddick,
1914–1945. | Woods, A. R., 1908–1976. | Crawford, William Harvey,
1835–1904—Family. | United States. Army—Biography. | Crawford family.
Classification: LCC E745 .W66 2023 (print) | LCC E745 (ebook) | DDC
355.0092273—dc23/eng/20230307
LC record available at https://lccn.loc.gov/2023008278.
LC ebook record available at https://lccn.loc.gov/2023008279.

British Library Cataloguing-in-Publication Data is available.

Printed in the United States of America

10 9 8 7 6 5 4 3 2 1

The paper used in this publication is acid free and meets the minimum
requirements of the American National Standard for Permanence of
Paper for Printed Library Materials Z39.48-1992.

to the memory of
Kate Riddick Crawford
and
Louise Crawford Woods

So nigh is grandeur to our dust
So near is God to man,
When Duty whispers low, Thou must,
The youth replies, I can.

—Ralph Waldo Emerson, "Voluntaries"

CONTENTS

LIST OF ILLUSTRATIONS

NOTE

As this is a work of nonfiction whose characters sometimes stray into fictional scenes, please note that the book seeks always to make clear what is real and what imagined; and may I observe that the lives of my subjects were flesh and blood before I consigned them to the page.

PREPARING THE BATTLESPACE

A House Older Than Canada, a Skirmish on the Trail

DISMOUNT.

The order is a whisper passed along the line. The men slide from their horses' backs, fluid as the flow of oil over stone. A young sergeant glances down the blue column stretched raggedly behind him, frowning slightly at the faint chime of a curb chain, but his stern look is pro forma. If there are rebels about, *ladrones*, there's little chance this jaunty band has gone unnoticed. After months in the islands, they are still a striking sight, tall men in blue jackets bright with gold straps or chevrons, mounted on powerful horses, bearing modern weapons of war.

The image of armed Americans moving through an Asian jungle will be a familiar one in the century to come, but the year is 1903 and these men are among the first.

The sergeant is a boy, not yet nineteen. Even so, he has been in the army for almost three years. Many of the men he leads are older than he, but in garrison or in the field they have learned to respect him. His orders are quietly obeyed. The problem at present is that he's unsure what order to give. So he waits, the Krag-Jorgensen rifle sinking into his shoulder like a heated iron bar. Mosquitoes swing from the brim of his sweat-soaked campaign hat. The malaria they carry will sicken him soon, but not today.

Just behind him, a private even younger than he gives way to apprehension. "Sar'nt, shouldn't we—"

"Be still. Stand to horse."

Silence. Birdsong. The sergeant shifts his weight from boot to boot. Rotten branches crunch softly. This is not the place to daydream, not the moment to lose focus or surrender full attention, but his mind drifts back to his last home leave, first to a doctor's examination that surprised him by uncovering a minor chest condition, then to a baseball game, to pewter steins of beer shared with old school friends, to a tranquil evening with his father, a Union veteran of the Civil War. This jungle trail feels far from Philadelphia. Of a sudden, the young man finds himself deeply happy to be standing on it.

Apparently, the order has come down to resume the march. The sergeant looks to his front, where the troopers have begun moving, sifting their horses into the green tunnel of strangler fig and buccaneer palm. He motions his squad to follow. They're foot soldiers now. Trained to saber and saddle, they will fight this day as dismounts, if they fight at all, which seems unlikely. The *ladrones* prefer action on their own terms and a full troop of US cavalry is a target too large to be tempting. But smaller units can be easy prey, and the fate of stragglers is gruesome to ponder.

The sergeant has heard the stories—decapitations, dismemberment, mutilation, worse. Americans have treated their captives savagely too, he knows. Shoot every male over ten, one general had infamously ordered only the year before. And then there were the stories of the water cure. This war is not quite what he had expected. Even so, the boy is mired in gloom at the notion that he may well return home without "seeing the elephant." Seeing action. He has heard his father, and other veterans, use the striking phrase.

He lets his thoughts return to Philadelphia.

The canopy of jungle cover thins as the trail opens out into a clearing. The lieutenant signals for a halt. The young sergeant tells his men to picket their horses and seek shade. He cautions them to drink sparingly from their canteens. Then he sits down in the shadow of a mahogany tree, resting his back against its crimson bark, rifle near at hand, and pulls the cork from his own flask. A corporal crouches, uninvited, beside him, a thin Irishman who gestures toward a low wall of broken limbs knocked to the edge of the clearing by a recent storm, a natural barricade.

"Good cover," the corporal offers. "Hold 'em there 'til hell freezes over, then fight on the ice."

The sergeant shrugs. Holding ground is not a part of the cavalry's mission. He takes a sip of warm, rank water.

Forty yards away, three men break into the clearing. The young sergeant sees the straw hats, the dark faces, the sweat-rotted jackets strapped to the small bodies by the bullet-laden bandoliers as though they were etched on glass. As if in a dream, he watches their leader raise his weapon and take aim. Later, the boy will try to remember, to savor, the impossible compound of terror and elation that floods him as he brings his own heavy rifle to his shoulder and touches off a round. But he's moved too fast, he has no clear target. Breathe, he tells himself. Steady down. He works the bolt and fires again. Sweat blinds him. Both shots go wide. The Krag jams. Cursing, the boy rolls behind the tree and tries to clear the action as the *ladrones* return fire, bullets sinking like hammer blows into the crimson sheath of the mahogany branch that shields him.

Around him the drumbeat of shots quickens. But if men are hit, wounded, dying on either side, their fates do not feel linked to his story. He is chagrined, set at naught.

Prone beside him, the voluble Irishman with whom the sergeant has shared guard mounts and rain-soaked bivouacs, saddle soap and cigarettes, rests his rifle on the branch and methodically takes up the business at hand. The fight lasts—thirty, forty seconds? an eternity—before the broken chords of fire fade into a forlorn rattle of shots as two rebels draw back into the forest.

Numbly, the boy studies his first battlefield. One Filipino lies sprawled at the edge of the clearing in a thin pool of blood already humming with flies. Americans are beginning to gather around the body. Supported by another trooper, a corporal shuffles slowly past them, dragging his shattered leg. The men begin to bray about the fight in ancient voices loud with victory. The consensus will be that the affair was an accident, not an ambush—a handful of hapless rebels had stumbled upon the cavalry position and tried to shoot their way out of it. Bad luck for the wounded trooper. Worse for the dead *ladrone*.

In camp that evening, the teenaged cavalryman, who was my grandfather, Louis Crawford, adjusts the mantle on the gas lamp inside his tent and makes a brief entry in his journal. *Skirmish on the trail today. Took two shots at a Filipino but missed. Riley had better luck.*

I SPENT MANY childhood summers in an antebellum Greek Revival house built on the banks of a tidal river that flows past a small town near the coast of North Carolina. The town, Hertford, which lies between Edenton and Elizabeth City, is the place Louis Crawford came to live when he married my grandmother, Kate Wallace Riddick, in 1909. The house, built in 1850 by a blacksmith named Lewis Richardson, was older than Canada, older than a *country*, a fact that filled me with wonder when I was a child. It had

been home to Kate's husband's family since shortly after the Civil War, then known in the South as the War between the States, and still referred to by my grandmother as "the late unpleasantness." The daughter of a country doctor and an aristocratic Virginian from a plantation called Glencoe, Kate had been born many years after the war, but its stories encircled her, inspiring a favorite of my own. During the Second World War, my mother told me, my grandmother wondered aloud whether Hitler could send a gunboat up the Perquimans River, and when her daughter told her not to be absurd, Kate retorted, "Why not? The Yankees did."

In this world, the newlywed young Scot from Philadelphia hoped to make his home, surrounded by Confederate ghosts.

His own ghost was a strong presence in that house. A formal portrait of Louis in the uniform of an Air Service captain, made some years after his Philippine adventure, hung in the entrance hall, flanked by his saber and the loop of gold braid that ringed his campaign hat. Tall cavalry boots stood below the sepia photograph, strapped into shining spurs. An American flag, furled tautly on its staff, lay propped beside the door, facing a delicate watercolor of three Confederate battle flags bearing the legend "Lest We Forget." This shrine might have been intimidating, but for the fact that my

grandfather's dark eyes held a merry light, and the slight smile above his
strong jaw was free of irony or guile.

Other photographs completed the gallery: Louis in the open cockpit of
an early army plane, a freshly minted aviator; Louis on maneuvers as an
infantry lieutenant with the Arizona National Guard; Louis on horseback,

patrolling the Mexican border during the early years of the Madero revolution. These were images of a wonderfully romantic depth that captured my
imagination before I was ten years old, and they sponsored stories I realize
in retrospect I must simply have told myself, gathering from the air facts that
furnished my grandfather with the cohesive career a different reading of the
evidence might have said had evaded him. That he had battled German aces
in the clouds above France seemed as certain to me as that he had crossed
swords with Moro horsemen in the Philippines and fought off rebels or
federales or both in Mexico. His widow and his daughter never challenged
my version of the past. I was allowed to create the grandfather I gloried in,
perhaps because my command of his story was not so very far from its truth.

In any case, these relics of a legendary life that decorated the hallway were
not the chief agents of my pleasure, whose main source was a vast army of
lead soldiers my grandfather had molded when he was a boy. There were
hundreds of them, confined to a deep wooden box lidded by a black canvas
top, waiting in silent bivouac for me to tumble them onto the dining room
table on the day my parents delivered me to Hertford for the summer. I had
toy soldiers at home in suburban Washington, but they were shoddy bits of
khaki plastic, designed for modern war and possessing none of the panache
of these two-inch heroes of 1864. The lead soldiers' poses didn't offer much
variety—the Union troops, rifles at the ready, knelt or stood, the Confeder-
ates advanced with their weapons at port arms—and time had chipped away
their brilliance: some had muskets broken at the stock, a few were missing
heads or limbs, and the silver metal of their bodies had gone a uniform dull
gray. But they inspired awe in their multitudes. Other boys might toy with
companies or platoons; Louis had commanded regiments of his own making, patiently pouring molten lead into the hinged, wooden-handled molds.
Modern parents would quail before this toxic hobby, but families in the
nineteenth century were made of stronger stuff.

I played with these soldiers hour after hour, scattering them through the
downstairs rooms, whose ornate Victorian furniture was easily turned into
forts. I engaged in trench warfare, positioned snipers on tabletops, marched
files into ambushes on Oriental rugs, scattered companies in disarray across
the polished hardwood floors. My grandmother might have allowed me to
take the whole lot back to Bethesda, but it never occurred to me to ask.
Part of the joy was in the nine months of waiting, and in any case, only in

that old house, on permanent station, could the little soldiers be entirely at home. Each year on the day we left for the north, I poured them back into their wooden barracks and marched them up to the attic, where they took their places beside an avalanche of crates and bins, steamer trunks, suitcases, valises, canvas grips, leather satchels, bags and baskets, cardboard cartons, safes, coffers, paper sacks, hat boxes, corner cupboards, gun cabinets, and every other imaginable receptacle an American family might use to casually store the scattered history it had accumulated in the course of more than a century.

My grandfather's artifacts were only a small part of this haphazard collection, but when I was nine or ten years old, they were the part that attracted me most strongly. Years later, I might pull a mildewed book from a dusty shelf, look through stereopticon photos of the "Holy Land," or study the Spenserian script of a Confederate forebear writing home from some Virginia battlefield. But while I was a child the toy soldiers and the entrance hall shrine fixed my attention to my grandfather, and in the attic I would come to find a great deal more of his story. It rested in a large black leather trunk bound in brass and labeled in resounding gold letters.

CAPTAIN L. R. CRAWFORD, USA

For some years I had been content with the lead soldiers, but one mild August weekend the summer I was twelve, when the heat had lifted long enough to open the attic to exploration and the Hertford days were nearly at an end, I raised the lid of the trunk and began rummaging idly through its neglected treasures. Soon enough I'd uncovered my grandfather's Hamilton wristwatch, a disc of silver tarnished deepest black; his steel Air Service ID bracelet; his captain's bars; his pilot's wings. Below these lay a small leather holster, stiff and dry with age, a spent brass artillery shell worked into floral designs, a small drawing on brown cardboard of a battle scene, a small wooden box of hand-drawn cards, a finely detailed model of an army biplane, and a heavy object concealed by oilcloth whose manifest shape caused my sixth-grader's heart to beat faster. Below all this I found a stack of photographs, a bundle of letters bound in a blue ribbon, a narrow red leather notebook, a few antique "women's" magazines—what were *they* doing there?—and a pile of typed pages whose print had faded to near illegibility where it had not been turned to lace by silverfish.

All of this corroded paperwork was more than I wanted to take on at the time, but I lifted the model biplane from the box, determined to trot downstairs with it and ask my grandmother to put it on display. Then, with a mounting sense of pleasurable dread, I peeled the oilcloth from the heavy object to reveal an automatic pistol with a long thin barrel and a wooden stock, stamped WAFFENFABRIK MAUSER just below the hammer, its menacing black steel body dull under a veil of cosmoline. Was the weapon loaded? I couldn't figure out how to spring the clip. The temptation was more than I could take. I pulled the hammer back until I heard it lock. Then gently, trembling, I lowered it slowly again until it rested on the firing pin.

There was a much smaller box beside the black trunk, wooden, its loose lid casually secured with a little hook. I opened it. In the box atop a fold of greasy cloth lay a 1911 Colt .45 automatic pistol. I knew at once what it was—most boys can identify a famous weapon. Fascinated but a little frightened, I studied the Colt with the hushed reverence a believer might accord a fragment of the True Cross. Then I numbly closed the lid and hooked it, my mind clouded with some imaginary battle reverie.

I rewrapped the Mauser with great care and sank it back into the box. I had no doubt my grandfather had tugged it from the grip of a dead Prussian pilot, although I would have conceded he might have acquired it as a souvenir from a veteran of Chateau-Thierry or Belleau Wood. What I knew for certain was that this was a relic my parents would never permit me to purloin. As for the rest of the remnants of Louis Crawford's story, they would wait patiently for my return the following year.

But the next summer, for some reason, we didn't go to Hertford, and the year after that I was more interested in fishing the river or swimming off the Outer Banks, whose bright beaches lay little more than an hour away. And there was a girl, of course: fourteen is not twelve. So the hallway shrine commenced to dim and the lead soldiers stayed in their box. So, too, the letters and photographs, the straps and chevrons, the tokens and traces of a life that lay beside them. I would come to explore these artifacts again, but more than fifty years would pass before I did.

LOUIS CRAWFORD'S was not the only story waiting to be discovered. His son haunted the Hertford house as well. A portrait of William as an implausibly beautiful West Point cadet hung in my grandmother's bedroom, and some of his childhood toys decorated her bookshelves—there was a metal model of the *Spirit of St. Louis* I was allowed to play with, long before I knew about the hero's flight it represented or even that it had been reverently constructed by one of Charles Lindbergh's most fervent youthful fans. And many of my father's archives could also be found in the attic, but while he was alive I took no interest in them, not because they were off limits but because it doesn't often occur to a boy that a man he sees every day might have had a life he's never seen at all.

HEIRS TO THE OLD house on our mother's death in July 2000, my brother Arthur and I struggled for some time to maintain it, but neither of us lived in Hertford nor were we ever likely to and the expense of propping up a weary dwelling over 150 years old became too much to sustain. We had been defrauded by contractors, beleaguered by tenants, robbed by antique dealers, and battered by storms, and we had seen fifty feet of oak foundation reduced to sawdust by relentless insect jaws. More deeply than Arthur, I felt the sentimental pull of the place, but when a flock of pigeons flew in through a broken attic window and took up residence on a lower floor I accepted defeat and in 2005, at my brother's urging, oversaw the house's sale.

The day before closing I walked through the empty rooms, absorbing the

feel of an unpeopled and unfurnished space that no member of my family had laid eyes on since 1870. All the movables, save for the little I intended to keep, had been shipped off to the avaricious antique dealer weeks before. I looked for the last time through the tall windows bright with hand-made glass pebbled by air bubbles that admitted the watery light of the river and studied the tiny Roman numerals marked on their sills to match the same numbers carved on the storm shutters that protected the glass from high Atlantic winds. An architectural historian who admired the old house had shown me those numbers and explained how the builder used them to achieve perfect matches between frame and blinds. He also fished from a strip of rotten wood three hand-forged iron nails and told me he had seen the same nails at Monticello.

I went up to the empty attic I had spent so many hours exploring as a child and carefully concealed two lead soldiers, Union and Confederate riflemen, in a place where the new owners of the house would never find them, leaving them on guard to protect the ghosts I was abandoning.

Within a year, I had divorced, retired, remarried, and moved to Pennsylvania. I sacrificed much in the debacle of the Hertford house's sale, losing memories along with material, because I would never have space for room after room of Victorian furniture, wall after wall of heavy paintings, towers of table silver, a library of English classics, mounds of bodices and bustles, high collars and frock coats. Besides, little of this loot aside from the books would have suited my aesthetic (my brother claimed no interest in any of it). It all looked well enough in the old house; it would hardly have thrived in the ramshackle domestic atmosphere I favored.

But my grandfather's black leather trunk came with me, as did some other provocative containers I had identified over the years. And it turned out there were two other reliquaries: a large aluminum trunk, dented from its travels, which proved to be the main depository for my uncle's story; and a plain green wooden box the size of a footlocker that housed my father's. Courtesy of my mother's care for the past, I knew their origins. The trunk had been fashioned from the wing of a wrecked DC-3 lost in the fighting in the Philippines, and the box built by mental patients at a VA hospital in Columbus, Ohio, where my father's father had served as medical director. In my house, even the storage told a story. But I did not yet know what that story was.

The things salvaged from the North Carolina attic went into a Pennsylvania basement. Vaguely conscious that I might be heir to a considerable history, still I let another decade pass before taking it on. In those years I sustained a serious illness that yielded a short novel, and with my new spouse journeyed a great deal, producing hundreds of pages of travel notes I thought vaguely of turning into a book. When I finally did open the boxes, it was with no notion that they might suggest yet another direction. I simply wanted to reacquaint myself with a past I had abandoned.

But that past almost at once began to take promising form. I discovered the giddy romance of my grandfather's odd epic, the classic arc of my uncle's career, and an account of my father's years as soldier and spy hardly less compelling than the adventures of the Crawford clan. Including as they did not only letters but official documents, maps, photographs, press clippings, weapons, badges of rank, and regimental patches, the Hertford boxes yielded up a bounty in which I could begin to read the stories of three very different men whose lives had been linked by the fires of three very different conflicts. I came to see that to recover their experiences would be in some measure to hold up a mirror to the American way of war and its impact on American families during the first half of the twentieth century.

The job seemed well worth doing, but its dimensions were daunting. Neither biographer nor historian, as a writer I am drawn primarily to fiction. I do have some interest in military subjects, but by temperament I'm not particularly inclined toward the exploration of family chronicles. So for some weeks, as I worked through the letters and the rest of the material, I was intrigued but resistant to the notion of committing years to a project whose shape and purpose I could only dimly perceive. But slowly my doubts were undone by a growing sense of curiosity. I kept coming across images that seemed gravid with stories, like a Rauschenberg combine: Korean flags, old silver watches, dance cards, trench knives, handguns, captain's bars, a West Point ring. And photographs: biplanes wrecked in a west Texas desert, Japanese paratroopers spotting the sky over Luzon, bronze Buddhist statues wincing above the Kodaks of American occupation troops. And letters: scores, hundreds, the hasty words of American officers finding comic moments in a firefight or planning missions that might put a modest twist into the history of their times. Three men going about their nation's business as they understood it to be.

Certainly, I had grown up with a vague sense of my forebears' service, but to uncover such charged specifics lifted the past from family lore into a larger history. At the beginning of my search, I had on my hands three boxes of unsorted memorabilia. At the end, I held in my hands three lives: one that led from the saddle of a war horse to the cockpit of a fighter plane; one that bridged West Point with high command and a Silver Star; and one that began in the infantry and ended at the sharp end of the Cold War CIA.

Here finally was an abundance that not only revealed an opportunity but imposed a task. These were at once ordinary and exceptional men, whose lives had been woven into some of the most compelling events of their times. I wanted to know their stories, and I knew the best way to know them was to tell them.

"THE ARMY IS NO PLACE FOR A SOLDIER"

Captain Louis Crawford Goes Looking for a War

Forty miles a day on beans and hay in the Regular Army O!
—Edward Harrigan and David Braham

LOUIS CRAWFORD'S passionate quest for a military life can't be understood apart from his father's story.

William Harvey Crawford, born around 1835 in Ayrshire, Scotland, a southwestern county on the Firth of Clyde, came of a lineage that included crofters, craftsmen, and minor nobility stretching back to the early Middle Ages.[1] Trained as an engineer in Glasgow, Crawford emigrated to eastern Pennsylvania some years before the beginning of the Civil War and there married a woman named Henrietta, a schoolteacher from the Isle of Man who had also concluded that her fortunes would best prosper in the new world. Their family grew to four children, a daughter and three sons, my grandfather Louis the youngest. It was William's second family and must have been precious to him—his first wife and five children died of plague while he was at sea.

There is a formal photograph of William Harvey Crawford taken in uniform on his birthday, April 8, 1863. His right hand is thrust between the brass buttons of his coat in a Napoleonic gesture popular at the time, his small, dimpled chin is framed in substantial mutton chop whiskers. I have that sunken chin, and other facial features that mark me as his descendant.

---

1. I've always cherished a story passed on by my mother about a remote ancestor named John Crawford who, sometime in the fourteenth century, announced a plan to build a mill on a spot that sheltered the bones of a saint. He was warned that if he followed through, the villagers would hang him. He did, and they did.

But what interests me more in this faded portrait is the distance between his calm demeanor and his ferocious story.

When the Civil War broke out, my great-grandfather was quick to offer his services. He signed up at first with an ad hoc cavalry unit formed by a local grandee, but ultimately became a company commander with the 61st Pennsylvania Volunteer Infantry, which saw action under McClellan in the Peninsula Campaign and Sheridan in the Shenandoah.

The regiment's list of battle honors is a long one: Fair Oaks, Seven Days, Malvern Hill, Chancellorsville, Gettysburg, the Wilderness, Spotsylvania, many others. Linger over the list. It is a crimson stream of American gospel. To a Pennsylvania boy of Louis's day, the very word "Gettysburg" would have held something close to sacramental power, for the battle was key to the final northern victory. And the price of victory was high, certainly for the 61st Pennsylvania, which, of officers alone, suffered more killed and wounded than any other Union regiment of the Civil War.

Captain Crawford first put his name on the casualty report at the Battle of Seven Pines, recovering from his wounds in time to rejoin his company at Antietam. It might seem that he had offered enough blood to his adopted country, but the navy stood next in line to request his services—given his training, William Harvey was much needed by a fledgling fleet short on technical officers. He was wounded a second time on Mobile Bay, serving under Admiral Farragut, and then again in a gunboat on the Mississippi River. He would die of his wounds in 1904. But they didn't prevent him from accepting appointment as chief engineer on the first steam vessel to round Cape Horn, or from building railroads for the Baldwin Locomotive Works in Japan, Palestine, and South Africa after his retirement from the navy.

This is an epic career by any measure, and in the glow of its example we are not surprised to find these avid lines in my grandfather's diary: "During my early childhood, when we lived in Valley Forge, I never tired of hearing Father and Uncle Robert tell of their adventures in the war, and my chief playthings were always lead soldiers. I can easily say that I was predisposed to a military life."

More than merely predisposed, Louis was passionate. When the war with Spain began in 1898, he marched straight to the recruiting office in Philadelphia, only to find the army wasn't taking fourteen year olds. His mother had been horrified; his father secretly amused. But two years later, still driven by a single dream, the boy graduates from high school. The conflict in the Philippines is slowly unraveling, and Louis is desperate to be in uniform before his chance to see action fades. He hopes to have his father's permission, but the old man's face is grave as he leads his son into the front parlor of the narrow row house on Green Street.

It is June 1901.

A cherished photograph permits me to offer an accurate image of that room. More than a century later, we can still see what Louis and William

Harvey would have seen: an elaborately carved Steinway spinet crowned with ceramic figurines, floral wallpaper crowded with pastoral art, heavy plush furniture, the mantle with its ormolu clock, the marble-topped table on which Captain Crawford's carved meerschaum pipe is resting. As to the event itself, I'm prepared to imagine it. The moment is too crucial to abandon to the silence of time.

Louis has, somewhat stiffly, requested the interview, choosing an hour when his mother will be away from home. There is much affection between the man and the boy, but at moments of possible discord each takes refuge in a studied formality. Thus William Harvey, after shaping a brief but heavy silence, begins in stately fashion.

"I expect I will not be surprised when you disclose the purpose of this conversation."

"I want to join up, Father."

"I see."

"Will you help me tell Mother?"

The old man smiles. The boy's ploy—the immediate assumption of paternal support—has been deft.

"I take it you have thought this through."

"Oh, yes, sir!"

"And you are certain it is what you want."

"For as long as I can remember," Louis says quietly.

"Sit down."

My grandfather sits on the edge of his chair, alert, expectant. He wears a dark suit and a shirt with a high white collar, a flowing tie, brightly polished boots, as though he expects to be released directly into the arms of the recruiting sergeant and wants to make an immediate impression. His father takes refuge in a bit of business with his pipe, tamping down the shag tobacco, dragging the pale flame of a match across the yellowing bowl.

"There are other options," William says finally. "I should be glad to see you apprenticed to my own profession. The business world holds many opportunities for an enterprising man. College is perhaps an even better choice."

Louis hesitates, then says:

"I know I've been a disappointment to you and Mother in some ways. I get into scrapes—"

"What boy doesn't? You're young, Louis. Time will amend your faults."

"The country is at war," my grandfather tells his father earnestly. "I want to serve."

"Not every thinking man is satisfied this war is just. In any case, we are told it has been concluded."

Louis brushes the objection aside. Both know sporadic fighting still continues.

"Son—"

"*You* served!"

This is the argument William Harvey has been helplessly anticipating. It can be countered, but only at the cost of undoing his own legend, which he is aware of having impressed into his son's imagination through a decade of stories shared with his brother Robert, an Annapolis graduate and navy captain who also fought through all four years of the Civil War. In the Crawford's house at Valley Forge, young Louis had sat by the fire night after night, listening in rapt silence to the laconic anecdotes of the two veterans, who, in deference to his youth, had heightened the romance and softened the violence of their tales.

Now the boy's father knows a passing regret at the imposition of a dark history on an enchanted childhood. But he does not regret, he has never regretted, a moment of his service or a single drop of the blood he'd shed or sacrificed. A Scottish heir to the promise of America, living in the long shadow of the city where the nation was born, how could he have refused the war? It was the condign task of his generation. And the Civil War *had* ended slavery and saved the Union. There was no fraction of self-deception in the thought. That the son should honor the father's valor in a great cause was well and good. But that he had come to see war itself as welcome adventure was another matter.

"What do you hope to find in the army, boy?"

"A name," Louis says promptly. And then, with no evident embarrassment, he whispers, "Glory." He is sixteen years old and an avid reader of the news of the day. He does not find it hard to speak the word.

"Ah."

Captain Crawford nods slowly. He knows something about glory. Glory was the young private, kneeling wide-eyed beside his commander in the dust at Fair Oaks, numbly trying to feed purple loops of soiled bowel back into the tattered fabric of his gut. It was the riddled corpses scattered through the cornfield at Antietam, the butcher's bill at Gettysburg. It was the sight of his own bright blood as he lay in the widening pool with a chunk of pig iron in his groin, thrashing about on the deck of a gunboat on the Mississippi River minutes after a rebel shore battery finally found its aim. From time to time, memories like these return to the old man with a vigor far more vivid than any of the ordinary incidents of an ordinary day, but there is no way to make them real to Louis even if he'd wanted to, in this quiet parlor of an old brick house in Philadelphia, with the afternoon light soft on the oriental carpet and the marble-topped tables, and no sound to be heard louder than the steady ticking of the mantle clock.

William Harvey Crawford draws deeply on his meerschaum pipe, fancying he can see each fragrant cloud darken the alabaster brow of the maiden whose carved tresses compose the bowl.

"I am not certain the army will, at your age, require you to have my approval, son," he says after a time. "I am thus the more gratified that you seek it, and the more inclined to grant it." He frees another cloud of pungent smoke. "I don't know that the service is the place for you to find yourself, Louis. But I'm not sure I should withhold my consent for you to try." My grandfather wisely says nothing. His father is moving slowly toward the benison of permission, but the moment is not quite yet there.

William Harvey at last gives his conclusion. "I do not feel I can entirely endorse your enterprise, son. But I will not oppose it."

My grandfather is ready to bolt from the room, as though delay might prove his father's consent fragile, though the engineer, who had over and over confirmed the value of his pledged word on many battlefields, has never broken a promise in his life. But he lingers long enough to hear his father say dryly, "I leave it to you to tell your mother. Let it be your first mission as a soldier to deal with that."

AND SO LOUIS Crawford went into the army. But not to the war, not to the Philippines—not yet. There would be many months of stateside duty before he could hope to hear the clash of arms. His first posting was with the 13th US Cavalry at Fort Meade, in Sturgis, South Dakota.

If Louis was a new soldier, the 13th was a new regiment, formed a month and a day after his enlistment on June 25, 1901. And it was a regiment prepared to take a modern turn. The birth of the century had witnessed an era of change in cavalry doctrine. General staffs in Europe and America debated

the proper use of horse soldiers, some holding them best suited as small raiding and reconnaissance parties, others clinging to the Napoleonic dream of
massed lancer charges. There were new drill routines and there would soon
be a new shoulder weapon, the Springfield rifle. There was a new complexity in tables of organization that fielded regular army, volunteer, and state
militia units in an uneasy mix all over the western plains. Some cavalry had
fought in the war with Spain, notably Teddy Roosevelt's Rough Riders,
though no mounted brigades were included in the initial occupation of the
Philippines in 1898. But the 13th would occupy the islands from 1903 on-
ward, and Sergeant Crawford would be among the first to ride with them.

In South Dakota, Private Crawford entered a new world—not only the
service, but the west. The Plains Indian wars were long past, but there would
have been old-timers in his outfit who could tell the tales and show their

arrow wounds. The setting was a perfect fit for the boy's fantasies: Custer with the 7th, Chard at Roark's Drift. He would work to make himself worthy of the fading bugle calls, the ringing steel of swords and the crack of carbines, plangent commands, boots and saddles, the real thing, a cavalryman. And he soon found favor in the eyes of his superiors, who sewed stripes to his sleeves as his merits were made manifest, private to corporal to sergeant so swiftly he must have begun dreaming of a brigadier's star.

Louis Crawford's assignments were not limited to Sturgis. He was here and there throughout the west, map-making in Montana and serving as a guard in Yellowstone during the period when the army controlled the national parks. He was part of the garrison at Fort Assiniboine, established to pen the northern tribes on their reservations. There he would have encountered the famed buffalo soldiers, Black troops who'd earned the ungrudging respect of the native American enemy who named them. And he was stationed for a time at Fort Keogh, established after the Battle of the Little Bighorn by Gen. Nelson A. Miles, a legendary officer under whom Crawford would later serve. If, in 1901, none of this quite counted as the old frontier, it was close enough, and it must have been heady stuff for a kid from Philadelphia.

It was not, however, war. And war was what Louis Crawford wanted.

HE GETS HIS WISH in the spring of 1903, when his regiment is at last ordered to the Philippines. Louis will have two weeks' leave before deployment. Determined to keep a journal of his active service, he acquires a thin red leather diary, 2½ × 5½ inches, stamped with the year in gold numerals in the upper right-hand corner. On the identification page, the boy writes his name with a flourish and gives his address: United States Army, 13th Cavalry. In case of accident or illness, the finder is asked to notify Captain William H. Crawford of 1612 Green Street, Philadelphia, Pa. There are spaces where the bearer can enter the make of his bicycle, the number on his watch, and his collar, cuff, and glove sizes. These have been left blank. The army will supply his clothes, replace his bike with a horse, and doubtless tell him the time should they feel he needs to know it.

The narrow pages of the little book are blank until mid-April, when Louis takes leave of his duty station in Sturgis, South Dakota, and travels east by rail to Philadelphia, with a stop in Chicago on the way. He idles at his family home, shops at Wanamaker's, and takes in a baseball game (Phillies vs. the Boston Americans, later the Red Sox). With his father and his Uncle Robert, both retired naval officers, he is present at the launching of a navy cruiser, the USS *Colorado*, and he finds time to travel to New York to see a musical, *The Silver Slipper*, then enjoying a year's run on Broadway. There are dinners, church services, visits with old friends. But if there are less decorous adventures, if there are romantic liaisons, they don't find their way into the journal.

Indeed, maddeningly little does. Writing only for himself, my grandfather feels no need to offer full descriptions; a fragment, reread years later, will restore a scene. So when he returns to South Dakota to rejoin his regiment at Fort Meade, we learn very little of how he spends the days before the 13th Cavalry sails for the Philippines. There is only a terse record of garrison routine: guard duty, prisoner guard (he loses a prisoner), stable work, a stint as charge of quarters, mounted and dismounted drill. Then on May 21, Sergeant Crawford leaves by rail for California, arriving at Oakland on the twenty-fourth, and marches with his troop from the ferry landing to the Presidio. In San Francisco, he dines at the Cliff House and visits Chinatown. But the time for tourism is short.

On June 1, he boards the USAT *Logan* and sails for Manila. The voyage will last twenty-six days. The diary takes faithful account of each day's weather. We are given a glimpse of a three-masted schooner, a detailed report on a refueling stop at Guam, and a view of Samar Island before the landing in Manila Bay and the trek overland to Los Baños in Laguna Province, where the regiment will be quartered while continuing to train for its ambiguous role as peacekeepers, advisors, possibly combat troops.

The routine is much as it was in South Dakota: guard duty, drill, inspections, an occasional holiday ("very little celebrating here"), a coveted assignment as acting post quartermaster sergeant. On July 8, nearly half the town of Los Baños is destroyed by fire. On July 20, the cavalry stables also burn.

These events are given roughly equal attention—that is, not much—as is the death of a horse and an incident on Laguna Bay, where, paddling about in a rowboat, Louis is run into by a steamship. He *is* happy to have two letters from home on July 7 ("my first in the islands"). Otherwise, the routine is as drab as his khaki, its repetitions so numbing that he ceases to make an entry each day and takes to scrawling "On duty" lengthwise across a page of weeks.

Louis is in that limbo all too well known to the garrison soldier, lost in the timeless rhythm of quotidian chores unalleviated by the spark of action. He has been in the army long enough to know the life, but perhaps not long enough to be wholly resigned to it. Fortunately, he has a diversion he can pull from his footlocker and turn to in his rare free time, a cracked cardboard box closely packed with rectangles cut from stiff paper, each measuring just under five inches by eight. This box of decorated cards puzzled me when I first found it in the leather trunk, but the mystery was solved as soon as I counted them. There were exactly 365; though the thing had the look of an oversized poker deck, it was in fact a handmade calendar. Leafing through the crisp pages, I came to understand that Louis's friends and family had painstakingly assembled this gift as a memento he might take with him to the Philippines, the idea being that on each day's service in the islands he could peel away a card to find a greeting that would instruct or amuse him, that would bolster his spirits by reminding him of home.

The first page of the calendar bore a beautifully executed watercolor of an American flag streaming in the breeze, and many other pages held expert pen or pencil sketches, precise calligraphy, or miniature paintings that offered the sense of a medieval book of hours were it not for the fact that they were often cartoons or caricatures. Collages of newspaper photos and magazine advertisements, portraits of Gibson girls, predominated. But most of the pages consisted only of text, and that largely quotation, and most of those quotations tediously hortatory—Sergeant Crawford would have to swim through an ocean of ponderous advice to find a drop of real amusement. Thus, under a photogravure of Teddy Roosevelt on his charger, Louis's sister Florence admonishes him to "be persevering, and a good soldier, and remember we are expecting great things of you." His Uncle Robert reminds him: "They only succeed whose courage and resolution increase with their difficulties." A friend informs him that "character is a poor man's capital," and his mother, Henrietta, insists he "cling to the moral good." Eugene Field and James Whitcomb Riley make inevitable appearances. Emerson, endlessly quotable, is endlessly quoted. After months of this stuff, the young soldier may have nodded agreement with a friend who writes simply, "Dear Louis, you are going to the Philippine Islands. Perhaps you will be better off there than you would be in Philadelphia."

But I must remind myself that my reservations may not have been his. Child of his times, my grandfather was capable of committing windy philosophizing himself now and again. And I admit I cherish, despite its tired air of received wisdom, one card written in his father's hand, simply because it *is* in his father's hand, a very rare page among the hundreds I would plunder. Disappointingly, like so many others, William Harvey Crawford confines himself to quotation; appropriately, the stern old Scot has recourse to Robert Burns:

> The fear o' hell's a hangman's whip,
> To haud the wretch in order;
> But where ye feel your honour grip,
> Let that aye be your border

Despite his present ennui, Louis knows he may be moving closer to combat. The poet's words, in his father's voice, will be his guide.

FOR THE FIRST time in his life, my grandfather is in a foreign country. The languages are new, the people strange, the culture deeply unfamiliar. From the jungle, birds he'll never see send calls he's never heard, plants undreamed of conceal creatures he can hardly imagine. Active volcanoes ring the horizon, typhoons and tsunamis linger out at sea. The day must be touched with wonder, but if Sergeant Crawford feels it, he may also be too burdened with routine to record it.

On August 23, this will change.

"*Ladrons* reported near Calamba, 100 strong," he writes. The next day, "*Ladrons* from Batangas coming north, 800 strong." And on the twenty-fifth: "200 *ladrons* from Cavite making total of 1100 outlaws in the mountains." His sense of excitement is palpable on the page. The following day, a contingent of Macabebe Scouts, native volunteers allied with the United States, arrives at Los Baños. On the twenty-seventh, the rebels take up positions near Santa Cruz, no more than forty kilometers from the 13th Cavalry base. On the twenty-eighth, raiding parties set out for the enemy camps. "Scouts under Bell and Smith advance toward Santa Cruz," my grandfather writes. And the day after, "Big battle raging."

The fighting continues for two days. Apparently his troop is left out of it. On the thirty-first, the *ladrons* retreat. Across that page, Crawford scrawls bitterly, "Duty at Los Baños. *Everything dull.*"

But his day will come.

On September 12, the regiment receives orders to reposition in Pampanga. For the rest of the month, the troopers will be largely occupied with constructing buildings for their new post, but patrols are sent out regularly and these are not always uneventful. On October 2, following a forced march to Mabalacat, H Troop, the young sergeant's own, takes on a task the diary describes with characteristic brevity: "Disarmed all natives in the vicinity. No resistance." Even so, Crawford exults in their valor: "Rise up, wolves, and howl!"

A comic misadventure will follow. On October 3: "Took platoon up to Republican River to join main column. Lost!" October 4: "Camped in jungle. Two men sick. Still lost." And, charmingly, on October 5: "Decided main column is lost instead of me." The last entry in the diary appears on the following day: "Pulled into Taal. Flying column had just passed through. Will catch up to it." Presumably, he did, though I have to suppose my grandfather's superiors must have found his map and compass reading skills left something to be desired.

But the entry that stands out from all the others appears a few days earlier, on Monday, September 28, when the patrol I began by conjuring makes the contact that would give Louis Crawford his first taste of war: "Skirmish on the trail. Shot twice at a rebel but missed. Riley had better luck."

More than with any other passage in the diary, I find myself chagrined by my grandfather's laconic account of an event that surely must have awed him—the moment of action he'd sought since the first day of his enlistment, the moment when he could step out from under his father's long shadow and claim equal status as a brother in arms.

THERE'S A POSTER on the wall of my workroom, handsomely framed and protected by museum-quality glass, that used to hang in the living room of the Hertford house. My mother came across it in the attic, safely rolled in a cardboard cylinder, sometime in the early 1980s, when she moved from suburban Washington back to North Carolina. In retirement, she had many old prints and paintings restored or reframed, fine colonial and Victorian furniture refinished. A trained artist with an excellent eye, she wrote identifying notes on the back of some photographs, an effort I'll always be grateful for, in part because her informative tags would come to my aid as I began to compose my grandfather's story.

But the poster was left to identify itself. A rectangle of shabby khaki paper, eighteen by twenty-four inches, it features a snapshot of Louis, two inches square, flanked by flags and framed by miniature portraits of the members of his troop, grouped in the shape of a horseshoe around him. The horseshoe evokes the cavalry, and forms a visual metaphor for the salutation that runs in bold type across the center of the page:

GOOD LUCK TO THE AMERICAN SOLDIERS
IN THE PHILIPPINES

At the time I was a little puzzled by the prominence my mother gave the poster, since it was in no way a work of "art" and it stood out sharply from the delicate Hiroshige prints that surrounded it. But she had adored her father, who died when she was twelve, and now I think that—even as Louis Crawford's widow had constructed the entrance hall shrine to his memory—his orphan, in her seventies, wanted to offer honors of her own. She had vivid memories of Louis, his kindness, his comedy, his affectionate teasing. More than once she spoke of how her father led her laughing around the cavalry paddock astride his own huge stallion and let her slip her toes under a border fence so she could say she'd been in Mexico.

No identifying tags, then—but the poster needed none. Once I'd learned a little about the war, I could see how packed it was with information.

Louise Crawford with her father, New Mexico, 1918

Crowned with a furious bald eagle, and filled out with a collage of military scenes, the faded lithograph is a proleptic frieze: blue-jacketed soldiers marching, fighting, making camp, standing guard, leading a supply train pulled by water buffalo beside a placid stream that runs along a thatch-roofed village where tranquil natives go about their chores oblivious to the presence of their presumed protectors.

Clearly the banner is a soldier's memento, like those satin jackets embroidered GERMANY or JAPAN that an occupying army could souvenir from overseas assignments after 1945. Doubtless any member of H Troop who wished could order a copy with his own picture predominant. But the work feels as well like part of a propaganda effort, a reminder that the war in the Philippines was the first to which an American administration brought a sophisticated sense of public relations. The action depicted is bloodless and vague. The native village that anchors the whole composition seems untouched by the war. And the young men staring out of the little silver photographs wear resolute but hardly bellicose faces, none more congenial than my grandfather's. No doubt the passage of over a century has further softened these anodyne images, but there are photographs and drawings from the Civil War that still stun us with their ferocity. In the horseshoe poster, the war in the Philippines seems little more than a benevolent dream.

It could hardly have been that to the troops who fought it or the civilians who suffered it, and there may be found in various archives a brutal photographic record that makes clear what the poster seeks to conceal. The two rounds my grandfather fired on that jungle trail had been locked and loaded four years before when an American soldier idly shot a Filipino who blocked his path, touching off a ragged battle that turned into a war. In the United States, the war was called an insurrection; in the islands, a revolution. Under any name, the struggle evolved as the ambiguous aftermath of a conflict with Spain that brought Americans to the Philippines as liberators and kept them there for decades as a colonial force.

In America, there was widespread enthusiasm for the new war at first, if some uncertainty as to how to wage it. Historian Stanley Karnow notes that senior officers and NCOs, whose experience had been formed by the Civil War and Indian fighting, tended to treat battle in the Philippines "as if they were still pursuing Apaches," while young volunteers, knowing nothing of combat, "had heard only tales of its heroics, which they were now eager to emulate." This contrast aptly depicts the collision between William Harvey Crawford's haunted memories and his young son's eager dreams.

It also accounts for the buoyant mood of the first troops to ship out to the Pacific. Entrained for California, Midwestern militia units passed through little towns bright with flags, loud with martial music, and wild with bloodlust. Adrift in San Francisco, soldiers drank, brawled, and absorbed the clap from an armada of prostitutes. Landed in Cavite, they felt themselves ready to face the remnants of the Spanish garrison or, if need be, a restive native population—the "goo-goos." Meanwhile, their officers waited for coherent orders from the McKinley administration, which seemed to have no idea what it wanted from the Philippines, if indeed it wanted them at all.

The Anti-Imperialist League certainly didn't. Its most famous member, Mark Twain, said that if his country sustained its claim to the islands, the American flag should be replaced by the Jolly Roger. Against the larger jingoism, this view could not prevail; still, by the spring of 1903, enthusiasm for the war had faded. A year later, its primary claim on the public's attention would be a crack Filipino drill team whose performance at the St. Louis World's Fair so impressed the crowds that the St. Louis Post-Dispatch felt it had to caution the city's women to show less enthusiasm for their exotic visitors.

On April 27, 1903, an atrocity report prepared by Gen. Nelson Miles, and kept under wraps for months by the Roosevelt administration, was

Louis Crawford, fourth from right, Philippine Islands

released to the American press, which largely ignored it. On that same day, my grandfather's leave of absence ended. At Philadelphia's Broad Street station, he boarded a train for Chicago and the west, the first stage of his epic journey to the fading embers of a war he had long wanted to fight. But by the time Sergeant Crawford stormed ashore on Luzon, the sword of empire was thoroughly tarnished, and by the time he returned from the islands, his hopes of a military career were temporarily thwarted as well. A first-rate soldier, he'd been recommended for a commission, but made a poor showing on preliminary tests due, he writes, to a bout of malaria. Then came his father's death in 1904, suddenly casting Louis in a new role as the main support of his mother and sister. Honorably discharged in 1905, he returned to Philadelphia, doomed for a time to negotiate life as a mere civilian.

IF THE ARMY could not offer him a career, what occupation could? In the years between 1905 and 1920, my grandfather found several ways to answer that question, but none could equal the military's mystic pull.

The foundations of his first civilian vocation appear to have been laid shortly after his discharge, when he becomes an apprentice draftsman at the Baldwin Locomotive Works in Philadelphia, where his father's legacy doubtless offered him entrée. But Louis's performance has spoken for itself by 1907, the year he decides to move west during a nationwide financial crisis that threatens to close the plant. In a letter of recommendation, the machine shop foreman, who had been my grandfather's supervisor, writes, "To whom it may concern, Louis R. Crawford served a two-year apprenticeship in Baldwin's 17th Street Shops. I found him to be a careful and intelligent young man of good family and was sorry to part with him." Similar praise is offered by his boss in Arizona, a master mechanic named Dawson, who finds Louis "careful in the performance of his duties. . . . I take pleasure in recommending him as a sober and industrious man."

Careful. The adjective appears in both letters. It might mean as much as *courage* to a soldier.

If such praise seems a pale commendation, we may recall that it is being used to describe the work of a draftsman at a time when technical drawing meant what it would have meant in the days of Leonardo—a subtle and exacting skill, not a few clicks on a keyboard or a gesture with a mouse. A survey of my grandfather's tools, many still gathering dust in the Hertford house attic, suggests the domain of their diligent employment: T squares, set squares, splines, compasses, French curves, protractors and proportional dividers, pencils sharp as scalpels, pots of dried India ink and pen points capable of the boldest lines and the most delicate shadings. Louis would have grown up not only in the shadow of his father's saber, but in the knowledge that the mastery of these instruments was another of the old Scot's powers.

Indeed, respect for blades and edges is a passion they may have shared. The only letter I've been able to find from father to son concerns itself almost entirely with the care and selection of drafting tools.

GIVEN THE INTENSITY of his devotion to the service and the urgency of his drive to make himself a place there, it's surprising to discover that Louis Crawford spent not quite seven years on active duty as a reservist or a regular. Even adding his time in the Arizona National Guard, which was about to become part of his post-Philippines experience, gives him fewer than ten years in the military—less than half his working life. But it was the half he drew on to provide the whole of his self-definition. His civilian employment doesn't even appear in the timeline he constructed and somewhat ponderously titled "File B"—another trophy of the black leather trunk—a detailed breakdown of duty stations that has eased my path in laying out his chronology.

The memoir he wrote for his children years later while stationed at Kelly Field is more helpful. It places him in Clifton, Arizona—a hardscrabble mining town in a setting of high cliffs and dangerous floods—as a draftsman for the Arizona and New Mexico Railway in 1909, the year of his marriage and the year before his first child is born. (Arizona was still a territory and Clifton still the frontier—my mother remembered being told that the legs of her crib were placed in bowls of water to keep scorpions from crawling up to the mattress.)

Work for the railway doesn't cause Louis to forget his military ambitions. By 1910, well qualified by prior experience, he has taken a commission as first lieutenant in an infantry company of the Arizona National Guard, just in time to see service along the Mexican border at the beginning of the Madero revolution. A platoon leader, he commands patrols in the region north of Agua Prieta and Nogales during summer encampments, alert for skirmishes between the rebels and government troops and doubtless hoping that a misstep on the part of either will give him the authority to engage. But actual combat between Mexican and American forces still lies some years away. Meanwhile, Lieutenant Crawford exults in being back in uniform and under arms, his body hardening as he hikes the pitiless arroyos, his spirit fed by the dusty pageantry of his citizen soldiers, though privately he is inclined to feel that guardsmen tend to be less disciplined and effective than regular US Army troops.

The summers on the border are largely uneventful, the withered horizon empty save for columns of tall saguaro and the tangle of mesquite and ocotillo that decorates the desert. It's a risky country even without a war—sidewinders and Gila monsters slumber in the shade, daytime temperatures often top one hundred degrees and summer thunderstorms can flood a camp. To Louis this severe world comes as a luxury, pulling him temporarily from the civil sphere, where he can never be altogether happy. He searches the arid landscape with a kind of greed, fixing his field glasses on the rare funnel of dust that shields a column of federal cavalry or a ragged file of rebel *caballeros*. But only once—so I imagine—does he witness an encounter. The forces involved are small, a squadron of soldiers and about the same number of Madero's men, somehow colliding on a low mesa vast enough to have concealed them both. The flash of their rifles is lost in the sunlight but the sound carries over the desert in precise small pops. Through the binoculars, my grandfather can clearly see the federal troops drop into position in gullies and behind boulders as the rebels maneuver to flank them. He watches one soldier stand, lift his rifle, and soundlessly fall.

A man slouched beside the lieutenant mutters, "Seems like a few rounds might have landed on this side of the border. We'd be within our rights to reply."

Lieutenant Crawford glances at his platoon sergeant, in civil life a rancher from Tucson. He shakes his head, though he's not unsympathetic to the notion of depleting the Diaz government's forces. Like many Americans, he has some admiration for Francisco Madero, whose populist revolt seeks to replace a grim dictatorship, but like any good officer he will not countermand his orders without cause.

The sergeant persists in his murderous ambition. "Got a fellow in the company was a sniper on Luzon. Could drop a goo-goo at five hundred yards. I say we shoot one or two greasers for Old Glory."

"Thank you, no," my grandfather replies, pleasantly enough, though his glance at the man is cold. A firefight is one thing. A national uproar over an international incident would be quite another.

ARIZONA OFFERS AN INTERESTING life, though Kate finds the ordeal of the frontier taxing—not too many mothers would welcome the chore of watching for rattlesnakes when their babies are put out to play in the yard. Anyway, Louis is restless, restless. After three years in Clifton he brings his work with the railway to an end, regretting only that his departure costs him his summer bivouacs with the Arizona Guard. By late 1912, he is again employed as a draftsman, now in Vancouver, Washington, until an eye injury enforces six months of idleness. He is also beginning to suffer from a chronic illness, never specified, that will haunt him for the rest of his days. By spring of the following year, he succumbs to his wife's pleas and moves his little family to Kate's North Carolina home. They will live with her parents in the old house on the river, an arrangement that produces the predictable tension Louis finally confesses in an explosive letter four years later. For now, he needs to find a job.

Instead he creates one. There's no work for a draftsman in Hertford, so, with absolutely nothing apparent in his background to prepare for or predict the move, he decides to establish himself as a writer, first placing short feature stories in the local paper, and ultimately publishing fiction in two national magazines and completing a novella that draws on his experience of patrolling the border. These are sterling as well as startling achievements, but his successes are sporadic and hardly promise a living wage. So he also toys with the notion of farming—the primary industry of the region—and even clerical work, though the first lies outside his capacities, and the second would have abraded his sense of style.

Then, in June 1914, Louis is elected superintendent of Hertford Graded Schools.

Of all the facts I've been able to unearth in shaping the civilian side of my grandfather's story, this seems the most remarkable. That a high school graduate with a largely technical education whose advanced training took place in the saddle of a cavalry mount should find himself in charge of a county school system asks for an accounting his history doesn't give. Louis perhaps felt the anomaly himself, since upon appointment he leaves at once for the University of North Carolina to take summer courses that will equip him for his work come fall. In any case, this new job is key to understanding my grandfather's place in small town southern society: while there's evidence he may have had to struggle to embed himself in Kate Riddick's family, it would appear that he was held in some esteem by his new neighbors and friends.

In the end, all these efforts are largely sideshows. Whether he wears the green eyeshade of a draftsman, the ink-stained cuffs of a journalist, or the seersucker suit of a southern school administrator, Louis is only marking time until he can get back into uniform again.

Meanwhile, it will be worth our time to take a more extended look at his fiction.

EVERYWOMAN'S MAGAZINE (vol. 1, no. 4) for February 1917, with its articles on fashion and home economics and its florid advertisements for corsets and millinery shops, would not have held the attention of the ten-year-old boy who had first laid eyes on it in 1954, but when I began to review the contents of the black leather trunk nearly sixty years later I assumed the yellowed pages must have been preserved for a reason. I found it on page 16—a short story, "Chevrons or Straps," by Louis R. Crawford.

If my mother had known her father was a published author, she never said so. I'd long thought myself the only professional writer in the family and was startled that she hadn't claimed a genetic root for my modest success. But Louis had been welcomed into print when his daughter was only seven, and there's every likelihood that Kate Crawford would have concealed even the most decorous romance from her innocent eyes.

I scanned the brief tale with no little curiosity, gratified to find it a fair specimen of the romance fiction of the era: a young army corporal risks disaster by paying suit to a daughter of privilege, whose hand he may claim only once he's earned a commission, and so on. The writing is fluent, though tainted with a beginner's devotion to adverbs and dialogue tags, and my grandfather's style is adroit enough to pull the reader easily into the story. And he's a master of the military setting. His officers and enlisted men ring true, and the armed exercise that forms the heart of the action feels authentic. Once we agree to the obligatory conflict (Corporal Warren must acquit himself of a charge of assault against an arrogant lieutenant who also seeks the lady's favor), we can enjoy the plot's formulaic unfolding.

And *Everywoman's* had something more to offer: a profile of the author that fills in a few details the other records scant. Admittedly, the brief note enhances his history, giving rise to the suspicion that the biography's subject may have had a hand in its composition. Thus we encounter the claim that malaria cost him his first try at a commission, though the official record names a failed history exam; also that he left the army and "returned to Philadelphia to take up newspaper work," though I can't find evidence of this enterprise; and finally that he took himself to Arizona to "become a Civil Engineer," though the facts say he held the more modest position of draftsman. But *Everywoman's* is accurate enough with the next stage of his story, placing him as a National Guard officer

on the Mexican border service during the start of the revolution that has now reached such a chaotic state. . . . During all this time he had been writing for the newspapers as a side-line, having always aspired to a journalistic career. In 1913 he launched out as a short-story writer.

He still corresponds as a freelance for the newspapers, and has had several short stories published in some of the leading magazines, *Leslie's*, *Everybody's*, etc. He has completed a first novel, *Viva, Madero!* a tale of the Mexican border, on which he has received very favorable editorial comment. Its publication is pending.

Hard not to smile. My grandfather is far from being the first hopeful novice to enlarge a publisher's cautious expression of interest into the dream of cash and a contract. Indeed, given the magazine profile's sometimes casual treatment of fact, I was ready to fear Louis Crawford might have been recklessly expanding a few pages of false starts into a nonexistent finished product.

But the book is no chimera. I found it in the black leather trunk.

VIVA, MADERO! is a thirty-five-thousand-word novella typed in faded blue ink on ninety-eight sheets of good bond paper that have held up better than many of the other items in Louis Crawford's footlocker against the ravages of time and silverfish. We can easily read every word of it, but not everyone will want to. I wanted to. And the more I studied the sheaf of worn pages, the more convinced I became that the forgotten fiction gave privileged access to my grandfather's story.

Too short to fill a book and too long to fit into a magazine, *Madero* belongs to a nearly extinct genre of boys' adventure stories whose remnants have long since been absorbed into action movies and computer games. Its earnest, enthusiastic prose is too often wearying. Its plot is risible. The clownish Irishmen and clichéd Hispanics who people its scenes would make modern readers wince.

But the novella's faults speak more to the tastes of the era than to the talents of the man. It has vitality. It's free of specious irony—we don't get the action delivered with a knowing wink. The author cares for his characters and he's committed to his classic theme, embodied in a hero, Jack Farnsworth, determined to "make good" by apprenticing himself to a demanding vocation. And the book fits firmly within a distinct literary tradition that stretches from the fiction of B. Traven to the films of Sam Peckinpah: stories of American adventurers defining themselves through violent ordeals south of the border.

Most importantly, we learn much about Louis from his creation. By abruptly transforming Jack Farnsworth from soldier to civilian, as he will do in resolving his ornate plot, Louis Crawford is doing more than fitting a surprise ending onto his story—he's imagining an alternative autobiography, forecasting a future in which his own best hopes lie outside the service. By 1917, he was far enough along in his competing careers to be able to pass judgment on his choices, and it's not much of a stretch to see Jack as a tool he could summon to examine them.

Viva, Madero! also supplements my initial picture of Louis's father, William Harvey Crawford, with a more nuanced one. It equips its protagonist with a backstory that suggests the trajectory of his creator's career may have been a product as much of chance as of deliberation. And it offers a sophisticated critique of the politics of the army, providing a rationale both for the hero's choice of a civilian job and for the author's relegation to one.

Madero has other merits. When he works from felt experience, my grandfather's prose is lucid and pictorial. "As the troop rode into Sturgis to entrain for El Paso, Jack was in his accustomed place beside the first four, the red and white silk of the guidon snapping from the lance held in his stirrup boot, the throbbing of his pulse keeping time with the rhythmic beating of the hoofs and the musical jangle of tin cups against picket pins that came down the column behind him."

There are other passages whose strings of prepositional phrases almost predict Hemingway. "Jack Farnsworth sat on an overturned cracker box at the door of the conical wall tent that served as a guard room for the little patrol and gazed across the Rio Grande at the irregular outlines, in the pale moonlight, of the Mexican shore."

If lines such as these suggest an approach to authentic style, Louis too often mortars the chunks of his story into place with phrases like "Slim emitted a low whistle of surprise," and he's not always confident in his pacing of dramatic and expository scenes. Such shortcomings are forgivable in a novice. We need also to remember that my grandfather, writing before 1917, had few modernist models to draw on, and that his largely technical education would not have exposed him to the few there were. What vexes me more than his uneven diction is his depiction of war, which he knew firsthand but describes as if he didn't.

But to a closer look at Jack's story.

The first page of the novella finds the young sergeant already in Mexico. The third paragraph plunges the reader into his origin myth.

Two years before, Farnsworth had enlisted in the US Cavalry, having decided that a military career was his particular calling in life. There had been two motives behind this step: first, of making good somewhere and wiping out a rather irresponsible past that had proved a bitter disappointment to his fond and slightly over-indulgent parents; and second, he took as naturally to soldiering as a duck does to water. Soldiers, like poets, are born and not made, and Jack's earliest memories were of marshalling his leaden platoons on the dining room table.

More than fifty years later, I marshaled those same platoons on that same table, but I think that even then my dreams were of telling their stories, not of fighting their wars. "Probably his military instincts were inherited from Farnsworth Senior, who had fought his way through the four years of the Civil War, and who would have re-enlisted in '98 but for the limp in one leg that was an ever-present reminder of the last Union stand at Fair Oaks." Which accounts for the second motive. As to the first, Jack has been falsely accused of a destructive schoolboy prank, on which his father "came down hard," causing the boy to flee his home in a rage at the injustice, "resolved never to return until he had shown 'the old man' he could make good." The army seems to be the answer.[2]

Having wedged Jack's relevant history into the text, the novella swiftly unfolds a melodramatic plot centered on multiple captivity narratives that require its hero to evade General Madero's troops and escape from *federales* as he makes his way illegally into Mexico, disguised as an officer, to rescue an American businessman falsely imprisoned as a rebel spy. The background of the action is the Battle of Aqua Prieta, a historical event my grandfather may have learned about from fellow soldiers present on the occasion.

Fought on November 1, 1915, the fight pitted the army of Pancho Villa against government forces that had been permitted by President Woodrow Wilson to cross American territory without Villa's knowledge. The result was a rout for the rebels, but also a piece of theater for the residents of the cross-border town of Douglas, Arizona. In *Viva, Madero!*, these gawkers earn the contempt of American soldiers who've been ordered to stay clear of the fighting unless fired on. "'If they want to go rubberin' around the side lines of a battle,' one sergeant remarks, 'it's their fault if they stop a stray

---

2. It's a stretch to assume this part of the account mirrors my grandfather's own story. He may well have invented the prank and its aftermath, even as I conjured the scene in which Louis seeks his father's blessing on his desire to enlist. We're both writing fiction, after all. But I'm convinced that either version captures the deepest truth—that my grandfather was entranced by *his* father's story, and supported by a youthful taste for adventure in his desire to emulate it.

bullet.'" History tells us this was indeed the outcome for a few, though only in my grandfather's fiction is an American family kidnapped by *federales*, prompting a fictitious character's fictional foray into Sonora.

Louis describes the battle in some detail, mostly of the arid kind that might be provided by a War College colonel offering a lecture on tactics: "With the opening volley the Federal right and left wings spread out as if to envelop the Rebel flanks . . . " He also lets himself compare the fighting to a football game. But this listless account is much improved by the introduction of a combat correspondent, who gives the author a chance to lecture the reader on American and Latin American combat styles: Latinos fight from cover, while Americans "fire a volley and then get up and chase the bullets." There is a faint imputation of cowardice on the part of the first though what's actually being posited is foolhardiness on the part of the second. At all events, in this livelier passage we meet an Irish sergeant, with his labored brogue, and the Associated Press reporter, whose trade receives a sympathetic critique from Jack and his colleagues. The war with Spain had seen the advent of the combat correspondent as a figure easily adapted for pulp romance, and Louis's careful inclusion of a representative specimen is one of the adroit touches that gives his story an authentic air.

When the battle ends, my grandfather records its indecisive aftermath with an accuracy that could hardly be improved upon by a professional historian:

> Douglas had quieted down again and the officials had apparently forgotten the incident of the fight across the line. For a few days, the yellow journals had screamed "Intervention!" in flaring type across the front sheets, and the people had anxiously awaited some action from Washington. But as the days wore on and the attitude of the administration seemed to be one of regret rather than anger, the citizens of the little border town resumed the even tenor of their ways.

The tenor of Jack Farnsworth's ways is anything but even. Convinced the sergeant, who's posing as an officer, commands a company of militia, the rebels free the American businessman and invite Jack to a banquet, where he gets drunk, poses for incriminating photographs, and signs unspecified documents that can only make his situation worse.

At this point, things turn stranger. Back with his regiment, Jack fears the repercussions of his adventure, so a civilian friend, Slim, fakes a telegraph from Jack's father that will fraudulently earn the young soldier compassionate leave. Jack and Slim dip back into Mexico in search of the dubious photos and papers, aided by a rebel captain happy to help the gringos out (the accent inflicted on his dialogue is an epic embarrassment): "Eet ees my plan at meed-night to attack while the *soldatos* sleep . . . " The two recover the documents during a brief firefight whose description causes the author to retreat to cliché—rifles "crack," muzzles "flash," bullets "whiz." My grandfather is recalling his reading, not his experience.

Wounded, Jack is taken prisoner by *federales*, but under cover of a rebel attack, he effects a daring escape, freeing at the same time another American prisoner, a mining engineer named Griffin, captured in his attempt to recover documents establishing his ownership of a stolen silver mine. As they ride for the border, Jack blurts out his tale, concluding by expressing his fears that his antics will have cost him his chance at a commission and earned him hard time at hard labor in a military jail. Griffin, somewhat mysteriously, offers reassurances.

After all this, Louis quickly wraps his story up, with a breathtaking disregard for plausibility. Not only does Griffin prove to be an old friend of Jack's commanding officer, who at the behest of the rescued engineer promptly dismisses all charges, but Jack's father appears on the scene as a deus ex machina to beg forgiveness for having falsely accused his son of the high school prank that led to the boy's enlistment. He also turns out to have been Griffin's commanding officer during the Civil War. The resultant bonhomie draws Sergeant Farnsworth into a lunch with his social betters, blithely violating yet another service rule. His reward this time is a job offer from Griffin, as the idea of a commission no longer appeals.

This sudden surrender of his dreams of martial glory may feel abrupt, but the author has skillfully foreshadowed it much earlier in the story when on page 24 Jack muses, "I've reached the conclusion that a man is a whole lot better off in some good business than in the Army in times of peace." And we've known from the first that his hopes for a commission are at odds with his wish to remain with his troop as long as there is the possibility of action.

The issue of Jack's future is smoothly solved by a question from his father and a comment from his CO.

During the luncheon, the talk wandered from the Peninsular Campaign, where Farnsworth senior and Griffin had followed McClellan to Fair Oaks and through the seven days retreat to Malvern Hill, to the Indian Campaigns in the southwest, where Griffin and Steele's father had pursued the wily Apache. The group heard of how Griffin, successful in some mining investments, had retired to follow a business career, and lastly, of Jack's stirring adventures across the border. When the meal was over and cigars lighted, Jack's father turned to him and asked: "Well, my boy, what do you intend to do? Still anxious for your commission?"

Jack admits he has begun to feel otherwise, and Captain Steele concurs: "I can confidently say that if a man has not had the advantage of West Point, he is better off if he stays outside the Army."

The question of just what sort of civilian job the young sergeant should have is resolved when he produces the documented claims Griffin had been searching for, having stolen them from a Mexican general's office for no better reason than that they were written in English. The engineer promptly rewards him with appointment as his private secretary at a salary six times greater than an army captain's, a rank Jack calculates he "would have had to work sixteen years to achieve." It's a fantasy of turning trauma into triumph in which a worthy but beleaguered young man is redeemed from a foundering career by a potent father figure who possesses both the will and means to save him.

To complete his victory, Jack is given a final prize—Griffin's "pretty niece and ward," the fair Kate, who has inexplicably arrived on the scene as suddenly as old Captain Farnsworth, and who expresses her interest in the handsome youth without hesitation when he proclaims that he hopes to prove himself worthy of her. "'You already have, Jack,' whispered the blushing Kate," though it's not clear how.

By the last pages, what *is* clear is that the creaking machinery of *Madero*'s plot has sacrificed any hopes the author may have entertained of maintaining the reader's credulity, and that, by this time, my grandfather has largely given up fiction for history: the senior Farnsworth's battles are those fought by William Harvey Crawford, and the junior Farnsworth's nubile prize bears my grandmother's name. But at the very end of the book, Louis manages a memorable line that gives him his final flourish and his grandson both a title and a theme. As Jack's troop entrains for New Mexico, they "cheer lustily for the smiling couple waving to them from the station platform," and for the last time the stage Irish sergeant speaks: "'He wor a foine lad an' had th' makin's of a good officer in him, but 'tis better off he is on th' outside,' adding as he turned to light his pipe, 'Sure th' Army is no place fer a soldier.'" I make no doubt the author took a grim satisfaction in his own bleak humor, knowing on the one hand that the irony housed an odd truth and on the other that there was, even so, no other place he wanted to be.

Viva, Madero! is datelined Hertford, NC, but no date of composition is given. Doubtless Louis wrote the book in the old house by the river, where more than half a century later his grandson would produce a first novel as well. But there's no way to know how hard he labored over it, or how long it took. Presumably he was for a time free of military duties or commercial prospects, and perhaps he hoped fiction could actually earn him a living wage, which in turn might explain his deliberate exploitation of the easy conventions of genre romance. I wrote my own book in about a year, and, as in childhood, though for different reasons, I could be in Hertford only in the summer. I still have vivid memories of nights on the screened back porch, kept up by coffee and kept comfortable by a fan, typing into the small hours—it was much too hot there to try to write during the day. It pleases me to think of my grandfather working away in the same place under the same conditions fifty years before, both of us drafting stories based on our army experiences, something I had no way of knowing at the time, though the black leather trunk containing *his* story sat silent in the attic two flights above my head.

THE FACTS OF Louis Crawford's career show his enlistment ending under conditions less sanguine than Jack Farnsworth's. I'll retrace that part of his story and fill in a few details.

Like Jack, my grandfather had been recommended for a commission but made a poor showing on the preliminary tests, due—he tells us—to a bout of malaria. He is further thrown off his stride by his father's death in September 1904, and when he fares no better on subsequent examinations—history is his stumbling block—he takes an honorable discharge at the end of his enlistment and in 1905 returns to Philadelphia to live with his mother and sister in the old family home on Green Street. He gets a job as a draftsman at the Baldwin Locomotive Works and meets my grandmother, Kate Wallace Riddick, an art student at the Philadelphia Museum School. Much in love, he follows her to Hertford on his first bewildered visit to the south. But it will be four years before they marry. In 1907, Louis loses his job at Baldwin when the plant closes in the financial panic of that year, and, in classic American style, heads west to the frontier to seek his fortune. The east is no place for a soldier.

JULY 1916 finds Louis once again in Chapel Hill, taking summer school courses to enhance his academic credentials. But he is also thinking of how to reopen a line to the army. The Great War has engulfed Western Europe and relations between the United States and Mexico are worsening daily. One way or another, battle is on the horizon, and this once and future soldier will not willingly see himself sidelined.

"War may not come," he writes Kate on July 2, "but I must say I cannot see how it can be averted. The tone of the Mexican government becomes uglier every day and all who are in touch with the situation feel that negotiating is only postponing the inevitable."

This is the beginning of a sixteen-page letter that, even more than *Viva, Madero!*, provides an invaluable key to any understanding of my grandfather. Here, as nowhere else, he lays bare the tension between his civilian ambition and his military dreams, celebrates his sometimes oppressive Scots thrift, counts the cost of chronic illness, dilutes his uxorious love with fretful chiding, and offers the stern rebuke to his aristocratic in-laws that has been simmering under his surface calm for any number of years. Under the pressure of his suddenly tapped emotions, the letter all but implodes, shifting from subject to subject as its author's moods impel him. But in the paragraphs that sustain his opening theme, he waxes almost rhapsodic, beseeching his wife to stand beside her warrior and confessing at the same time the powerful influence of his father's example before he strikes the note of a Christian crusader, which he follows up by evoking faith and family pride:

Do you know what war means to a soldier? To one with a fighting line of ancestors?

To one whose earliest recollection is of looking at his daddy's saber on the wall? Have you heard of Gethsemane? That's what it is when the troops march off and a soldier is left behind.

You say I've served my country enough. Kate, dear, you understand love.

You know a lover, spurned, still falls at the feet of his adored one. So it is with me. My country cast me off, but I love it—and that old flag I've been taught to take my hat off to.

And he has a final card to play. "Why, Kate, could I look my little boy in the face in later years when he is learning the spirit of citizenship and patriotism and say I was not willing to go?"

I don't know whether my grandmother resigned herself to his zeal or tried to counter his points through a reasoned appeal to his other obligations. In such an effort, I doubt she would have succeeded. If Louis Crawford felt called to the colors, Kate and the children would have to tag along. After all, though America is not yet at war, he has already begun to cast about for a commission. "They have called for a Company of Engineers to be in readiness here and I've tendered my services to them. There'll be big work for the Engineers in the reconstruction of Mexico."

Abruptly, Kate's young husband shifts subjects. Most of the rest of the long letter will take up themes of domestic life, finances first, then a darker note:

Now about the household management question. You say my illness is no reason why we should change the way we've been doing things. That's just it. Illness brought me to the realization that we can't go on as we are. Being sick costs money. I get a raise this year but the expenses are outstripping the income. The children were growing you said—would I deny my baby milk? Probably not, but it has to be paid for.

And Louis is in no doubt as to where his hapless wife has learned her profligate ways: "Your mother's system will last just so long. 'I intend to pay for that' is all right but sooner or later someone has to put up the money. This robbing Peter to pay Paul never works."

We need no reminder that we're eavesdropping on a deeply conventional early twentieth-century marriage: the husband is the breadwinner, the wife runs the household. But if her management skills falter, he will step in to make the necessary course corrections. Much more than money is at stake here, and after several pages that read like bank statements, Louis finds his way to the true source of his growing distress: "I don't mind staying at the old house but in the past as soon as I'd yield an inch I'd be crowded a foot. I don't enjoy having to fight all the time for what should be mine without a struggle."

Again abruptly, he turns his attention to his new career as though he had not just announced his plans to return to an old one: "School affairs in Perquimans are in an awful state. It's going to take a damn hard fight to straighten them out. When I come back this fall I'm going to start the fight and for a man with some opposition to begin with that may mean a fierce battle and I want a line of retreat open." At this point he parallels the purported failure of the school system with disorder in his adopted family:

> The fault exists right in your own home where people are living on
> the reputation of how life was ordered long ago. Bluntly, your family
> have not adjusted themselves to the needs of the present.
>
> I want to stay in Hertford. There is the finest field for school work
> there that exists in the whole State, but it means a hard fight, single-
> handed, against people who are strongly entrenched behind their
> undisturbed complacency.
>
> That's why I want a happy home. To strengthen me for the fight.
> I couldn't stand it like it's been—fight all day for what is right in my
> work and then come home to fight for what is right there, for what is
> no more than intended by God in either place.

Nineteen sixteen seems a late date to be claiming the divine right of hus- bands, and I feel it unlikely that on calm reflection Louis would have insisted his life and work carried the Almighty's personal imprimatur. But his heated language is a measure of the passion he brings to a topic that may have been too often suppressed.

And he isn't done. Lest Kate be in any doubt that changes are about to be made, her husband ends with a considerable fanfare, softened only by an affectionate close:

> I love you, dear heart, but you know I've had some sacrifices to make
> and it hasn't always been easy. Whenever the choice came to you,
> you always chose the old home in preference to the one I tried to

make for you and by and by I gave up trying 'tho it was hard. But there is a new generation coming and I don't intend to wait until I am grey-headed to get the wife and helper that God gave me seven years ago. She's mine by all rights 'tho I've tried to share her and in return have been pushed ever further away from her and the things I loved her for.

That way of living is ended now.

It's nearly midnight. I must take this down as they post the mail before I rise in the morning.

God bless and watch over you, for I love you.

Your own Lou

Too much may be made of the conflicts revealed in this letter. Tensions within marriages rooted in the competing demands of extended families are hardly unheard of, and the perceived failure of one partner to meet the unexamined expectations of the other is a familiar story. But in its inordinate length, its scattershot construction, its broad focus, and the high fever of its language, the July letter becomes a singularly valuable document in my attempt to unpack some of the potent contradictions in my grandfather's psyche. Here I find confirmation of my sense that his father's valor provided the engine of his own model of achievable manhood, and that in his father's several careers he found evidence of more than one way forward. Here, too, Louis shows himself a demanding as well as loving parent, a frustrated as well as passionate husband. And here, as nowhere else, he reveals the nearly erotic force of his love of country, and of the army, and his determination to make his dedication overcome his disappointments. It's a lot of self to show in a sheaf of unguarded pages.

Of course, it's also only his side of the story. We can easily imagine that Doctor and Mrs. Riddick, even after the birth of grandchildren and years of proof that their daughter had made a sturdy marriage, may still have carried their initial image of the brash young Philadelphian as a carpetbagger, a Snopes to their Sartoris, a chaotic Yankee who seduced a child of the South and followed her home to continue the plunder. And it takes only a little sympathy to suppose Kate a passionate girl whose heart had been tugged in two directions. How startled she must have been to open a long letter so much more forceful than her husband's usual sentimental offerings. In all his correspondence before, strenuous notes are rare; few will appear hereafter.

And certainly nowhere else, and never again, will we find him in a state of siege with every element of his life: at war with himself, at war with Mexico, at war with Germany, at war with the school board, at war with the service, at war with his best beloved, and at war with the august Dr. William Moore Riddick and his haughty patrician Virginian plantation-bred wife!

Ten months later he is back in the army.

European empires have been fighting for over two years when the interception of the Zimmerman telegram prompts Woodrow Wilson to ask Congress for a declaration of war against Germany on April 6, 1917. Louis Crawford is quickly commissioned in an army suddenly desperate for experienced men. In May, he is ordered to Fort Oglethorpe, Georgia, to train as a platoon leader destined to fight in the trenches. His cadre includes a young captain, Dwight David Eisenhower. And among his classmates he will find an aspiring writer, Second Lieutenant Francis Scott Key Fitzgerald.

I think they knew each other.

F. Scott Fitzgerald was stationed for most of his brief army career at Fort Leavenworth, Kansas, and Fort Sheridan, Alabama, where he met Zelda Sayre. But at least one historian places him in Fort Oglethorpe at the same time as my grandfather. And when I tie that fact to the remarkable parallels between their lives I feel pretty confident of my case, and still more confident that some sense of their probable encounter can enlarge our knowledge of an unknown soldier and a famous writer as they set out to engage in the war to end all wars.

SCOTT FITZGERALD'S life is too well known to require review, but I'm the custodian of my grandfather's story, and I had to open that black leather trunk before its details leapt out at me. Once they did, I discovered a man for whom the soon-to-be famous novelist might have been not only a fellow soldier, but almost a double, a secret sharer.

See them side by side: two young men of good family and comparable social origins, Yankees uncertain of their welcome in the South, both Celts, both in love with southern girls they feel in some ways unequal to, both movie-star handsome, both bright but uncredentialed, both survivors of some vague chronic illness, both Civil War buffs, both infantry officers poised for battle. And if this is not enough, each was an eager apprentice to the art of fiction. Indeed, at the time they would've met, Louis was Scott Fitzgerald's senior in the world of letters as well as in the army—he'd published short stories in *Frank Leslie's* and *Everywoman's*, two of the time's major markets, before Scott ever made his way into print. And he had finished a first novel, *Viva Madero!*, a romance of the Mexican war. The two would have had a lot to talk about.

And to write about. Their literary styles have little in common, but they might have scribbled each other's letters from camp. "I've taken Regular Army exams, but haven't heard a word from them yet," Scott writes on September 26, in a line that could have been lifted verbatim from one of my grandfather's letters to my grandmother Kate, just as Louis's pride in the Allied victory ("Men, who a year ago were clerking in stores . . . have defeated an army that has been in training for years") could easy have been recorded by Scott, who shares his brother officer's eagerness to fight: "We have no news except that we're probably going inside of two months, and, officers and men, we're wild to go."

Wild or not, Scott Fitzgerald didn't go, and felt the lack for the rest of his life. As for my grandfather, the medical officers were already looking with concern at his X-rays. Awaiting the results, Louis offers Kate a meditation: "Somehow, dear, I look on this war as a great test, a readjustment of the world. All of the old sham and false glitter seem to be gone." His words would been endorsed by Fitzgerald, who in one letter notes: "Every man I've met who's been to war, that is this war, seems to have lost youth and faith in man." The two positions neatly capture postwar attitudes, my grandfather's emphasizing the pensive optimism common to the era, while Fitzgerald is beginning to shape the romantic cynicism whose chief spokesman he will soon become.

Fearing his commission may cause his mother worry, or worse, trigger a display of public pride, Scott writes her, "About the army please let's not have either tragedy or heroics because they are equally distasteful to me. I went into this perfectly cold-bloodedly." To a cousin, he asserts his indifference to the notion of dying for his country. "I may get killed for America —but I'm going to die for myself." Louis has already countered Kate's objections in another way. "You say I've served my country enough. But do you know what war means to a soldier? It's hell when the troops march off and a soldier stays behind." Different motivations, even allowing for the bravado in each case. But they work toward similar ends, locking each writer into his separate commitment to the war.

In Scott Fitzgerald's published work, the war does not loom large as a topic. In the tattered stack of my grandfather's letters, it comes up again and again. But the letter I would most like to see—I've dug around in the footlocker to find it—is most likely one never written: "Dear Kate, met a very interesting young man at the club today, an aspiring author from St. Paul, Minnesota . . . " And while I'm ready to imagine a connection, I'm not prepared to invent a correspondence. But I will invite Louis and Scott to the Fort Oglethorpe Officers Club for a final conversation.

The US Army in the early twentieth century still hewed in some respects to its British origins, and the club I envisage at Fort Oglethorpe would have been familiar to any subaltern of the Raj. In the long low room regimental honors hang from whitewashed walls and polished oak surfaces shine under the dim chandeliers. Negro servants, enlisted men in crisp white jackets, pass silently among the linen-covered tables, bearing platters of raw oysters and cracked crab, slabs of rare beef, dusty bottles of Burgundy, cold pitchers of beer. Scott is already at the bar, studying his second whiskey and soda, when Louis strides in, taking a moment to find his new friend in the cigarette haze.

"Lieutenant Fitzgerald."

"Lieutenant Crawford. What will you have?"

"A small bourbon would do."[3]

Scott signals for the bartender. When the fresh drinks arrive, he lifts his glass. "'Now God be thanked—'"

Louis nods somberly as he completes the toast. "'—Who has matched us with His hour—'"

They have talked about the poem before, Rupert Brooke's sonnet sequence "Peace," one of the best-known works of the war. But while Louis Crawford would have been fully in accord with the poet's vision, Scott Fitzgerald would have been armed by his sense of irony against it; indeed, in 1920 he will go so far as to draw on Brooke's verse to find an epigraph for *This Side of Paradise.*

They touch glasses, making the crystal chime.

My grandfather says, "So . . . what did you think of that captain on the pistol range today?"

---

3. It's vexing not to know whether my grandfather drank. But he soldiered in some pretty rough settings and lived at a time when hard drinking was the norm, so I feel comfortable pouring him a glass.

"Eisenhower? Not much."

"He's a West Pointer."

"Some of them are all right."

"He seems a little bleak."

Scott laughs. "Well, hell, he's stuck in Georgia in a training camp. Us, we'll win medals in France. There won't be much future in the army after the war for men who didn't get over. Not that I plan to stay in—no offense."

Louis shrugs. But the irony is bitter. He wants nothing more than to "stay in" as well as "get over," but this very day he's been ordered by a medical board to an upstate New York sanitarium to see whether some troubling health issues can be resolved. Scott, who is leaving in the morning for his next post, is unaware of this. But Louis knows it will be a struggle to convince the medicos he's fit to face poison gas.

The conversation turns to other things. To literary, not military, matters. Scott, suitably impressed by his companion's status as a published writer, presses him about his method, asks how he refines his sources, selects his material. The junior partner is mildly surprised that Louis has confined his fiction to tales of the Southwest and the Mexican border. After all—over the days at Oglethorpe they have learned a fair amount about each other— doesn't his colleague have his father's Civil War tales to draw on, as well as his own life of action in the Philippines, his American travels, his Philadelphia childhood, his tumultuous southern romance?

The questions aren't idle. Scott has made a start on a novel of his own, drawn from his Princeton experience. He's intensely focused on finding the alembic in which life is transmuted into fiction.

Louis's reply is uncertain. Though he has placed some stories, he doesn't really feel like a true professional. Most of the time, and certainly now, he's too involved in his life to step back and see it as material, and the protagonist of his unpublished novel is modeled so nearly on himself that little alteration can be said to have been made. Still, the subject is fruitful enough to carry them through another drink, after which the talk returns to the profession of arms, to the drills and fatigues they've endured, to the classes on tactics and war aims they've drowsed through, to the progress of the Allies and the probable evolution of the war. Matters less grand are touched on as well, Fitzgerald—a little drunk—confessing a lingering irritation:

"Can't believe they've retired dress blues for the duration," Scott grumbles, fingering the tight collar of his olive drab blouse.

"Well, it's a modern war," Louis consoles him. "Can't go over the top wearing finery."

"A fellow would cut a better figure in the club, though." The younger man sighs. "At least I had my kit made up at Brooks Brothers."

"My compliments to your tailor."

"One more?" Scott asks.

My grandfather glances at his watch and shakes his head. "Marching a platoon to the rifle range just after dawn. I'd better turn in."

Scott Fitzgerald nods. "Why don't wars have banker's hours?" He offers his hand. "Well, I've got my orders for Fort Sheridan. We'll meet again in France."

"Count on it."

"Good luck over there, Louis."

"And you, Scott."

"We'll have our next drink in Paris."

"Hell," my grandfather says, "Berlin."

REFLECTING ON their conversation, it's easy to imagine Fitzgerald's envy of the experience Lieutenant Crawford was already able to draw on. For Scott, life is material—if he survives the war, he might write the big novel about it.

Years later, innocent of combat service, it would still have been within the Princetonian's power to imagine convincing combat scenes but, wincing in Hemingway's shadow, he wouldn't have dared. Instead he offers an uncommon conjecture in *Tender Is the Night* in the form of a speech Dick Diver makes to the ingénue Rosemary Hoyt as he guides her across the rubble of one of the great battlefields of the war, entreating her to imagine "a whole empire walking very slowly, dying in front and pushing forward behind." In the novel, Fitzgerald understands the Great War as a conflict of ancient social certainties—he calls it, memorably, a "love battle," contrasting its conduct to the "mass butchery" of the War between the States. Crawford, whose father fought that war with grave elegance and died of his wounds, might have held a different view.

Like my grandfather, Fitzgerald was destined never to serve in France—it's small wonder that, when he took the war as a subject, he reduced it to an abstraction—but also like my grandfather, he retained an abiding interest in the Great War and its social consequences, writing with fine hauteur to Edmund Wilson in January 1917, "This insolent war has carried off [another friend] in France, as you may know, and really is beginning to irritate me—but the maudlin sentiment of most people is still the spear in my side."

I somehow doubt my grandfather would have compared himself to Christ, and his writings suggest he'd have been quicker to condone maudlin sentiment than condemn it, but the image of the war's ongoing waste would have seemed congenial, though he might have replaced Fitzgerald's irritation with a certain willingness to share in the slaughter that was, after all, said to be making the world safe for democracy, just as his father's war had kept America safe from a darker version of itself.

Scott Fitzgerald's writing rarely touches on the event that shaped his generation. There's a passing reference in *Gatsby* and that noted scene in *Tender Is the Night*. But the author fully encounters the theme only in a 1936 *Esquire* story, "I Didn't Get Over," an underdeveloped vignette in which four college friends of the class of 1916 meet for their twentieth reunion. When talk turns to wartime experiences, it develops that only three saw action, but the fourth, Hibbing, tells the tale of a stateside training accident that carries the consequences of combat ("Of course, that's nothing to what you fellows must have seen"), even as one of his classmates admits he spent his time in France as a prison guard. There are other twists to the story, but the multiplying ironies aren't enough to save Hibbing from his vague shame at having been on the "safe side of the ocean." As the biographer Arthur Mizener concludes, "Training camp was a hopelessly inadequate setting for the heroism Fitzgerald had imagined." Bold feats of arms would have to remain fantasies for the author, who finished his service stateside before his discharge in February 1919.

My grandfather's story has a different outcome.[4]

---

4. I can't leave this antic sidebar without an apology to two ghosts. In the fall of 1970, I had dinner with F. Scott Fitzgerald's daughter Scottie. In retrospect, I wish I'd been able to ask her if her father, reminiscing about his army days, had ever mentioned running into a dapper Yankee soldier from Philadelphia possessed of a flair for romantic prose. But at that time my grandfather's story still slept in the attic of the Hertford house. Scottie was good company, but my enchantment with Scott Fitzgerald's work led me to a curious act of which I've long been ashamed. The occasion on which Fitzgerald *fille* and I met was a literary dinner in Washington, DC. We both had new books out, mine a first novel about the army (like my twin subjects, I'd served in wartime but "didn't get over"), hers a memoir of her father, which she autographed to me. I was so awed to possess a signature so close to the royal blood that I took the book home, scissored out the inscription, and pasted it in my copy of *The Letters of*

When Fitzgerald left the army shortly after the armistice, Crawford was already serving at Kelly Field, and my imagined encounter between them no longer has space to expand. It is in any event no more than a small romance of my own. But the scenario seems entirely plausible, and I've permitted myself the pleasure of developing it because, like Lieutenants Fitzgerald and Crawford, I derive some part of my understanding of the world from the realms of unapologetic imagination.

Still, the story has taken us far afield, though to good purpose. At the least, it has both exemplified, and offered a reflection on, ways fact and fiction may travel in harmony; and picturing my grandfather in cocktail conversation with Francis Scott Key Fitzgerald has somehow made me feel I know him better. But the historical facts robbed both officers of their infantry dreams, and Lieutenant Crawford's next move opens onto a field of action he has never remotely considered.

CRAWFORD SOLDIERS hard at Fort Oglethorpe. His prior experience stands him in good stead. He gets high marks for his knowledge of tactics and strategy, for rifle and pistol marksmanship, for skill with the saber, for clarity and strength in troop command. But at the end of the course a routine physical detects a shadow on his lung and an army medical board sends him to recuperate at a spa in upstate New York. Though the furlough appears to restore his health, a second board confirms the findings of the first, denying him a combat assignment. In his diary, he records his "bitter disappointment." But though Lieutenant Crawford's stamina is too fragile to enable him to face poison gas, he is somehow able to convince his superiors he isn't too ill to stay in the army.

For he will not give up his dream of active service. He travels to the War Department in Washington, DC—perhaps there is a friend at court?—and comes away with a posting to the Signal Corps's newly formed aviation wing. "I was to be known as a Ground Officer," he writes. "I had never even thought of entering the Air Service before."

The end of the war seems in view, but perhaps there is still one last chance for him to find a path to the fighting.

F. Scott Fitzgerald as though Scottie's own work could be of no interest save insofar as it led to the temple of her father. Of course, I'd signed my book for her. I hope she threw it away.

ON NOVEMBER 26, 1917, Louis Crawford reports for duty as officer in charge of maintenance at Kelly Field, near San Antonio, Texas. The base, which had opened only the year before, would train most of the American fighter pilots who served in France, as well as many of the mechanics who supported their efforts. Lieutenant Crawford, still smarting at being sidelined from the war, nevertheless commits himself to his work, which soon grows to include duties such as salvage officer in charge of wrecked planes, officer commanding summary courts, and finally chief caretaker of Kelly Field's troop of carrier pigeons, clever birds with tiny tin cups under their wings who serve as the only means pilots aloft possess of contacting their base.

In May 1918, he is promoted to captain in recognition of his worth, but he frets over the routine nature of his chores. He is, after all, a man who has seen active service in the Philippines and on the border, and the passions of the Great War still run very high. On a trip to review a damage claim at Marfa, a west Texas town with a large German community, he rebukes a man for speaking the language, and one night at dinner with fellow officers, he hears a newsboy in the street hawking an extra with the cry "No armistice!" In his diary Crawford happily notes, "We celebrated." So I can easily envision the new captain—after months of salvage and maintenance work, staffing courts-martial, and tending to birds—standing one day at the edge of the field closely watching the fragile biplanes of a fledgling air force trudge down the rutted dirt runway with their sagging wings and shaking fabric before suddenly falconing into the sky and later that day writing in his diary, "I realized for the first time that it could be done."

He gets his chance. In August 1918, the army opens flight training to ground officers, and my grandfather applies at once.

He is not a natural pilot. His journal and his letters home document his struggles to master a startlingly new skill. But his competence is manifest, and his courage never in question. Once he notes, "I find that I do not ever think of the personal danger while flying, my chief thought being not to smash up the ship," and one of his instructors remarks, "Captain Crawford seems to disregard the ground." Then too, his grace on horseback would have contributed to his aerial intuition, and his training as a draftsman to his flair for mechanical things. Even so, the aircraft, and the air, are challenges.

He flies the Curtiss JN-4, the Jenny. It is a plane with a large place in aviation history. Fitted with skis, the JN-4 can land on ice; with pontoons,

on water. It sees service as an ambulance and an observation plane and can even be fitted out with guns: armed Jennies fly south with Pershing's punitive expedition into Mexico. But the aircraft's primary use is as a trainer, and virtually every American and Canadian pilot sent to the front will have spent the requisite time in the Jenny's dual cockpits.

Captain Crawford's hours in the plane prompt the most detailed writing to be found in his pages. It is as though he were replaying every moment of one flight in order to correct its faults in the next. And he's very self-critical, indicting himself not only for technical flaws but for matters of style: "Banked for the turn too close to the ground. No harm done, but bad form." His instructors say little, which causes anxiety, but they move him along in a steady progression of increasingly demanding tasks. Within a week of his first flight, his teacher will casually kick a plane into a spin at twenty-five hundred feet and wait for Louis to find his way out of it. "I did pretty well," he reports, "but I learned the danger of it, for on one trial I could not centralize my rudder soon enough and we got to revolving very rapidly and fell 1000 ft. before I could level the ship. On another one I tried to level before the spin had developed and actually kicked the ship over on its back. This had me guessing for some time before we described a half loop to come out."

"It's a lot of fun," he insists, then adds honestly, "when your instructor is along to give you nerve."

One of Louis's instructors, a Lieutenant Merrill, sets the fledgling pilot a series of stunts designed to increase his confidence. In the first, a power spiral, a steep bank throws the Jenny on its side, shifting the rudder and elevator positions. "It's hard to remember the change," Louis writes, "but if you make an error in your controls you are apt to go into a spin. I cut several of these spirals but found them very difficult."

He masters the difficulty and soldiers on, though each day presents its challenges. Some are contrived by the instructors, some by the sky itself.

I had a thriller in the air today—bumps like never before—with all controls held neutral, the ship would roll and toss just like a small boat in a high sea. You had to keep fighting it all the time to stay right side up. I have never worked so hard as I did. The air pockets were fierce. It's a queer sensation to drop fifty feet or shoot straight up, to feel the bottom of the ship drop out from under you.

And there is at least one moment of manifest danger when a new instructor, Lt. Ed Funck, twists the plane into an Immelman, and Captain Crawford experiences "an eclipse and a deluge," a stream of oil that sprays back across the fuselage and into both cockpits.

It completely blotted out the windshield and my goggles. I pulled them off and got a faceful of oil. . . . The ship, in the meantime, had dropped out of the loop and was volplaning [gliding without power] down. What happened was that the strain of the loop in the high wind had broken a feed pipe in the motor. If it had happened to me alone, I think I would have lost control before I discovered the trouble, because I was blinded for several seconds. The instructor was half-blinded, too. He pulled his goggles off and landed with one eye closed.

Temperamental aircraft, demanding teachers, muddy runways, and rough weather are not the only barriers standing between Louis and his coveted gold wings. Flying no more than an hour or two a day, he is expected to keep up with many of his regular duties, and his health continues to be fragile. He may indeed have been touched by an early instance of the postwar Spanish flu whose global epidemic slaughtered tens of millions worldwide and saw

Kelly Field quarantined on more than one occasion. Or the malaria he'd acquired in the tropics might have recurred. Or the illness that kept him out of the infantry. As usual, the letters and journals never specify the malady they occasionally mention.

But none of these things is as great a threat to his ambition as the calendar. On October 30, tells his diary, "I now have my back to the wall. The time allotted for dual instruction has expired. I must solo tomorrow."

On the next page, he begins to describe this elemental rite—at which point the silverfish have consumed most of the paper. The novelist in me can applaud this complication; the novice biographer is dismayed to lose the fine detail. But we know the ending. At the bottom of the page, a single word—"Celebrate!"—survives. And in the pile of photographs that litter the black leather trunk I find one of my grandfather, posed smiling beside his chief instructor, the left breast pocket of his tunic crowned with a pilot's wings.

This exultant snapshot is one of many. To it he will add a few dozen more. "I'm going to have my picture made for you in helmet and goggles," Louis writes Kate shortly before his solo, adding scornfully, "So many here are taken that way of men who never go near a plane."

He speaks of photography only the once but submits to the camera with disarming frequency. He's photogenic, and he knows it. A small, slender man with obsidian eyes, a strong jaw, and a generous mouth, he shows up like a film star in formal portraits, casual snapshots, and group poses—indeed, to admit a tempting anachronism, there is a considerable resemblance to the 1940s matinee idol Tyrone Power.

The folder of photographs even includes a comic tableaux vivant, in which Louis stands with two buddies beside a parked JN4, belly bloated with a pillow, portraying a fat Prussian foe, a tiny German helmet propped atop his head. This booty is "one of the 100,000 dress helmets made in Germany in 1915 for their triumphal entry into Paris," Captain Crawford notes on the back of the photograph. How such a sample of the spoils of war made its way to Texas, we aren't told. But I've held that helmet in my hands—part of the bounty of the attic of the Hertford house.

Other casual poses find him lounging with brother officers outside his quarters or standing proudly beside the post baseball team he managed. And there are multiple copies of the one he promised his wife, a head-and-shoulders portrait in goggles, helmet, and leather flying jacket—nothing is

Louis Crawford (at left), manager and coach of the
Kelly Field baseball team, 1918

missing but the white silk scarf. But the most dramatic shows my grandfather in the cockpit of his plane, turned toward the viewer with a reluctant smile, as though willing to grant his posterity only *this much* of a reflective pause before springing into action.

FLYING NOW BECOMES one of his regular duties, and one of his greatest delights. Small wonder. Captain Crawford enjoys a style of aviation largely unavailable in the present day. He rides an open cockpit, guided by a compass and a handmade map, following roads, railroad lines, and riverbeds. He knows the strength of his craft through the drumming of the sturdy motor and the treble notes of the wind. The wire, wood, and canvas feel alive to him, as well they might to any soldier whose prior beast of burden was a horse.

Ever alert to its dangers, Louis can find comedy and irony in powered flight as well. In a feature story for the Hertford *Herald*, he observes:

My favorite stunting ground is a couple of miles south of San Antonio, selected because there are several good fields available in case of trouble. One borders on the State Insane Asylum. Frequently in coming out of loops or Immelmans while hanging on my back for a second several thousand feet up with only a thin safety belt between me and the hereafter, I have imagined the inmates on the porch beckoning and saying: "Come on down, you qualify."

Here I was up in the air, alone above the clouds, a mile above the natural haunts of man, trying to fly a mechanical thing that had peculiar ideas of its own, and my only companion, a pigeon, designed by nature to fly, was strapped to the seat behind me.

Assigned his own plane, he names it for his wife: K8.

Meanwhile, his administrative work continues unabated, and as the war enters its final months, his frustration with being out of combat intensifies. On July 31, he writes: "The Germans fight hard and fight on. They will have to be annihilated to be beaten. I've read where they are using American uniforms to deceive our troops. Oh, for one crack at them! Give me a Lewis gun in the cockpit of a fast fighter plane and I know that I'd be satisfied with life."

Such satisfactions as he can take in his present circumstances are marred by rotten weather and failing health. In August he notes in his journal: "For a solid week we have had no flying . . . rain, rain, rain. I'm due for a routine physical tomorrow and dread the probable outcome. My eyes are swollen, I can't breathe or talk. I can't get seem to get warm. I'm flirting with the flu and feel miserable. I don't think I ever felt so miserable in my life before and the hard part is, there is no sign of a let up."

If Kate is unhappy with his saber-rattling, she can take comfort in the knowledge that Louis's condition makes it unlikely he'll be called on to draw his sword. "Tonight the adjutant's office is working overtime," he tells her on September 25, "making up personnel lists for two bombing squadrons to leave for England right away. Reckon you'll think that sounds ominous. But I'm not on the roster."

As the war struggles to its conclusion, a more practical question is Captain Crawford's place in retention and promotion files. He dreams of a major's gold leaf but is realistic about his prospects: "The officers I get along with have a habit of leaving. Our new CO is reluctant to recommend others for promotion to his own rank. Then, too, you know such promotions are now made in regular order from Washington except in exceptional cases." He has been told by several superiors that his *is* such a case, but their words seem somehow weightless.

From the day of his arrival at Kelly Field, Louis has kept up a steady stream of mail. His letters are usually sentimental, often patriotic, and occasionally pious. This can make them feel impersonal, as though they carried only the tone of the times. But they're never unconvincing. The earnestness and ardor that shines out of the photographs shows up in the prose, which is especially appealing when he lightens the tone with gossip: "More scandal here. Mrs. Cavendar has left her husband, with Mrs. Ewing, whom I think you knew (a very young-looking girl) named as correspondent. Also, Lieutenant Mills is implicated—he lives next door to me now—his wife's away. The Colonel has ordered the whole crowd to vacate the field in 48 hours. He won't stand for scandal at the post."

And Louis can be glumly funny, as when, briefly disheartened by slow progress in the air, he signs himself "Mud Lark," having been "Sky Lark" in the letter before. But his flair for drama sometimes causes him to strike a disconcerting note. Usually seeking to calm Kate's worries as to the dangers of his work, he will nevertheless write on one occasion, "Know, darling, that if I crash, I'll be thinking of you as I come spinning down." Having mastered a maneuver called the "falling leaf," he sketches a Jenny slip-sliding down the margin of one page. "It's a grand sensation—think of me cutting such a stunt 2,000 feet in the air!" Cheerfully but not altogether reassuringly, he adds, "If I keep at it, you'll have a real live flyer for a husband, or an angel."

Unsurprisingly, most of his mail is addressed to his wife. Of letters to his children, I have found only two. A postcard to his son William, postmarked Columbus, New Mexico, July 7, 1919, offers a sepia photograph of a mounted color guard passing down a dusty western street. The scrawled message is terse: "National and regimental standards of 12th Cavalry on parade July 4. Daddyman." But I expect my uncle was pleased. The card would present a stirring image and a manly greeting for a boy of five.

To his daughter Louise on January 30, 1919, the fond father writes a long description of his work with the carrier pigeons. The letter's tone is affectionate and lightly teasing. He admires a painting she's sent him and admonishes her "not to put the paints in your mouth." Then he introduces the child to a bird he's named for her, praising the creature's ability to "deliver a message faster than a letter, and sometimes faster than a telegram."

"The other day," the child's father confides, "Lieutenant Blakely flew 100 miles up country and sent me a message by Louise. He turned her loose at 10 am and the message was on my desk at noon." My mother is invited to join him in marveling at this avian technology, and I can picture her delight at learning the straightforward way the pigeons are summoned to their chores. "When they're all out flying and we want the call them in, we rattle an old tomato can filled with pebbles and they come straight home." The bird Louise, he tells his daughter in conclusion, "after carrying the message to me laid a little egg to celebrate the occasion. I have the egg for you if Blakely don't eat it." The event reminds Crawford that the army isn't always clear as to the gender of its winged messengers. "You may remember George—the government sent him here listed as a rooster, but every now and then he lays an egg. This puzzles all of us, as of course the government can't be wrong." A lengthy description of the construction of the pigeon coops need not detain us; it adds little to the meticulous drawing that forms the letter's postscript. But the letter itself is more than a kind gesture to a waiting child—the sheaf of pages tells readers a fair amount about the army's management of its carrier pigeon corps.

Twelve days later, Louis receives in reply a valentine for which Kate has composed a photograph. She has evidently been experimenting with the androgynous beauty of her children, as her husband's response acknowledges. "Billy makes a dandy girl and Louise a fine boy." While it might seem tempting to read some psychological quirk into this performance, the custom of the day kept boys in dresses at least until the age of three, and there was a sense of relaxation about gender in early childhood that was about to vanish into a century of Freudian anxiety. It seems to me my grandparents are to be commended for their playful spirit, though I must say I wish my mother were alive so I could ask whether she remembered the occasion and if so how she might have understood it.

Though Louis's wife is the main recipient of his surviving letters, she is not quite the only one. In addition to the several pages to his daughter and the postcard to his son, I find a message to the sixth graders of the Hertford grammar school that had been part of his realm as superintendent. Written less than a week after the armistice, it naturally seeks to draw lessons from the war. "Just think what the American soldiers have done," he reminds the children. "Men, who a year ago were clerking in stores, working on farms and going to school have defeated an army that has been in training for years, and what makes it all the more glorious is that the Germans had victory in their grasp when the Americans started."

As a pilot, he is quick to pay special attention to the achievements of the Air Service, in whose valor he sees the stuff of Arthurian legend:

> The airmen on both sides had a great deal of respect for each other because they observed the rules of war. When a ship got out of control, they stopped shooting at it so the pilot would have a chance to save his life. Whenever we brought down a German flyer, our planes flew over next day and dropped flowers on the crash site. And the German flyers buried young Roosevelt with full honors after they shot him down. The reason for this fellow feeling is that air combat is single-handed fighting—man to man—and that brings out the best there is in a man.

If there's rank sentimentality here there is some truth as well, and a reminder that to the end of his days my grandfather understood single combat as the final test of manhood. The daily sight of his father's saber on the wall had left its mark.

It's understandable that, in writing to American schoolchildren, he celebrates American feats of arms, but the letter does seem tacitly to claim that the United States, late to the party, had engineered a single-handed victory over the Boche. Such would not have been my grandfather's considered view. Proud of his Scots heritage and a thoughtful student of the European war, he was saturated with British patriotic poetry, if we may trust the evidence of a much-worn anthology I found in the black leather trunk. He quotes Kipling's "If" in full at the beginning of one of his letters and seems to have been fond of a passage in A. E. Housman's *A Shropshire Lad* that speaks to a subject close to his heart, the passing of the sword between father and son.

> Oh, God will save her, fear you not:
> Be you the men you've been,
> Get you the sons your fathers got,
> And God will save the Queen.

Above all, he would have endorsed the wild sentiment of Brooke's sonnet "Peace," published in 1914.

Now, God be thanked who has matched us with his hour,
And caught our youth, and wakened us from sleeping!
With hand made sure, clear eye, and sharpened power,
To turn, as swimmers into cleanness leaping

For untried troops and sentimental civilians, the first year of the war might just support the majestic tread of these familiar lines. But the "cleanness" these swimmers were leaping into was Verdun, Passchendale, and the Somme. Present-day readers will look with a kind of horrified awe at an imagination capable of seeing, in the vile mire of the trenches, the crystal waters of a healing stream. My grandfather, however, would have been fully in accord with the poem's vision. From Kelly Field, he muses in the long letter to Kate referenced earlier, "Somehow, dear, I look on this war, with its attendant risks and troubles, as a great test, a readjustment of the world. All of the old sham and false glitter seems to be gone."

Still, he is more apt to summarize events than ponder their meanings. On October 21, he writes:

We are following the news very closely about the American drive in France. Today it seems the Germans are delivering a counterblow. Their position looks bad but they continue to fight with unreasonable fury. I don't know how long it will take to bring them to their knees. They are being driven out of Belgium in rapid order, and their retreat is almost a rout. But they may make a strong stand when they reach German soil.

I can see him papering his office with maps of the battlefront and tracking the positions of the armies with colored pins and bits of ribbon. His war may lie in training other men to fight, but a steady professionalism draws him to the study of strategic detail. And he never altogether gives up hope of a combat assignment until November 11, when the guns are stilled.

AFTER THE ARMISTICE, the cadre, crews, and trainee pilots at Kelly Field are not spared the radical reductions in force that sweep the services. Nearly a quarter of a million men have gone through the base during the war; the number stationed there now shrinks to ten thousand. Countless aircraft are surplussed, forming the spine of civil aviation in the postwar barn-storming years. But while many bases close, Kelly Field remains open, though it cannot support its wartime staff. My grandfather must have considered his own position relatively safe—he'd been recommended for promotion to major and transfer to the regular army toward the end of the war. But Headquarters Southern Command determines his unit to be over strength, and in the chaos of paperwork that follows his name appears mistakenly—this, admittedly, is Louis's account—on the list of those to be discharged. The collapse of his career must have stirred the ghost of past failures, but he has never before called it quits with the army and he won't go without a struggle now.

He holds an ace, but it is Kate who plays it, quite possibly without her husband's knowledge or consent. Louis's sister Florence had married the brother of Gen. Peyton March, Army chief of staff, and Kate solicits this remote relation on her husband's behalf, begging him to ask March to intervene. The brother is amenable, and writes the general on November 26, 1919, supplying my grandmother a copy of his letter, which runs in part:

> I wish very greatly you would interest yourself in the case. Captain Crawford has been from boyhood tremendously anxious to be a soldier. He enlisted in 1900 at the age of 16 and seems to have won steady promotions and to have all sorts of good letters from his commanders. He has been dropped from the retention list by what appears to have been pure accident and everybody connected with him is eager to see him back.

The younger March notes that Mrs. Crawford "insists she is not asking for special favors," though the claim is difficult to reconcile with her bold request; at all events, the chief of staff apparently found it inappropriate to intervene.

Even so, Captain Crawford manages to keep bars on his shoulders. Expecting to become a major of aviation, he accepts appointment as a lieutenant of cavalry, and finds himself in command of a troop stationed in Columbus, New Mexico, the border town Pancho Villa had raided four years before while Louis was enduring one of his occasional periods of exile from the service. His old outfit, the 13th Cavalry, had taken the shock of the raid and he had to watch from the sidelines as his comrades crossed the border with Pershing's "punitive expedition," losing two troopers at the Battle of Panal. He's more than content to be in the West again but his service in New Mexico is interrupted in October 1920, when he is ordered to the Cavalry School at Fort Riley, Kansas, for additional training.

Whatever his thoughts about the contingencies that continue to deform his prospects, Louis Crawford is happy to be working once more with army horses, the beasts upon whose backs his career began. "I like the mounted periods best when the horses are good," he confides from Fort Riley on November 16. "This afternoon I rode Jim for two hours and led Kino for exercise. I was anxious to take the kick out of him. Kino behaved beautifully and I complimented him so much Jim got jealous."

This pastoral is not destined to last. A week later, a brother officer will be thrown by a rank mustang and hospitalized with a shattered skull. "Last night they tied the outlaw in with Jim," Crawford writes, "and he kicked my horse so bad that Jim is now in the hospital himself. To make things harder, the major assigned *me* the outlaw. My beautiful Jim Horse is crippled and I have to ride the wall-eyed goat that did it." To these hammer blows is added an increasingly painful congestion in his throat. "I can't get near the damn animal," he laments, "and I can't go on sick report to have my throat treated because they'll think I'm afraid of the horse."

A concern for his reputation is never far from my grandfather's mind, and this is not the first time he has made a reckless choice in order to protect it. "My back's against the wall," he confides to his worried wife. "Got to go on my damn guts again and it gets tiresome. But I'll ride the piebald son of a bitch or make him ride me." The vow gives way to a transient moment of despair. "When in God's name will something go the right way with me? My morale is about zero."

This defeated note is rare in his letters. Louis Crawford's usual response to his troubles is to soldier on. But his illness is beginning to undermine him. He may suspect that even if he survives it, his career will not. Still, he manages to turn in a credible performance of his duties throughout the rest of the year and well into the next, but by the end of March 1921, there is no way of concealing his debility. The Fort Riley doctors consign him to Fitzsimmons General Hospital in Denver, where he rallies briefly, writing to Kate on March 29, "I think I'm getting on the winning side of the fight now, though the doctors say it will be a slow one."

Still, he is realistic about his prospects. "Where do you think we should relocate if I can't stay in the army? I might want to get in the mountains or go back west. Seems like swamps won't be much good to me."

Swamps.

Hertford.

Restless under hospital discipline, he finds his bedridden state distasteful, but it does give him the chance to let his mind, ordinarily curbed by the myriad details of duty, drift into a reverie. His thoughts touch on religion, with greater modesty than they had possessed when years before he railed against his domestic conditions and the civilian world. "It has come to me that the ultimate cure will come through faith in God. Somewhere in the haze of things I see Him distinctly but can't grasp the full faith . . . Well, we won't talk any more of the dark side."

With or without faith, no cure is forthcoming. His plight deepens. The doctors are down to providing such comfort as they can. On April 7, my grandfather manages a final letter:

> Not able to write often as I still feel pretty weak. Can't say much of my condition and don't like to. Also learned today that this means almost sure retirement. The diagnosis is enough. Take best care of yourself. Don't worry or grieve. Remember I love you. Too tired to write more. Love to the babies. God bless you.
>
>   Your own Lou

Louis Crawford died on April 9, 1921. He was thirty-seven years old. From *The Rasp*, a yearbook published at Fort Riley, Kansas:

> During the months he spent at Fort Riley, even during the early stages of his illness, when he was severely handicapped by his physical condition, he struggled to keep up his work at The Cavalry School. The news of his illness and death came as a distinct shock to all his classmates. His loyalty to the Service was but one of the many characteristics that drew respect and deep friendship from those around him.

The hospital would have given the cause of death. *The Rasp* does not. And its reporter seems unable to settle on the duration of my grandfather's illness, calling it "very brief" in one paragraph, and referring to its "early stages" in another.

The Rasp is not alone in its circumspection. Over the years, Louis Crawford's correspondence has made occasional mention of a chronic illness without ever giving it a name. The danger is apparent. Discussing plans with Kate in July 1916, he adds "if I live," suggesting his condition is understood between them and needs no further comment. Even his last letters from the Denver hospital, whether hopeful or resigned, couch his affliction in vague terms. "The doctors sound my lungs occasionally and I suppose have found some trouble, but not much." It is as though he does not want to give his illness a name for fear of giving it a home.

His service record unlocks the mystery: the upstate New York town where my grandfather rested between medical boards in 1917 was Saranac Lake, home to the most famous tuberculosis sanitarium in North America. Louis Crawford had been living for years with the most feared disease of the day: widespread, contagious, much feared, always dangerous, often mortal, and suffused in the public mind with both romantic fantasy and repugnant dread. Dealing with its recurrent assaults during the last months of his life, Lieutenant Crawford may have been called on to find as much courage as he would have needed on those European battlefields he'd dreamed of, and been denied.

I FOLDED my grandfather's last letter and laid it back in the trunk with the others.

In the end, his correspondence could not be called comprehensive: apart from the flood of mail from Kelly Field, I had learned most from the long, impassioned letter of July 1916. The lighthearted note to his daughter, the terse message to his son, and the patriotic appeal to his students were largely footnotes to his story, though they did illustrate his paternal side. Larger revelations came through other treasures, especially from his brief but fertile journal from the Philippines, from the concise family history and personal fragments he had laid down for his children, and, above all, in the text of *Viva, Madero!*, which I was increasingly convinced provided a shadow autobiography of whose confessional nature its author had remained largely unaware. Other icons—his boots and spurs, his officer's dress sword, the box of lead soldiers that foreshadowed his future—told their tales as well.

Then there were the photographs. And over the weeks I worked on his story, I was even able to explain the things in the trunk that had at first puzzled or mislead me. The German pistol, the semiautomatic Mauser, I now knew, had not found its way to Hertford from a European battlefield; it was a weapon in common use by *ladrones* on Luzon and by both rebels and *federales* in Mexico. He might have found it after any firefight. The holster wasn't army issue, but part of an Arizona cowboy's gear, a stock item from Sears, Roebuck hand-tooled by its original owner with the brands of the ranches he had worked for. Louis had doubtless picked it up in Clifton as a souvenir. The engraved artillery shell was a fascinating example of trench art, embossed with the Cross of Lorraine—it *had* come from France, perhaps sent to Texas by a comrade in the American Expeditionary Force. The most arresting artifact was the drawing, an original sketch in pencil and white chalk on brown cardboard depicting an intimate battle scene of the Philippine war, which proved to be the work of Gordon Grant, a prominent illustrator of the day who had served as a combat artist for *Harper's Weekly.* How the drawing came into my grandfather's hands I don't know. He paid thirty dollars for it.

All these things went into Louis Crawford's story. Did they tell me who he was? I could never be certain but I thought I could rest content with what I had learned.

WHEN I WAS a child, I knew my grandfather through the photographs and artifacts in the hallway of my grandmother's house, through a box of toy soldiers, and through my mother's affectionate memories and her mother's rare reminiscences. He was a myth, a shadow, an unfinished sketch I could complete with any colors I liked. Inevitably, I made him into a towering emblem of warrior romance. He returns to me now as a less-imposing figure but a far more appealing one, a man whose urgent quest for self-definition threw him into wildly varied pursuits, to all of which he brought an unstudied élan. He found modest success as a technician, as a journalist, as a fiction writer, even as a kind of rural academic bureaucrat.

But the army was his life.

It seems to me that his hunger for service stands unsurpassed. If he couldn't enlist at fourteen, he'd manage it two years later. If he couldn't go off to war at once, he'd wait until a war came calling. If he couldn't be an officer, he'd be an NCO—if not a sergeant, then a corporal. Commissioned, he wore captain's bars and expected his majority, but offered a lieutenant's job, he'd take it rather than resign. If not cavalry, then infantry. If not infantry, then Air Service. If not Air Service, then cavalry again. He wanted combat but would agree to a desk job, wanted to be a regular but would accept appointment to the reserves, wanted the army but would bide his time in the National Guard. He could ride a horse or shoe one, fly a plane or fix it, draw a sword or raise a rifle, lead or follow, command or obey. He seems to have been something close to every shape of a soldier, though his career kept falling into fragments and his ambitions were thwarted first by circumstance and finally by failing health.

No paragon, he came to remind me of Saul Bellow's Henderson, a man of fundamental decency beset by a passion for experience that often outran his capacity for judgment. His somewhat chaotic civilian vocations parallel the hectic drama of his military career. He adored his wife but may never have made peace with her family, and he certainly never understood his marriage except in the most conventional terms. He was an awed but uncritical son, a loving but often absent father. And he wasn't altogether free of bitterness as he pondered the shape of a life that may well have disappointed him. He had hoped to match his father's legacy. Instead, though he never knew it, he did something more. He created his own.

He was a sentimental man, a welcome quality in that it served to temper the stern imperatives of the received American masculinity of his day. And despite his devotion to the army, I can't altogether see him as a warlike one. Beyond doubt, he yearned for the test of battle. His father's life seemed to ask no less. But the stories I've heard, the letters and journals I've read, and the photographs I've studied are suffused with a grace and good humor that form no part of the makeup of a bellicose personality. A taste for military pageantry, a sense of family pride, and a foundational honor linked to buoyant patriotism—these things drove him. Many a good life has been built on less.

But I don't want to take leave of Louis Crawford on the sweat-soaked sheets of his deathbed. It's no place for a soldier. Instead, I admit imagination for a final time, envisioning his last day at Kelly Field, and I risk the move for the largest possible reason: to give my grandfather his meaning, his purpose, his destiny, his due—his telos: not his ending, but his end.

So . . . I see him standing by the flight line in flying boots and leather jacket, helmet and goggles, pulling on a pair of supple deerskin gloves. For the last time, he studies the beautiful ships that are no longer his, war birds that have housed his hopes. Then he strides toward the shabby hut where flight schedules are maintained and tells the sergeant in charge he wants a plane—*his* plane, K-8. The noncom hesitates—he has no orders concerning this unauthorized flight—until my grandfather, normally genial with enlisted men, favors him with a cold stare that elicits quick obedience.

Captain Crawford straps himself into the familiar Jenny, its seat shaped to his slender body, its stick alive to his touch. He signals for a spin of the prop. The engine coughs and catches. The pilot opens the throttle gently, feeling each rock in the rutted runway as the plane begins to move toward the low blue hills at the far end of the field. Buildings flow past, hangers, barracks, the machine shops, a water tower. He sees troop columns on the move, brother officers sauntering, a few hands raised in greeting. He salutes loosely in return. More power. Wind fills the wings as the Jenny lifts. Captain Crawford climbs, banks, heads west. He has no flight plan other than a dream of altitude.

THE FINAL SEAL

Colonel William Crawford and the Battle for the Philippines

It doesn't matter how tall a man's father is. He's got to do his own growing.
—Irish Saying

WHEN THE ATTACK BEGAN, Lt. Col. William Crawford was standing outside his tent eating an ice cream cone.

He watched the approaching planes without much interest. They were obviously American C-47 transports, holding a tight formation though flying strangely low. Yellow puffs trailed after them—fading bursts of anti-aircraft fire, some trigger-happy navy gunner shooting at his own side. It happened.

As he watched, the puffs took on strange definition. Figures swayed below them, like men clinging to clouds. For a long moment, the colonel's mind refused what he was seeing. For days, intelligence had been picking up radio traffic hinting at a large move by the Japanese, but this was breathtaking—an airborne assault on the division's base camp.

Bill Crawford admired the precision of the paratroopers' exits, the orderly way the sticks tumbled free of the planes. He could see the small men dangling from the billowing silk, working the risers as they waited for impact. And he understood with complete clarity that within five minutes he would be in sustained close combat with the best soldiers in the Imperial Army of Japan. The falling men would draw him into a zone as personal and intimate as love. Later he would say it was the only time in the war that he ever felt fear.

During his weeks in the Philippines Crawford had witnessed a good deal of the war, though usually at a certain remove that caused him to say in one letter home that it was much like a movie—"in color, with good sound effects." From the beach he had seen kamikazes slipping down the

sky like thrown darts to embed themselves in navy ships in the harbor. He had watched Zeros and Corsairs braiding invisible tapestries around each other until one tumbled toward the ocean on a rug of flame. He sometimes sketched these striking images in a notebook he carried always. Though untrained, he had a steady hand and eye, and enjoyed keeping a graphic record as others might have kept a diary. In the jungle, he had tracked tracer rounds probing enemy positions, and had heard the rattle and snap of rifle and machine gun fire boxing the compass, since the war was happening on all sides. Once, cutting his way through heavy bush with a short machete, he had come across the rotting corpses of an American soldier and a Japanese marine linked by their plunging knives in a tangle of limbs. It was an image he found hard to shake, though you were always in the presence of the dead.

But this was different. For weeks, the war had been on his doorstep. Now it was through the door.

But he was goddamned if he would let a pox of Oriental infantry rob him of the pleasure he was taking in his ice cream cone.

He was finishing it when a young lieutenant trotted up, a butterbar named Gray, probably not twenty yet, one of the L-4 pilots. The boy clenched the stub of a thick cigar in one corner of his mouth. He was carrying a Thompson submachine gun with a drum clip at port arms. His eyes were poisonous and his eager grin had been stolen from a wolf.

Crawford smiled. "Eddie, you look like a gangster."

"Got to find our clerks and cooks, sir. Here's where they earn badge pay. Where do you want us?"

Bill Crawford hesitated. There were plans in place for dealing with infiltrators but nobody had anticipated an assault on this scale. Reaction forces would have to be improvised wherever there was a salient. Mostly the Japs would be scattered but Crawford had seen one stick land in a group behind the mess hall. "Send everybody you find down there. Tin pots, standard loads—no, all the ammo they can carry."

"On my way, Colonel."

The young officer was staring at Bill Crawford with open awe. The ice cream cone. Then he sketched a salute and took off.

Back in the tent, Crawford gently placed the remnants on the corner of a map table; a trickle of vanilla bled into the white reaches of the map, staining an image of the island he was fighting for. The colonel switched his Swing cap for a steel pot and buckled on a web belt hung with his canteen, first aid kit, Colt .45, and M3 trench knife, a six-inch dagger with a needle tip and razor edges on either side of the matte black blade. He had found the knife a bit theatrical at first since he didn't plan to fight a modern war with a weapon from the Middle Ages. Then he had seen men coming in from the field carefully wiping blood from their knives before sliding them back into the scabbards.

Armed, he turned toward the pale light pouring into the tent through the open fly. The drone of the engines was fading—the Japanese were on the ground. He heard the crump of a grenade and the stutter of small-arms fire. Headquarters was beginning to give an account of itself. Hoarse cries, boots pounding.

Something strange happened. He felt as though his own boots were mired in the tent's mud floor. His arms felt heavy, too, as though his hands held an unseen burden. For a moment, walking through the tent was like leaning against a wall of water. He kept going. The moment passed. By the time he stepped outside, he felt light, agile, clearheaded, full of power. He racked a round into his carbine and turned toward the sound of the battle.

The butterbar with the cigar and the Thompson gun lay on the ground fifty feet down the path, his body like a shattered statue's dragged through a pond of blood. The lieutenant was motionless, beyond doubt dead, so the colonel let his path be blocked by a sergeant he recognized, a man from the motor pool, a slight figure in soiled khaki trousers and a brilliantly white T-shirt whose spectacular cleanness seemed unreal. The sergeant was wild-eyed, but, Colonel Crawford thought, just short of hysteria. He held a Garand rifle loosely in his right hand, far away from his body, as though he wanted to give it to someone.

"Jesus, Colonel, there's Japs all over the area!"

If panic was contagious, so might sangfroid be. The G4 put a steadying hand on the man's shoulder and gave him a hard Hollywood smile. Two guys on a hunting trip. "Well," the young colonel said, "maybe you'd better lock and load."[5]

BILLY CRAWFORD was born September 6, 1914, in Hertford, North Carolina. He grew up in the house where I spent my childhood summers, the old house on the river where his father, Louis, settled to commence his marriage and consider his civilian career. Given Kate Crawford's penchant for salvaging every scrap of paper her son's life threw off, the boy's early years

5. The language feels right but may be an anachronism. There's no certainty that the phrase "lock and load" was current during the Second World War. John Wayne uses it in *Sands of Iwo Jima*, which is set in 1945 but was made in 1949. On the other hand, one version of the order—"load and lock"—could date to the Revolution and its flintlock muskets. It's still not an "official" military command, though I heard it often enough on the rifle range during basic training at Fort Dix in the fall of 1966—"on the firing line, lock and load one 12-round magazine." And by now it has gone into civilian discourse as a way of preparing the hearer for just about any kind of heavy action.

seem to have left surprisingly few traces, freeing us to imagine a rural idyll shaped by his mother's doting and his father's drive. There were fields and forests to wander, the river and swamps to explore, and the pleasant poky little town itself (a *New York Times* reporter once called Hertford "a place as comfortable as an old dog asleep on a porch") where Billy would have gone to school, played sandlot ball, met his friends for Cokes at the soda fountain, flirted with the girls, and paused in any of these pleasures when- ever a motor's drone above the horizon signaled the approach of a plane, some ragged barnstormer crisscrossing the country to offer access to the heavens for a dollar a ride. For just as his father had grown up in the shadow of William Harvey Crawford's sword, this boy's proudest possession was Louis Crawford's silver wings.

Early on, Billy showed a mechanical flair. At five he was tinkering together models that by fifteen would become plans for planes. Louis encouraged his son in his passion. Kate, who steadily held before the boy a mirror that reflected a young prince, would have been happier with a hobby that offered a smaller element of risk. Louise kept her doubts to herself. Kate and Louise had to anchor the boy in an everyday world, as Louis's military calling often took him from the family home, and he died when Billy was seven.

It is not altogether a formula for a happy childhood, but I think he had one. The old house would have welcomed him with its magical spaces and stories, just as it did me thirty years on. And his family would have enjoyed a protective prominence in the little town, his father for his military bearing and exotic origins—a Philadelphian!—and his mother for her family's cen- turies-old plantation sovereignty in the Albemarle.

I also have the sense that that childhood was largely solitary, by Billy's wishes. Handsome, athletic, and social when he chose to be, my uncle would have had no difficulty becoming the center of a circle of friends, though he was indifferent to hunting, one of the chief pleasures of the region, deer, waterfowl, even black bear being plentiful. Louis didn't hunt so Billy didn't either. Indeed, he disliked guns. But when I look at his later life, where the record is much fuller, I find a repeated note of stoic isolation that can only have developed out of a temperament established early on.

The summer I was fourteen, while conducting one of my annual explora- tions of the attic of the Hertford house, I came across a copy of the Septem- ber 1929 issue of a magazine called *Aero Digest*, a thick yellowing pulp filled with vivid color advertising, technical articles, industry notes, profiles of

pilots, and pictures of planes—and a letters page, where I was stopped by a photograph of a pensive Billy Crawford, who looked about my age and who appeared to be sporting his father's fleece-lined flying jacket, leather helmet, and goggles. Billy's letter, addressed to "Uncle Cy," takes up much of the page with its account of some of the boy's adventures as a fan of powered flight, a model maker ("my sister sat on a de Havilland and crushed it"), and a veteran of a few short rides in a war surplus Jenny over the Carolina cotton fields. I carried *Aero Digest* downstairs to show the crusher of de Havillands the letter and photograph and ask who Uncle Cy might be.

"Oh, God," my mother said. "A very odd man your uncle somehow got mixed up with. Your grandma Kate let Billy go up to New York to spend some weeks with him, but it didn't end well."

"Why?"

"I'm really not sure." Louise studied the photograph fondly, then handed *Aero Digest* back to me. "The trip wasn't wasted. Before he came home, Billy was able to spend a day at West Point. After that, he had his heart set on becoming a cadet." She paused. "I think Daddy always wished he'd gone there himself. I know he wanted it for Bill."

That brief exchange could have been the end of Cy Caldwell's potent

place in my uncle's story had I not uncovered several more documents more than fifty years later, including a handful of letters between the man and the boy written before their ill-starred meeting, and an illustrated journal Billy Crawford kept of his New York trip. These told me much. But what proved invaluable was a long, strange, abrasive letter from Cy Caldwell to Kate Crawford about the boy's visit. In that thick sheaf of typed pages, I surely met "a very odd man." But it took a bit of digging to get the measure of Cy Caldwell.

The years between the two world wars have been called the golden age of aviation. Rapid developments in motors, metallurgy, and airframes made the sky hum with eccentricity, genius, glory. Experimental planes dangled from the clouds like Christmas baubles as civil aviation and strategic bombers found their champions. The cast of characters composed a pantheon of the brave, the brilliant, and the deeply strange. At its summit, Charles Lindbergh and Amelia Earhart possessed of a fame—social media be damned—unimaginable today.

Their supporting players were no less vivid. Wiley Post, who died with Will Rogers in a crash in Alaska. Colonel Roscoe Turner, who set speed records with a lion cub in his lap. Wrong-Way Corrigan, who landed in Ireland looking for Long Beach, California.

Howard Hughes.

Their stories captivated Billy Crawford, who had long dreamed of following his father into the air. We can't wonder that he rejoiced in his initial contact with Cy Caldwell, whose name belongs on the notables list. A minor luminary in an era when aviators enjoyed the celebrity today accorded only to pop stars or pro athletes, Caldwell was the kind of emblematic figure John Dos Passos might have profiled in *USA*. And Billy happened on the flyer at the peak of his fame.

Born in Nova Scotia in 1892, Caldwell taught himself to fly in 1915 and led bombing raids over Germany as a captain in the Royal Flying Corps. After the armistice he returned to Canada as a pioneer in new techniques of fighting wildfires from the air. In 1922, he arrived in America as a test pilot and salesman for the Glenn Martin Company and began to write for aviation magazines. At least one version of his story has him making, rather by chance, the first flight of what would become Pan American Airways, a mail run from Key West to Havana. He also found time to toy with a career as novelist, drama critic, and playwright, while staying in the news as a participant in air shows, speed trials, and distance races. On one occasion, he emerged as something of a hero, rescuing several people from the Lake Erie crash of a commercial amphibian, a craft equipped to land on water or land. On another, he earned renown for leading a fruitless search for French transatlantic flyers lost over Newfoundland.

Despite his prominence as an aviator, Caldwell seems to have concluded that tamer pursuits offered a better path to fame and fortune, and he turned his attention to the popular press of his day. His books included a melodramatic novel about a Caribbean revolution, a life of Henry Ford, and a study of airpower produced early in the Second World War.

Throughout the 1920s, Cy Caldwell wrote a regular column for *Aero Digest*, to which Billy Crawford was a loyal subscriber—stacks of the old magazine crowded a shelf in the attic. On July 6, 1929, the boy introduced himself in a letter whose jubilant claims caught the journalist's attention: "I've been studying correspondence courses and anything I can find anywhere about airplanes. I've been writing an editorial column for a newspaper. I've built six radios and a scale model of a de Havilland, but my sister sat on it and wrecked it. I am working on an invention for changing motors in the air, and I've written Mr. Edison some of my ideas."

These claims sound wildly inflated, but I found evidence confirming most of them, including a telegram from Thomas Edison expressing polite interest in a young boy's project. As to his claim to build radios: vacuum tubes, capacitors, wires, and knobs crowded a dusty wooden crate of parts. And I'd seen files of Billy's chirpy contributions to the local press. As to the correspondence courses, aviation instruction was only part of the loot that must have tumbled daily through the Front Street door. Leaflets, pamphlets, booklets, and brochures on barbells, bodybuilding, X-ray waves, piano playing, shop tools, salesmanship, survival gardening, and the secrets of the ancients were just part of his regular reading. The 1920s was a great age for mail-order instruction, and to an active boy in an isolated town it must have seemed miraculous that a three-cent stamp could bring such manna.

"There is a flying boat factory near Hertford," Billy Crawford's letter concluded, "and an airfield will open here as soon as the watermelons now growing on the land are sold."

Caldwell was intrigued. In reply, he praised the boy for "writing like a grown-up" (on other occasions he would contradict this view) and showing a good deal of knowledge, especially of aviation, adding: "At first I imagined you were a pilot yourself." Billy accepted the accolade with a certain complacency. "I wrote the Wright Aeronautical Corp with some questions on mechanics. They thought I was a grease monkey and sent me the installation blueprints for a J-5 motor." Caldwell then pulled back a little—this self-confident kid is verging on cockiness. "You have rotten penmanship, Bill," he chided, apparently unaware that he himself wrote a sprawling, nearly indecipherable hand.

Such censure did not ruffle Billy at all—he thrived on attention, noting that where his projects were concerned, his mother was usually too busy and his little sister too bored. The boy included in his next letter clippings of brief comic squibs he had contributed to a local paper. Caldwell relented. "Billy, you're a writer and a damned good one. And you're my kind of kid. I *like* you." The boy returned the compliments—he'll model his own writing on Cy's. Indeed, in his range of interests and activities, with aviation always at their center, Billy might seem a carbon copy of his mentor; but when he expresses admiration for the older man's varied and active life, Cy backs off again. "Getting old and tired. Life is no longer an adventure. I've been an adventurer for twenty-three years, but the end of the trail is in sight. I kind of like you, Billy," he repeats.

Contemporary readers might be too quick to find a sinister motive in Cy Caldwell's share of this exchange. I gave some thought to the possibility, especially after reading Caldwell's angry denunciation of Billy following the fifteen year old's visit to New York in 1930. Yet there's no convincing evidence of anything illicit—to make the charge is to read our times into theirs. There's no convincing evidence of illicit passion, while there *is* reason to believe that Caldwell's influence—pompous, abrasive, and self-important as the man could be—helped shape the boy's character, if only by giving it a wall to hurl itself against.

But Cy Caldwell's praise for Bill Crawford's writing gave me pause, as did his suggestion that journalism might be a sounder career choice than aviation. Though Caldwell himself had known some success at both, Billy's gifts seemed to me clearly technical and mechanical, and his juvenile prose struck me as labored, especially the attempts at humor, something Caldwell had singled out for praise.

From their frequent correspondence an affinity grew, and in June 1930, the aviator invited Billy Crawford to visit him for an extended stay at his home in Island Park, New York, a Long Island town that by the 1920s had become a popular place for New Yorkers seeking summer houses. Proximity to Manhattan, the beach, and the Valley Stream airport commended it to Cy Caldwell, by then an American citizen. He made his base there, overseeing enterprises prosperous enough to enable him to maintain an office on West 42nd Street, where he became "Cy Caldwell, Incorporated." Billy Crawford bounced back and forth between these spots during his visit, experiencing urban life as well as the chance to fish, fly, sail, and swim.

To Billy, Cy's invitation must have looked like an opening to a world he had only dreamed of—the world of the city, the crowded sky, the society of airmen. We can't know what family debates took place in that summer before Kate Crawford approved her son's adventure. But on June 26, the boy departed for New York on the Norfolk steamer, and on the same day he began a journal he would keep faithfully until his return.

Along with his pistol, his paratrooper's knife, his jump wings, and the other relics of my uncle's later life, I found that journal in the aluminum trunk. Reading it was an intimate experience. The words shaped a voice from Billy Crawford's adolescence, a voice chatty and cheerful and yet somehow guarded. It gave me some of the feeling I got again while working through his letters from the war. He seemed informed, observant, engaged with the life around him, but there were intimations of a shadow text, the unwritten account of an unspoken story. Each page lay covered in large block pencil letters, the lines woven throughout with cartoonish illustrations, almost as though he were attempting in 1930 what would become known as a "graphic novel" or *roman fleuve* sixty years later.

Like his father's novella of the Mexican War, Billy Crawford's journal requires patience; unlike *Viva, Madero!*, it doesn't altogether reward it. Of course the comparison is unfair. The one is a work of fiction by an adult, the other the exuberant diary of a kid. I had hoped for more, had hoped to find in the penciled pages some unguarded insight into the boy's evolving character. But there's little self-reflection here. Even so, I did meet an earnest and engaging youth, one able from the outset to charm his way into off-limit areas. Aboard the steamer, he prevails upon the chief engineer to take him on a tour of the boiler room, and he gets the captain to let him stand on the bridge as they enter New York Harbor. He shows a keen eye for aircraft, identifying whatever he sees, in the sky or on the ground. Alone, he explores New York fearlessly: Wall Street, the Brooklyn Bridge, Times Square, Chinatown. At the Bronx Zoo he sees a "rinoscherous," noting his own doubts about his spelling. He goes to the movies—Gary Cooper, Clara Bow—and to a vaudeville show. To Coney Island, where he rides the Cyclone. Unselfconsciously, he strikes a note in which he shows himself clearly to be a southerner in a northern city: "They sure celebrate the Fourth of July here more than they do in Hertford."

But if he had hoped for a month of flying, he must have been sorely disappointed. He seems to have managed no more than a single joyride in a Curtiss Robin from the airport at Valley Stream, where Cy Caldwell had come to renew his pilot's license. There's no evidence that Caldwell himself flew with the boy at all. Apart from that one hop—which Bill Crawford illustrates with a well-drawn aerial map—his experience of the air was confined to forlorn sightings from the ground.

But he got in a lot of swimming. Hardly a page of his journal lacks references to a dip, and the account makes clear that Billy is an absolute beginner, struggling to master his fears as well as his strokes. The day he learns to float, he notes the achievement proudly, and his first dive is recorded in thick block letters. But anxiety is threaded through his efforts—he's never quite comfortable in water over his head.

Living on a river, why had he not learned to swim much sooner? Pollution might be one answer. Well into my own childhood, the Perquimans was rainbowed with leakage from oil storage tanks. Snakes might be another; in her old age, my mother still remembered the day as a teenager she was trapped on a diving platform by a swarm of water moccasins weaving around the pilings. In any event, these daily swims in Island Park were new in the boy's experience, and they also appear on a checklist—"a final report"—Cy Caldwell mailed to Kate Crawford barely two weeks into Billy Crawford's trip.

"I am glad to say I have practically eradicated Billy's fear of the water," the boy's host intones. "I have made him swim out a few feet from shore into water over his head, and at last he can really swim. But he needs to get more confidence in himself—to improve his stroke—and learn not to grow frightened and lose his composure."

It is one of the more temperate remarks in a typewritten letter of six single-spaced pages, a bizarre document whose prolixity may be explained by the fact that it was "dictated but not read" but whose contradictory assessments seem all but impossible to reconcile. Billy is found guilty of "blind imaginative jumps" and a "lack of reasoning power," though he also has "a good mind" and is "a perfect gentleman." Even that quality is flawed because it's a product of his "very sheltered life," though Caldwell concedes the boy's adult knowledge of technical fields like radio and aviation and sometimes admits that he shows promise.

The question of a military career was apparently raised. Cy's conclusion: "If he went to West Point with his present mental outlook, he would fail before he had completed a term."

Such scorn seems irrational because it lacks a context. If we had other accounts of Billy Crawford's Island Park visit, if we knew more about the connection between the boy, his mother, and his irritable mentor, the letter might appear less jarring. But there is one hint that could explain Cy Caldwell's distress: "From his letters I imagined a little boy. I was astonished to meet a young man."

Astonished, and perhaps not altogether pleased.

I tread cautiously here. That Caldwell might have been enlisted to fill a void in the life of a fatherless boy is obvious. But that Billy could have represented to Cy an opportunity for a forbidden encounter seems not altogether impossible—indeed, a contemporary understanding might be swift to conclude the likelihood of some psychosexual darkness, especially given the irrational anger of the letter and the disquieting preoccupation it displays with young Crawford's "sexual development." The probably unanswerable question lingers: Did Cy Caldwell invite other promising lads to spend weeks with him in his fortress of solitude? The record is silent on this point.

I'm open to the possibility of serious trouble, although there isn't a whisper of discomfort in Billy's perky diary, and Kate Crawford was apparently able to master any doubts she may have felt. But a more innocent scenario is hardly less painful: a man in his thirties and a boy of fifteen, each filled with a hope swiftly tattered by inevitable disappointment, can't find the language to soften their collision. Caldwell would have understood himself to be a public figure who had earned his stature through epic efforts, and he would have seen Billy as a reckless boy destined either to fall or to achieve a glowing future through unmerited grace. Billy would have felt himself a rising hero, a warrior prince poised to carry his father's sword in battle, thwarted in his dream of finding a noble guide.

I have to admit that when I first read Cy Caldwell's letter, it stirred my ire on behalf of a woman long dead and a man I never knew, and thus put me at risk of repeating Caldwell's mistake and crafting a reaction based on too little knowledge.

So it's necessary to add that his critique is not entirely without merit. From a lifetime of experience, he cautions the boy about the dangers of the homemade airplane Billy is building, but his warnings are shrugged off. He expresses reservations about the immaturity of Billy's writing, and the journal partly bears those out. He complains that his houseguest fails to do his share of the chores, which may well have been so. And he hazards a few observations about the boy's character, which there's no way of confirming, but which seem consistent with what might be expected of a fatherless fifteen year old raised in relative isolation by devoted women. "He is unduly old in little ways," Caldwell writes. "He is too serious and lacks the ability to play as other boys do."

There seems to be no area of Billy's life Cy Caldwell is reluctant to pry into. He calls the boy "ignorant of literature" (evidently meaning the sort of secular self-help Caldwell favors) and "interested in odd things." Billy's interests apparently don't include girls, and his mentor invests a certain amount of solemn thought in the question: "I believe that he is sexually immature, for certainly at his age he would normally be evincing some interest in girls and he is not doing it, although I have thrown him in the way of an attractive one at the beach for the purpose of arriving at some conclusion as to his stage of development."

There is something creepy about these lines. And why does Cy Caldwell feel called upon to render such judgments? Or even feel free to? He's neither an old friend nor a family member, and the honorary "uncle" Bill Crawford's journal begins with vanishes almost at once from its pages. Cy had known Billy only briefly, and he seems never to have met Kate Crawford. But it is she who in the end becomes the target of his most vitriolic onslaughts: "Billy is very much of a mollycoddle and you are very much to blame. If you had thought less of making a martyr of yourself and had looked around like a normal woman and gotten yourself a big rough man that would have been much better for your children."

The persona Cy Caldwell reveals in this diatribe looks grotesque now, but in 1930 it represented the conventional posturing of a prominent self-confident male. Sadly, far from being angry, Kate Crawford would have felt justly rebuked. If Billy had seen the letter, he might have risen in his mother's defense—which would have only confirmed Caldwell's conviction that he was dealing with a momma's boy from whom little fortitude could be expected. It is not the irritable aviator's finest moment.

Still, in the end, I can find a vein of sympathy for Uncle Cy, or at least a modicum of understanding. Because hiding behind the strutting and lecturing was a profound disappointment. Caldwell had expected a docile child who would trot after him adoringly and absorb his every chance remark. Instead, off the boat stepped a stubborn boy of nearly sixteen, trained to good manners and grateful for the opportunity to enter the famed aviator's world, but fully prepared to defend his own ideas and wishes. So I think, as

I've suggested, that their quarrel did amount to something more than the old story of a young ram and an older one locking horns.

That being so, I'm grateful to have this letter. Apart from a hoarder's load of English papers and math exams—Kate saved so much of her son's schoolwork I couldn't decide whether it was an embarrassment of riches or just an embarrassment—few documents from Billy Crawford's youth survive. And apart from Cy Caldwell's letter, none contests the legend I grew up with—of my uncle as a golden boy, a Galahad, a noble native ghost whose aura informed the Hertford house even more profoundly than his Yankee father's could. He *was* perhaps those things—but he was also an unruly kid, stubborn and single-minded. Caldwell's censure may not have been wholly unjustified.

Yet the very qualities the aviator shrank from made me like my uncle more. I'd become so enchanted by what I'd learned about Billy's eager vivid striving father, with his shattered dreams and scattered energies, that the son's life had a certain chill perfection to it, at least in the version I'd been offered as a boy. This strange sidebar to his story showed me a welcome measure of disorder at the root. And it showed me something more: a way of reaching my ancestor's psyche through the sudden recognition of an unexpected parallel in our backgrounds. Billy Crawford had been shepherded through early childhood by three devoted women, just as I had—and by the same three women.

More than eighty years after it was written, the letter still stings. It must have devastated Kate. Even so, she kept it. And she kept it in the metal trunk, that strange reshaping of an aircraft's wing, along with all the testimonials to her son's triumphs, as though she wouldn't absolutely dismiss what she couldn't altogether disprove.

BILLY CRAWFORD'S VEXED visit to Island Park finally draws to a close on Saturday, August 16. In the morning Cy drives him to Kingston, where he will take a ferry to Rhinecliff for the train to Peekskill. We may imagine an unhappy silence sifting through the ride. In Peekskill, the boy will be staying with friends of his mother's, a family named Arnold, who have arranged for his visit to West Point on the following day. His excitement is scored deep in the final pages of his journal, which are festooned with exclamation points and decorated with one of his stylish little sketches—cadets on dress parade on the plain.

"The men move like clockwork," Billy notes approvingly. He meets several, some no more than two years older than he. He's awed by their poise and their affable manners, by the crushing power of the grips he struggles to return. The setting where he encounters the gray-clad student soldiers possesses a silent power of its own—the granite Gothic towers, the emerald green of the parade ground nailed down by ancient cannon and bronze heroes on horseback. He is granted a quarter-hour's conversation with his new companions and learns a little about the daily life of a cadet. He's also afforded the chance to witness "beast barracks," in which plebes undergo the ritual ordeals that introduce them to the ethos of the academy: Spartan physical training and a barrage of army doctrines and traditions framed by rigid restrictions on the way the men sit, stand, eat, move, breathe. He learns some of the time-honored fragments of arcane knowledge the plebes must possess: the West Point anthem and the football fight songs, General Schofield's definition of discipline, the number of lights in Cullum Hall and the number of gallons in Lusk Reservoir. Plebes memorize the chemical definition of leather and are taught one specific way to characterize a cow: "She walks, she talks, she's full of chalk." None of this organized mayhem is pointless, and perhaps Billy Crawford begins to grasp the point: to instill in hapless civilians habits of thought and action that will equip them first to follow, then to command.

Academics aren't neglected. He visits a French class taught by a Major Finley, who invites the boy to his home for dinner that evening. A veteran of the Great War Billy's father had struggled so hard to serve in, Finley has a trove of combat stories Billy Crawford follows avidly, as well as a perspective on the academy from a faculty officer's point of view. The boy combines what he hears with what he's seen, and in his imagination there begins to chime the academy motto: Duty, Honor, Country. Words his father rarely spoke, but always lived by. We may picture Billy as for the most part a dutiful son and an honorable child—always granted a spirit touched by willfulness—and Louis's legacy has given him a simple-hearted love of country, necessarily colored by the experience of a southern boy well aware he's also heir to the Lost Cause.

But here the old, worn words have real metal in them. It's even possible that the boy is beginning to understand that he may discover at West Point an aspect of his psyche in need of nourishment, something to anneal what's listless in his character with a vision of service and strife. We can't know whether he had been most moved by single moments or had felt the two days coalesce into the image of a destined path, but by the time he was on the Monday train to Norfolk, he had made his father's dream his own.

PERQUIMANS COUNTY DIGNITARIES—lawyers, bankers, the American Legion's minor lords—were easily persuaded to write letters to congressmen supporting young Crawford's bid for a nomination to West Point, and these letters have as much to say about his family's position in the region—at once lofty and diminished—as they do about the young man's manifest qualifications.

Kate Crawford preserved copies of all of them, though she may have felt faintly humiliated by a sponsor who writes, "I come to you on behalf of a struggling little woman who is in desperate straits. Miss Kate Riddick married a fine young chap by the name of Crawford, a captain in the Army Air Corps, who died and left his little widow with two children. Her only hope of educating her son is through an appointment to West Point." Determined to leave no tear unshed, the writer concludes, "If you can bestow any available appointment on Billy Crawford, you would give wings to the drooping spirit of a fine woman, who, all alone in the world, has battled bravely and against great odds to preserve the good name and noble traditions of a grand old family." Other writers, happily, placed more stress on the candidate's accomplishments, calling him "a young man of unusual ability and fine character." He was presented as a "clean, wholesome, ambitious youngster . . . from excellent stock on both sides."

The connection with Louis Crawford was repeatedly made. "Billy's father died while in service in the World War, which deserves consideration in making an appointment of this kind." That fudges the dates a bit but isn't as blatant a falsehood as another letter that had Louis actually killed in the war with Germany. There's no reason to think Kate Crawford approved these deceptions, unnecessary in any case. Then as now, children of soldiers who died on active duty might have an edge over equally qualified candidates. The point is that William Crawford enjoyed an entire community supporting his ambitions, less in celebration of his merits than in recognition of his father's service and his mother's need. Nor, in so time-bounded and traditional a world, would it have passed unnoticed that Kate Crawford's mother's maiden name—Wallace—had been prominent in the Albemarle for some two hundred years.

The nomination was duly made, though in the end Billy received the greater honor of a presidential appointment. But West Point considered his academic qualifications a little thin and recommended an additional year of preparation, which he spent at Stanton, a military prep school in upstate New York. That postgraduate year left few traces, but it did introduce the focus on physical conditioning that would become a law with him, and it revealed a boyish appetite for war. There's also a nice comic note: still not wholly certain of his welcome at USMA, Crawford explores in schoolboy Spanish the possibility of admission to the Academia Militar de Argentina. And he follows the world's war news with something close to glee, writing to Kate in the fall of 1932, "That Chinese Army is sure getting along fine. I've read—in the *Times*—that wounded Chinese soldiers soak their clothes in kerosene, rush into a house held by Japs, and light themselves with a torch—human firebrands. I'm pulling for the Chinks. I hope they win. . . . Maybe I'll be fighting in China someday," he muses. "But that's a long way off. Meanwhile I'm working to stay in shape for whatever war they want to send me to."

The letters from Stanton frequently mention hours spent in running and weight training, and one expresses satisfaction in his waiter's job because of the stacks of heavy dishes he's constantly hauling. He knows West Point will be physically demanding and welcomes the council of a Stanton student admitted to the academy two years before. "Get your legs in good condition before coming here—we double time everywhere." The yearling's letter contains other bits of hard-won wisdom. "Don't bring any fine clothes. Develop a sour, military expression—smile at nothing. (This helps a lot.) Don't use cadet slang."

The Stanton year successfully concluded, William Riddick Crawford is granted admission to the West Point class of 1937 and takes his place in the long gray line.

IT WAS THE HARD SCHOOL, THE FORGE. To enter you passed, that first day, into an inferno. Demands, many of them incomprehensible, rained down. Always at rigid attention, hair freshly cropped, chin withdrawn and trembling, barked at by unseen voices, we stood

or ran like insects from one place to another . . . some had the courage to quit immediately, others slowly failed. It is the sounds I remember, the iron orchestra, the feet on the stairways, the clanging bells, the shouting, the cries of yes, no, I do not know, sir!, the clatter of sixty or seventy rifle butts as they came down on the pavement at nearly the same time. Life was anxious minutes, running everywhere, scrambling to formations. I remember the sweating, the heat and thirst, the

banned bliss of long gulping from the spigot. At parades, three or four
a week, above the drone of hazing floated the music of the band. It
seemed part of another, far-off world. There was the feeling of being
on a hopeless journey, an exile that would last four years.[6]

This passage from James Salter's elegant memoir *Burning the Days* sums
up the shock of one's first day in the army, which even for a draftee is always
numbing. The shock of one's first day at West Point—in 1933!—must by
many orders of magnitude have been more severe. Beast barracks, which
Bill Crawford had seen only for a day and only as a civilian, sinks plebes in
the fires of the forge. And it lasts for weeks. In four years, the academy will
not offer a more strenuous ordeal. The army means swiftly to learn who will
harden, who will break.

"They don't ease up on us here because of heat, or for any other reason,"
New Cadet Crawford wrote after the first few days. "We go as hard as we
can for as long as we can and if we fall out we're hauled to the hospital. The
life is hard," he adds, "but I like it." Though this may be only bravado, it
sounds to me as though the youth is beginning to match his training with
his temperament. Even so, there's relief in his conclusion: "I think most of
the worst is over now."

He would not have been as sanguine at the end of that first overwhelming
day, though he retrieved from it a small victory. Stumbling toward the showers near midnight, Crawford collided with a naked upperclassman whose
wordless glare was enough to freeze him in the rigid posture of attention.

"Definition of leather, mister."

In his first visit to West Point, my uncle had noted the arcana he would
be expected to master. In his year at Stanton, he had rehearsed it. Somehow,
despite his exhaustion, the answer floated intact to the surface of his mind.

"If the fresh skin of an animal, cleaned and divested of all hair, fat, and
other extraneous matter, be immersed in a dilute solution of tannic acid—"

"That'll do." The naked man studied Crawford for a long moment. "Are
all the buttons on my robe buttoned, mister?"

"I . . . see none unbuttoned, sir."

"Post, dumbjohn."

The senior cadet had remained expressionless throughout the encounter,

6. James Salter, *Burning the Days*, 1st ed. (New York: Random House, 1997).

but on Recognition Day he will be the first upperclassman to seek out Bill Crawford, shake his hand, and offer his own name.

That moment is months away. Now, after lights out on his first night at West Point, New Cadet Crawford lies rigid on his narrow bunk, clad in issue pajamas. His mother had offered to pack his favorite pair.

"I couldn't wear them if you did," he'd told her. "We have to be in uniform all the time—even in bed." Sleepless, he lies as still as the catafalque of a medieval knight. The stunning moments of a seemingly endless day pass in review: the pounding boots, the shouting voices, the crash of steel on concrete, the rapid questions, and the only permissible replies, *yes sir, no sir, no excuse sir!*

He had begun the day feeling well prepared and confident. He ended it utterly depleted, convinced the army would never find a use for him.

As Bill Crawford sank into a coma, he felt the letters "US," printed on his olive-drab blanket, tattoo his flesh.

WEST POINT SEEMS a granite monolith, a changeless presence in American life, but its survival has not always been assured and its history sparkles with controversy. The academy's home is an old fort high above the Hudson, from which in 1775 Washington's artillery was able to command a bend in the river and so halt British progress up the valley. After the Revolution, it seemed a natural spot for a school for soldiers, but there was no general agreement that such a school should even exist. Many Americans were suspicious of the idea of a standing army; the war had been won by a civilian militia, after all.

George Washington took a different view. Aware that his best commanders had been French and Prussian professionals, he reasoned that the new country would do well to commission its own military caste. Thomas Jefferson at first rejected that view, but eventually came to share it, and in 1802 he made a federal military academy a reality. But West Point would saunter down a rocky path over the next hundred years, at times little more than a finishing school for gentlemen, at others a warehouse for a rabble of rebellious youth. Its future was often in doubt. More than once, Congress threatened to defund it.

In 1846, the Mexican War confirmed the academy's worth. American troops under West Point officers performed brilliantly in battle. These commanders would meet again less than twenty years later, leading with terrifying effectiveness and panache on both sides of the Civil War.

Conceived largely as an engineering school, West Point supplied officers who would build the country's railways, roads, and bridges in the years before that fratricidal conflict. The immediate postwar era was marked by a struggle to reintegrate southern cadets into the academy, to deal with the practice of hazing, and to make a faltering beginning at drawing young black men into the Corps. Only the first of these issues showed signs of easy resolution. At the same time, boys both northern and southern who sought a broad field of studies were largely immune to West Point's appeal; as a technical training school, the academy had failed to show wide academic range.

But in 1919 a new superintendent—Brig. Gen. Douglas MacArthur, who was to hold the post for only three years—began to introduce the reforms that would shape West Point into the institution Bill Crawford entered in 1933. Humanities attained something closer to parity with the sciences; athletics found new prominence; and military training joined the twentieth century, reflecting the lessons of the First World War. But hazing continued, and the plight of black cadets showed no signs of easing.

Despite these changes, USMA remained still very much a trade school, very much a men's school, and very much a national institution that largely drew its students from a regional base. "West Point was a keep of tradition and its name was a hallmark," James Salter notes. "It drew honest, Protestant, often rural, and largely uncomplicated men." This is a fair characterization of my uncle, who thrived at the academy in part because he was one of those for whom it had been made.

MAJOR GORDON FINLAY was a competent and courageous battalion commander in combat and a ranked scholar of Provencal song. He kept a more-than-casual eye on Cadet Crawford during that first year. The young man's seeming perfection puzzled the major. You could see it in his deportment, his studies, his devotion to duty, his steadiness. It was as though Bill Crawford never once doubted his place in the Corps of Cadets, and that meant—a paradox if you will—the Corps had failed him. To feel to the depths of your dark heart the despairing determination that you must quit was one of the lessons of plebe year. You came to see that not only could you not hack it, you didn't *want* to. If that moment never came, you were probably not a West Pointer. And as far as Major Findlay could tell, the moment never came for Bill Crawford.

THROUGHOUT HIS YEARS at West Point, Bill Crawford's letters draw on a small set of themes—cadet life, family relationships, academics and tactics, furloughs and future plans—but they hold interest because each topic is evoked with increasing maturity as time goes by. In his first year, the young plebe frets continually over minor debt while resolutely declining offers of assistance; later, he solves the problem with jobs taken during summer furloughs, looking especially for manual labor that will help him stay in peak physical shape. As a plebe, he languishes in isolation; a yearling, he makes elaborate plans for visitors, often providing them hour-by-hour schedules of activity. In this, he repeats the pattern of the cadet day, shaped as it is by drum rolls and bugle calls. The regimen suits him—as he says, "I like an ordered life."

Another favorite topic is his eyesight, too weak to permit him to qualify for flight training after graduation. The Air Corps is his goal, and he stubbornly undertakes a program of visual exercises in hopes of amending his deficiency. He laments classroom struggles, where he fumbles the conversational French an officer must have and complains of being required to read *The Mayor of Casterbridge.*

Technical subjects are a different matter. He has no problems with physics, chemistry, or analytic geometry, and he positively shines in engineering and mechanical drawing. Like his father, he has a flair for draftsmanship and, like Louis, he often illustrates his letters with cartoons, vivid little sketches on the margins of the page that sometimes substitute for anecdote.

Still, if *techné* draws him, military science lies at the center of his study. In brightly lighted classrooms with their rows of highly polished wooden desks and timeworn chalkboards, Cadet Crawford and his fellows sit at attention under the lash of their instructors' voices and take careful notes on the strategies of the Punic and Napoleonic wars, of the Civil War, of the vast muddy struggle that had shattered Europe only twenty years before. Poring over maps and bent over sand tables, they begin to acquire theoretical mastery of infantry technique. Tasked with planning for units of all sizes, they shape frontal assaults and pincer movements, ponder breakthroughs and holding actions, learn how to exploit salients and develop counterattacks, how to marshal reserves and fashion supply lines, how to minister to the wounded and give rough burial to the dead. All these things a young officer must know; all of them Bill Crawford commits to learning. But it is in the field that his passions are fully engaged.

"Last week we had a three-day sham battle," he writes on April 14, 1935:

> It involved an advance of twelve miles through woods and rocky fields and crossed deep creeks. I had to run hundreds of yards at times, always wearing a pack and carrying my rifle with fixed bayonet at high port arms. We at the point—the advance element—had to keep harrying the enemy so the main body could maneuver freely behind. We stayed at a dead run, attacking from unexpected spots. Once a Blue soldier—we're the Red and Blue armies—popped out of the mist so close to me that neither of us could fire. I knocked aside the down stroke of his rifle and pinned him through the chest with my bayonet. The bayonet was in its scabbard, of course. But it all felt very real. Hand-to-hand combat is damned exciting.

Cadet Crawford cheerfully confesses his shortcomings. "I got off five or six well-aimed shots but none of them counted. After the battle, the Blue sniper who shot me pointed out that I was dead before I opened fire."

The sunlit life, the spit and polish, the endless training, the bugle's blare, boots and saddles, the rigid discipline, the hoarse commands, the military élan, the ring of steel, small triumphs, dread, pressure, exhaustion, dark epiphanies, all the elements of the hard school—Bill Crawford thrived on them. And his days in the field, under arms, lost in war games that came as close as the Point could come to war, were the days that told him where all the rest was headed. He had to wonder how he would perform should the real thing come along.

Throughout his time at West Point, Bill Crawford had urged his sister to visit him, and she finally succumbed at the start of his first-class year. Louise was a great success at a dance, which pleased her brother. "Always now you'll know some men in the service," he wrote in August 1936, adding gravely, "Eventually, of course, they'll hold positions of high command." My mother gave a repeat performance at her brother's graduation hop; before she arrived, he reassured her of its informality. "The ladies don't wear garden party clothes. It's more like a dog fight."

William and his sister, Louise, c. 1940

IMAGES OF WEST POINT haunted the old house in my childhood—steel engravings of the Gothic towers, framed photographs of my uncle in his Napoleonic uniforms, an album of 78 rpm records boxed in black and gold from whose scratchy surfaces lifted the powerful voices of the cadet choir.

The Corps! Bareheaded salute it,
With eyes up, thanking our God—
That we of the Corps are treading
Where they of the Corps have trod

Hearing the songs sometimes made my mother tearful. She had happy memories of her brother's graduation hop, of dancing with his attentive classmates, who paid only the most respectful court to their friend's lovely young married sister. But Kate Crawford never mentioned the place, though she never banished its relics. And although my uncle, in one of his last letters from the war, had happily supposed that his new nephew might follow him to the academy, I never shared the fantasy. Unathletic, innumerate, and anarchic by temperament, I would have been as bad a fit for West Point as my uncle was a good one. It's improbable I would have been appointed, implausible that I would have succeeded, and inevitable that, had I somehow made my way through the program, I would have mislaid parts of myself I would have had to seek out for years thereafter. This, I think, is what happened to James Salter. It was precisely his triumph in the world of the alpha male that slowly revealed to him what that world was missing. I don't think my uncle felt that much was missing or regretted anything. He moved through the academy as he moved through the army, sunlit, ever rising.

His father's ghost is a close companion. "Could you send me one of those little pictures of Daddy as an aviator?" he requested at the start of his first year. And mention of Louis will appear from time to time in the letters thereafter, whenever young Crawford exults in a victory he knows his father would cherish or bemoans a failure that would cause the fallen warrior chagrin. Most noteworthy are a few lines from the spring of 1937, written shortly after his commissioning. The son had packed Louis Crawford's dress saber off to an English swordsmith for refurbishing—a costly graduation present from his mother—and the result delighted him. "The saber has come and looks wonderful. They did a beautiful job. Hard to believe it's the same sword but I can tell it is. I'll be so proud to use it—a reminder of Daddy."

The sword that linked the lives of these men hung in the hall of the Hertford house for many years. It is on my study wall now. When I was a boy, I was permitted to treat it as a toy. The risk was less to me than to the steel, though a dress saber is a dangerous weapon, and indeed to this day the blade is marred with a fretwork of nicks inflicted by my childhood fights with doorframes and newel posts. In retrospect, I'm startled that I was allowed to draw such an heirloom into my imaginary world, but there was not much my grandmother was prepared to deny me.

ON JULY 16, 1933, Cadet Crawford made a detailed sketch of his quarters, positioning the sparse furniture—cot, table, straight-backed chair—with an architect's exactitude. Then he outlined an hour-by-hour schedule of his day. "I hope all this junk is interesting to you," he adds modestly, "but I can't see why it should be."

I can. The ferocious small detail is the heart of the story, the path of transformation. "White gloves must be spotless. We change them every half-hour." Add to this the weight of his studies, whose relative values may be tracked by an offhand remark: "Had to buy more books: two on analytical geometry, four about Napoleon, and five on the Civil War." Of this college library, only two volumes have survived: *Tactics and Techniques for Infantry*, volumes 1 and 2, which I discovered not in the aluminum trunk but on a tower of shelves in the hallway of the Hertford house, flanked on one side by some technical manuals from the Baldwin Locomotive Works that had belonged to his grandfather and on the other by *Kelly Field in the Great War*.

Bill Crawford was hardly an original writer, but he was a pretty good sketch artist, and sometimes captured a quick observation in words as well: the muzzle of an old cannon thick with verdigris has a "green eye," and an exhausted cadet shows a collar "edged in sweat stains." His ear is similarly acute when he describes an evening maneuver, drawing on memories of his voyage to New York as well as on his first encounter with the precision of cadets at drill ("The men move like clockwork"). "One night in the rain they marched us through gravel a long ways. Everybody was in perfect step and the crunch-crunch-crunch kept up so regularly and monotonously that we felt like some square-shaped machine, like the engines on the Norfolk ferry."

Not every young man would rejoice in regimentation, but I think that in this instance my uncle—like some Italian Futurist—has tapped into its aesthetic dimension. (I've been on rainy night marches where the misery of wet boots and ugly weather was eased by the staunch rhythm of the column: *crunch crunch crunch*.)

He mentions swimming several times in his letters. Doubtless recalling his struggles with Cy Caldwell, he sounds a note of triumph in his final report: "I have qualified in every stroke required here. Now all I must qualify in is distance, and I'm not worried about that."

Water will be his combat environment. But if he had feared water as a boy, it retreats to the background once he is a man.

At the academy, time passed in tones of black and gray and silver. "The days here are much the same," the cadet observed placidly in the spring of 1934. Still, they did admit of some variety, and when in June a film company appeared on the plain, Bill Crawford, now a yearling, was given the opportunity to enjoy the diversion. "Warner Brothers are shooting a movie called *Flirtation Walk* here. There are cameras all over the place. I've talked with a few members of the crew and picked up some pointers on motion picture production."

At the age of twelve, Billy had tinkered together a projector from spare parts, an achievement that inspired him to commandeer a room of the Hertford house for his grandly named Flash Theater. He set up folding chairs, hung a screen, rented old comedies and westerns from mail order services, plastered playbills to the walls, and sold tickets to his friends and neighbors—real theater tickets, also ordered by mail. So he was pleased to be at the academy the year a film was being produced there, but when he finally saw *Flirtation Walk* he was unimpressed. The following February, he wrote, of the annual cadet production of a comedy review, "I've been in the Hundredth Night show. It's not *the* big event of the year, as the movie would lead one to believe. And they failed to include any winter scenes—no cadets with frozen ears."

He might have extended his objections to the movie's stiff acting and sentimental story, and to its failure to depict West Point as anything more than a montage of marching men. It strikes me as invidious to treat an august institution as a mere backdrop for broad comedy. *Flirtation Walk* finds its place easily on the short list of movies about West Point, none of which amounts to much. The West Point movie remains to be made.

It isn't surprising the young cadet's letters home are sparse, nor that, in their ordered march, they measure his thriving. Even after the harrowing first year, when the academy ordeal had lightened up a little, he hardly had many hours of free time, and Kate was not his only correspondent. Still, a careful reader gets a good sense of his days—his struggles and successes with classwork, his growing mastery of military skills, his rare moments of relaxation with friends. Above all is the sense of his pride at flourishing in a supremely demanding environment. Toward the end of his second year, he noted: "As the work grows harder— the academics, and the Army side—I somehow feel more equal to it. At the center of the chaos, there's an odd calm. I don't really know how to account for it."

I think I do. Shorn of his indulgent family, he planned to make a home in the army. Separated from self-selected tasks and civilian pleasures, he would embrace those West Point sets before him. *Amor fati* was his watchword. His strength becomes suppleness, his restless intelligence finally an instrument of ambition and will. Like his father, he is beginning to love the army, although, also like his father, he never deceives himself that it will love him back. Still a youth, he is coming to find the adult vocation he is determined he must.

Some degree of social life must have been possible even for a plebe, because by the winter of 1934 he has met Mary Shelburne, a fellow North Carolinian he will marry five years later. Openly worried that Kate may be jealous, he promises her he is not engaged, and suggests that mutual friends be enlisted to vet the girl and assure the family of her sterling qualities. "I know you will countenance and advise me in my affairs," he tells his mother, "and I will confide in you." Oedipal drums are sounding here. Their noise will deepen.

"You should be glad I have a girl back home," he pleads in a subsequent letter. "It keeps me from getting in any affairs up here!" These reassurances apparently fell on deaf ears, because only a few days later Bill Crawford felt compelled both to shift his argument and to frame it more forcefully. "I'm here to become a soldier and that's what I'm going to do. Everything else is secondary. As you may know, there will probably be war in Europe within the next year. If we're drawn in, I'll have more on my mind than marriage."

Still, he cannot shake the fear that to insist on a life of his own was to sabotage the one he and Kate had shared since she had become a widow. The guilt continued to plague him into his second year. "I have a chance to ship out with the navy on a midshipman's cruise this summer," he wrote that spring, "but it would mean forgoing any furlough in Hertford." Aware that his choosing career over kin might plunge his mother into gloom, he added, "But twenty-six months from now I'll graduate, and then we'll be together for years and years." In making such an unlikely promise, William Crawford is setting aside a probable war, a possible marriage, and his indenture to the

US Army. And there's no escaping the fact that this is language that belongs between lovers.

But perhaps it could not have been otherwise. A lonely widow since her husband's death, Kate almost inevitably fixed her emotional life on her only son; a solitary boy shy around girls (I think we may trust Cy Caldwell here), Bill Crawford was equally destined to be overnourished by his mother's love. Indeed, I think he may have found at West Point the best way to flee Kate's smothering devotion, though he could never altogether escape it: she had no hesitation about touching the levers of power if she believed she could advance her son's ambitions. In January 1938, some maternal request made to the commanding officer of the new lieutenant's first post drew this resigned plea: "In things concerning my own little career, please don't presume you know better. This army is a funny racket. For God's sake let me have the security of mind of *one headquarters only*."

Six years later, Kate was still at it.

"She drove General Swing crazy," my mother once told me, naming the commander of the 11th Airborne Division, "but Swing thought the world of Bill and never held it against him." Those who doubt that a major general would permit his life to be invaded by a determined little lady from the rural South need only recall Kate Crawford's bold attempt to have her husband Louis reinstated in the Air Service in 1918. (Kate's readiness to reach deep into the lives of her children was a source of concern to both well into adulthood. Evidence of their mother's controlling will crops up again and again in their letters to each other, first alarming Bill and Louise, then amusing them as their mother's grasp weakens.)

The absent or oppressive father, the adoring but controlling mother—themes like these pass down through the generations, and while I have only the most tender memories of my grandmother Kate, who died when I was eleven, I also remember my mother once telling me, "I tried to fill the hole left by Bill, a grotesque thing to do. I gave you to your grandmother as a consolation prize. Of course, she spoiled you rotten." And of course I lapped up the love, though the relationship carried psychological costs—as it had for Cadet William Crawford.

THERE ARE TWO main ways a father can fail a son: by being so powerful that the boy must submit or rebel, or so passive that he may spend a lifetime searching for a substitute. But there is a third way, which may inflict the worst kind of wound. When Louis died in that Denver hospital, Billy at the age of seven was left to make his way in a world of women, much loved but at a loss for male guidance. His problems would emerge in his adolescence, when he would have to carry the image of Louis as officer and aviator without being granted the option of entering into open struggle with his father's dream. Bill Crawford became what he beheld because he couldn't behold an alternative. Childless, he found compensation only insofar as a leader may be a father to his men. To a field commander, that possibility is open, but for a staff officer it's blocked, and for a first-year plebe it isn't even an option. Because his father had gone AWOL early, he had to father himself. He got good at it by bringing Louis back to life as an avatar.

"Sometimes when I run into a wall—a field problem I can't solve, a tactics instructor I can't seem to satisfy," he noted on one occasion, "I ask myself how Daddy would handle it. Usually I come up with an answer. Of course, these are problems specific to a future infantryman. They wouldn't arise in a civilian university."

Perhaps not, but he can sound like a college student as well as a cadet, an eighteen-year-old boy as well as a prospective officer. Many of his letters reveal eager plans for his brief furloughs, broodings over his romance with Mary, worries about money. Such common touches warm me toward him. I can see him as self-absorbed, overconfident, and sometimes a bit too conscious of his merits. I find similar faults in my own late adolescence and tend to think our common tutelage provides the link: for better or worse, Kate Crawford, Louise Woods, and Pearl Hill, who served my family for nearly fifty years, were for both of us guides to the men we were to become.

This shared experience is my passport to Bill Crawford's inner life. Early on, I hadn't been captivated by my uncle's story in quite the same way I was by his father's: Louis Crawford's life seemed so varied and compelling, so full of twists and turns, that each new packet of letters I pulled from the black leather trunk promised to let me join him on a new adventure. There was something less engaging, more reserved, about his son. It was strange—of the three soldiers whose lives I was learning, Bill Crawford had left the longest record and the largest legend. He was the consummate professional, the only veteran of sustained combat, and the most highly decorated of the three, as well as the man who gave me two-thirds of my name. But I was finding him hard to get close to.

"One year ago today, I entered West Point," the rising second-year cadet reflected in July 1934. "I'm mighty glad I did—I'm a better man for it."

In many ways, he was. Stronger, sharper, and more self-disciplined, he had measured his powers against a Spartan program and found them equal to it. Yet in other respects he might have been better off at a civilian college like UVA or Princeton, frequent destinations for a Carolina bravo. At the very least, liberal studies would have prompted him to challenge his prejudices, which couldn't happen in a trade school designed to endorse them. But the humanities were not his strong point. Just as Louis Crawford had been forced to abandon his first try for a commission because he failed a history test, so William Crawford would stumble over the same hurdle. "Well," he observed blithely at one point, "I didn't come here for an education."

It isn't that he lacks interest in the history being written in his own day. Convinced the United States will be drawn into a European war within five years, he makes cogent observations on preparations for defense. His sympathies are with England and France, and he has no doubt America will support these allies. But, he briskly informs his mother, a regnant Germany offers the world's best shield against "Russian barbarism," and he suggests that Adolf Hitler, whom he rather admires, may indeed represent the highest hopes of the German nation. To underline his seriousness, he asks for an early Christmas present—a copy of *Mein Kampf*. I found it in the aluminum trunk.

This does not come as an unqualified shock. During the Spanish Civil War, Bill Crawford had supported the rebels ("a better sort of people"), and a disdain for Soviet communism crops up from time to time in his letters. But what follows is an ugly surprise: Cadet Crawford sternly cautions his mother not to let her view of Hitler be shaped by "Jewish newspapers" published in New York. Such frank anti-Semitism is sickening to find in a man whose memory I'd been taught to revere. Its counterpart is racism, and here there can be no surprises. William Crawford, a small-town southerner raised by the remnants of plantation aristocrats, lived in an America racist to its core and served in a military where segregation was endemic, nowhere more than at West Point.

My uncle had little hope of abandoning his ingrained attitudes. But at least once his grudging recognition of merit almost lifted him to a higher plane. Of a black cadet in the class just before his, Bill Crawford remarks, "Davis is a good soldier—strong physique, solid intellect, military bearing. He's earned his place at West Point. But," my uncle adds with awful candor, "I just don't like it." He has no problem with men of color from other nations filling out the ranks of the Corps—they're exotics, after all. But a homegrown American darky?

As it happens, the cadet Bill Crawford refers to was Benjamin O. Davis, Jr.,[7] who would go on to command the Tuskegee Airmen through more than sixty combat missions and cap a distinguished career by becoming the first African American general officer in the air force. But in his four years at West Point, with the full connivance of the faculty, Davis was "silenced"— never spoken to except in the line of duty. He lived alone and dined alone, shunned and isolated, still managing to graduate high in his class before commencing his exemplary career. A remarkable man—but had the black cadet turned out to be a nonentity, my uncle's surrender to the collective cowardice of the Corps of Cadets and the contemptible behavior of the officers who sanctioned it would have been no less reprehensible. I remind myself that it's easy to take the moral high ground when you risk nothing in doing so. Standing alone against the savage will of two thousand young men secure in the mantle of their ignoble behavior might not have been so simple. In the matter of Benjamin Davis, my uncle was a child of his times. I wish he could have been more. But he wasn't.

RACISM, PROFASCISM, ANTI-SEMITISM—it was a misery to learn that my uncle had held these views, however weakly or for however short a time, and there was little solace in reflecting that only two letters in two hundred voiced them. If only Kate Crawford hadn't kept those letters with the others, if only I had somehow overlooked them as I rummaged through the pile. . . . Afterward I had to struggle to maintain my sympathy for the person I was discovering. To stay with him, I would have to trace the origins of his attitudes.

The racism seems all but inevitable. Born in 1914, Billy Crawford was brought up in a small southern town where the social order governing relations between black and white would have stood unchanged since Reconstruction. The anti-Semitism is at first more surprising—were there even any Jews in Hertford?—but a passing reference in a letter to Cy Caldwell suggests a source. "I listen to the radio a lot. Do you know Father Coughlin?

7. Davis was not the only cadet of that era to know a measure of fame. One of William Crawford's roommates was Colin Kelly, a future legend of the Second World War, widely though erroneously believed to have been awarded the Medal of Honor for sinking a Japanese battleship with his B-17 in a suicide dive.

His program is very interesting." Edward Coughlin, a Roman Catholic priest whose radio show commanded a vast audience, spewed anti-Semitic vitriol over the air through much of Billy's childhood. He couldn't have avoided it and he seems to have found no way to challenge it.

Another likely influence is Charles Lindbergh, whose pro-Nazi sympathies and anti-Semitic platitudes were on open display throughout the 1930s. And Henry Ford saw no shame in this deadly posturing. To Billy, both men were heroes.

A letter he wrote his mother at the age of eighteen is extremely hard to stomach. "If Hitler had a bodyguard, I'd volunteer," he notes gleefully, on a page decorated with tiny swastikas. Nothing can defend this; but youth, ignorance, and the spirit of the times can at least account for it: when the Fuehrer came to power, he struck even some mature minds as a leader who might bring Germany out of the economic chaos of the Weimar Republic and restore a measure of justice to a nation humiliated by the Treaty of Versailles. The potted history Billy learned from the pro-German propaganda he encountered would have been convincing to a kid whose rural high school education was sufficiently limited to require a postgraduate year of preparation for West Point.

All of this may be parsed. None of it can be countenanced. But the boy of nineteen who admired the Nazis was not the man of twenty-nine who made war on them, and the cadet who scorned a classmate was not the officer who came to admire the black troops he saw in action. In the end, the best I could manage was to put my uncle's failings down to his provincial youth and the relentless pressures of his culture, and to remember that, when the time came, he was ready to hazard his life fighting the forces that had seduced him as a boy.

THREE YEARS HAVE passed. At the beginning of their final year, graduating cadets are awarded their class rings in a formal ceremony. Bill Crawford orders his from Tiffany & Co., an oval of black onyx set in a massive hoop of gold engraved inside the band with his name and his fiancée's initials. The ring arrives in an elegant miniature black leather box lined with white silk. No symbol of achievement will mean as much to him until his shoulders sport gold bars.

For first classmen, the tempo slowed a little. Training was still arduous—long lecture hall hours, tactical field problems, rigorous close-order drill—but there seemed to be more space in the days, time to walk with your girl at Trophy Point, drink coffee in the lobby of the Thayer Hotel, even take the train down the river to Manhattan for a precious weekend leave. Above all, there was time to think about the future after West Point. For Bill Crawford and his peers, the very idea seemed strange. For almost four years there had been nothing *but* West Point. Now these young men would enter the larger world of the army. (It's 1937. There are no young women.)

Questions loomed. What branch of service should the graduate elect? What duty post or further schooling should he seek? Though class rank will enlarge the possibility of choice for some, most of the newly commissioned officers won't have much say in these matters. But in one area they do command their fates, and it is not an unimportant one.

Second lieutenants leaving West Point were expected to purchase their own apparel, military and civilian, and as June Week approached the academy took a paternal interest in its graduates' choices. "Do not buy shoddy or ill-fitting civilian clothes or uniforms," a stern memorandum warns the cadets. "They are more expensive in the long run and it is unfair to yourselves to give a poor first impression." At the same time, the army will be providing some funds, and does not want to see them wasted. In the hotel suites where bespoke tailors and English bootmakers gather to display their wares, tactical officers are stationed to give council to the firsties. "Be careful and circumspect in placing your orders. Salesmen will try to make you spend your money."

Cadet Crawford has always been careful with his money, but he has no intention of hazarding a poor first impression. (His fastidiousness emerges in a letter thanking his sister for the gift of a necktie: "The tie is a beautiful pattern woven of blues of 'different hues, luminosity, and saturation.' I like the way it's made—the ends not folded under but unwoofed for a quarter inch. It goes very well with my suit.") For some months his letters home have read like a Brooks Brothers catalogue as he solemnly envisions a wardrobe in which navy-blue blazers and white flannel trousers will share space with mess jackets and dress blues. "Evening clothes," he notes, "are a necessity for an officer." The cost of all the finery he covets might seem daunting, but in 1937 a dinner jacket could be had for fifty dollars. Of course, that is 1937 dollars.

Blouses, breeches, boots, spurs, riding crops, foulard ties, fedoras, canary-colored cotton gloves—there seems no end to the list. Correct attire was a serious business for the rising aristocrats of a prewar army that held its share of formal dinners and regimental balls. Bill Crawford's sartorial concerns are as much a part of his evolving career as a command of conversational French, fencing, and horsemanship, none of which might play a role in modern war, but all of which still mattered in the making of a West Point officer.

At least there is no need to buy a sword. He has his father's.

IN 1937, THE HOWITZER, West Point's yearbook, printed a vivid sketch of my uncle:

> Quiller—always interested and always interesting. Ardent militarist
> and jingoist—private first class with drill spec'd cold. A proud goat
> with four stars. Poor in French but capable of repairing an engine or
> putting across a business deal. Interested in construction, he knew by
> name the workmen on the post and was familiar with their work. A
> self-confident, hard-headed, critical Scot; but he never oiled the wheels
> of his own progress at the expense of another. Generous to a fault.
> Took it easy and learned much not found in books. His well-balanced
> menu and evenly tempered attitude are invaluable assets as later
> events will prove.

There were surprises, starting with the nickname, which never appears in his letters, was never used by his family, and seems to have vanished altogether after his graduation. "Quiller"—the etymology is vague. One source calls it a rare, obsolete term for an unfledged bird, another traces it to the Old French for a spoonmaker, and so by implication for any other sort of craftsman or smith. Both meanings work as glimpses into character; it's impressive that a pack of teenagers was astute enough to come up with the name.

In the silver trunk I found a little khaki booklet distributed to cadets upon arrival.

Official Courtesy and Customs of the Service tacitly admits that not all young men enter West Point as gentlemen and may require tutoring in the niceties of civilian life as well as military protocol. The 1934 edition Bill Crawford was issued possesses a sort of faded, Fitzgeraldian charm. We can't read it today innocent of the knowledge that any meticulous discussion of how to choose a tailor, set a dinner table, or judge the quality of an opera hat would be rendered moot within a decade by the dark pageantry of global war. Nevertheless, the guide stood my uncle in good stead as he prepared for graduation, enabling him to address with confidence the myriad small details of the life that lay ahead.

One such detail was calling cards, part of an officer's punctilio in reporting to a new post. "These should be of moderate size and in good taste as to design and lettering," the elegant guide advises firmly. "If in doubt, follow the example of someone whose judgment in such matters is beyond question. Never use any but engraved cards."

Crawford makes his selection. When the little ivory box arrived from the engraver, he must have prized it open and gazed raptly at the elegant tribute to four years of hard work and harrowing ordeals:

William Riddick Crawford
Second Lieutenant
United States Army

James Salter, also seeking a second lieutenant's commission, entered West Point ten years after Bill Crawford under an accelerated program designed to produce officers for service in the Second World War, but his experience would have been entirely familiar to his older brother-in-arms, which is why I didn't hesitate to let Salter's first day on the Hudson stand as proxy for my uncle's.

It seems to me that both young men, arriving at the academy along different paths, reached similar conclusions about its transformative power. I think they came to see that the image of manhood—the notion of character—proposed by the army might yield selves superior to those they had earlier conceived themselves to be.

At West Point, James Salter had a conversion experience. Something similar happened to Bill Crawford. In the first instance, transformation was called for; in the second, mere refining. But in both cases, the lesser man becomes a classic version of his romantic self. And it is the academy—less

through its specific course of instruction than in the tenor of its daily life—
that fashions the change. These are the fires of the forge.

Salter's father was a West Point graduate. It was a schooling he had always
wished for his son. But the younger man—"seventeen, vain, and spoiled by
poems"—felt himself destined for Stanford and the lotus land of the California coast. He took the West Point entrance exam at his father's urging and in
something of a fugue state drifted onto the path of his father's bidding. His
only preparation for the academy was a background of cultured ease. The
world he entered was like none he had ever known.

Salter somehow survived his plebe year, though in a barely suppressed
state of rebellion. But the ethos of the place was seeping into his soul in
unexpected ways.

"I began to change," he writes, "not what I was truly but what I seemed
to be. Dissatisfied, eager to become better, I shed as if they were old clothes
the laziness and rebellion of the first year and began anew."

The poet in Salter never vanished. At the end of his years of service, the
writer would be born in answer to those years, as though aware that the
world of military honor alone could not satisfy his conception of a full self.

William Crawford did not have so profound a transformation to effect.
Poetry was not in his blood, and the paternal wishes Salter at first resisted
Crawford had long embraced. But he too had a distance to cover, an inner
change to achieve. I can trace it in his letters, which become both lighter in
tone and more serious in purpose over the four years. But I see it most clearly
in two photographs—the first from his early teens, which shows a sulky
boy whose soft features are suffused with self-love; and the second from
the year of his graduation, in which the face is candid, cheerful, resolute,
outward-looking. If anything, this face is more striking than it was in louche
adolescence, but with the hard gaze of tested maturity. It's a face James
Salter wore and would have recognized: the mask of command.

THE NEW LIEUTENANT had his heart set on the Air Corps. Flying, after
all, was his first love. We have seen that his father created this passion, and
that Cy Caldwell set up the obstacles that confirmed him in it. But his eyes
weren't good enough for the army. Though he sought medical treatment and
persisted in vision exercises, he failed the eye test more than once. In the end,
there was clearly no hope. But he was a flier already. He'd been piloting light

planes since his teens, borrowing them from friends and skittering around the Carolina countryside as happily as any barnstormer, once remarking that he really ought to get a license someday. This insouciance didn't sit well with the Air Corps, which informed Second Lieutenant Crawford that he would not be piloting fighters or bombers for the government of the United States.

But he was well qualified for other options. He had graduated comfortably close to the middle of his class, not the worst place from which to commence a career in an institution as conservative as the army. His academics were adequate, his military toolkit strong. His record would neither dismay his superiors through evidence of weakness nor put them off by displays of suspect brilliance. West Point had presented the service with a young officer ready to take on almost any military task, one who could serve successfully in any branch but aviation.

Cavalry—by that time, armor—or mechanized infantry were equal in his mind as second choices, but subsequent schooling intervened. He went where they sent him, uncomplaining, always alert for an assignment to the combat arms. And at last he got one, when he was posted on September 8, 1937, as a platoon leader in the 12th Infantry Regiment at Fort Washington, Maryland, a tough foot soldier's outfit where he could ease his disappointment over the Air Corps by practicing the profession he'd been trained for. And the location offered Lieutenant Crawford a welcome opportunity to test his social skills. Twenty miles from Washington, DC, Bill Crawford's new post allowed an easy drive on a weekend evening to the stirring social life of the capital. Tall, trim, blonde, well spoken, and dashing in civilian clothes or uniform, the young lieutenant found himself much in demand at dinners and dances from Georgetown to Chevy Chase. *Courtesy and Customs of the Service* stood him in good stead as he called on his tailor, chose a wine for his hostess or flowers for the debutante de jour. He liked to dress in civvies, carefully matching ties to shirts, suits to shoes, confident that his military bearing would always shine through the tuxedo. Hosts, though, often begged him to arrive in dress blues. There was something about a soldier.

Two days after Christmas 1939, Crawford was invited to a dance at the White House. In a letter to his sister, he doesn't mention meeting the president, but did chat with Eleanor Roosevelt. "I was impressed by her—a fine woman, smart, a strong personality. Unfortunately, she slipped while doing the Virginia reel and sat down in the middle of the floor."

Lieutenant Crawford, reviewing troops, Fort Washington,
District of Columbia, 1939

The first lady's minor gaff was not the most disappointing part of the evening. Crawford is appalled by the dregs of the governing class he encounters.

Louise, if what I saw is a fair cross-section of New England aristocrats, I want none of them in my army in time of war. Bluebloods or sons of some Mrs. Ritchbitch, they were neither neat nor clean-cut looking. Hair too long or Joe College short, they stood with their heads shot forward about half a foot so the backs of their necks never made contact with their coat collars.

It's a social detail worthy of Tom Wolfe.

Nor are the ladies spared. "Never have I seen so many beautiful dresses on so many homely women." The black-tie crowd's decorum is roundly faulted as well: the men are uncouth, the women improper, and neither group shows sufficient respect for their august surroundings. "Really, I could have made money in a sideshow with the bunch I saw there. The men didn't even look like men. Now I know why the Vassar girls come all the way down to West Point. Hell, I'd take any infantry outfit at Fort Washington over this White House crowd. Our men may be Polacks, Hungarians, Lithuanians, etc.—but they're *men*."

The lieutenant's xenophobia—we've seen it at West Point—is once more on display. Nevertheless, his words *are* a mark of the richer experience that was beginning to carry Bill Crawford from the backwater of Hertford through the cloisters of West Point into a wider world. As for his anger at the callow dancers, I think it may have had something to do with his unspoken awareness that war was on the way and these unfinished figures were the ones who would send him to fight it.

At Fort Washington, he was eager to put his West Point training to practical use. Younger than many of his men, he needed to balance command presence with tactful regard for those he led. Replete with classroom knowledge and carefully scripted field experiences, he had to adjust to the gritty realities of life in a rifle platoon. He worked with sergeants whose respect he had to earn, under a captain whose evaluation he would rise or fall by. He did his work well, and soon was tested by additional duties: "Too tired to write much now, as I've been on all-night maneuvers and have had no sleep for the past 48 hours. But the maneuvers were interesting—very realistic—I learned a good deal. I'm becoming a better educated officer from a professional standpoint." He has been appointed battalion S-2, combat intelligence officer.

> With a 12-man section to aid me, I had to determine location, strength, and disposition of the enemy, which meant I had to know all the roads and trails so I could position the companies at the battalion CO's orders. This involved interpreting aerial photographs and evaluating field reports, discounting some, acting on others, and constantly updating an operations map. It's a nerve-wracking job, but I thrived on it. And of course I kept thinking about how, and how well, I would perform this task in a real war, under fire.

Though Billy's skills as a leader of infantry were steadily developing, he still dreamed of flying. "I'm strengthening my eyes," he wrote Kate on April 3, 1938. "I've got the color blindness licked, and I'm working on the near-sightedness. I'll take the exam in May, and with any luck be in Texas"—Kelly Field—"shortly thereafter. I'm not giving up on this," he insisted. "I want the Air Corps more than any other branch."

The records don't show that he ever became a fully qualified military pilot, but his persistence did bring him a measure of flight training. He spent two weeks in December 1938 on temporary duty with the 3rd Observer Squadron at Langley Field, Virginia, and in the summer of 1939 was posted

to the civilian Alabama Institute of Aeronautics as a student officer. But pilot's wings never appear on his uniform, and his episodic training never leads to an Air Corps appointment. Instead, he's ordered on brief courses at two other army schools—Quartermaster and Motor Transport—before assignment to Fort Benning as a vehicles maintenance officer on January 3, 1940. In effect, he has reversed his father's progress from horse soldier to pilot, an irony perhaps not lost on a man who, like his father, wanted, more than anything, to fly.

You go where they send you. As he had at Fort Washington, Bill Crawford did his work with professional aplomb, but he was well aware of the embers of war glowing fitfully on the horizon. If it comes, he has no intention of riding out the firestorm in a stateside camp.

Meanwhile Kate Crawford had been up to her old tricks again, and this time her reach was truly breathtaking. "I hope we'll get the FHA loan through soon," her son writes her at one point, "but *please* leave Mrs. Roosevelt out of it. If I asked her aid, I'd be marked PI—Political Influence—in the War Department, a distinct disadvantage in the service. May I earnestly ask you to steer clear of the White House in matters pertaining to private concerns?"

In a letter of July 4, 1940, from Fort Benning to his sister Louise, he bellyached about their mother's most recent manipulations, and diffidently noted his promotion to first lieutenant. Then he mentions his growing interest in airborne training for the first time:

> Things are popping in the army now. We're so busy organizing new units that the post stays in a constant turmoil. To me, the most interesting development is a parachute platoon, just forming. I tried my damnedest to get placed in charge of it but didn't have enough pull. I left my name on the volunteer list. I think this is going to be something new in warfare, and I want to be part of it.

Though the army had yet to develop a coherent airborne doctrine, Lieutenant Crawford was already at work on his own: "Parachute troops would be used to take landing fields in South or Central America, or to drop down and oust any enemy outfit that had seized a base there. The parachutists would be followed by air infantry units flown in and landed. Such units promptly placed would be worth many divisions later."

This vision of future war in the southern hemisphere seems startling at first, but perhaps Crawford was pondering the possibility of a Nazi *Blitzkrieg* that would have to be countered by a rapid American response. And it's worth noting that he was already thinking strategically about airborne doctrine before a credible airborne force even existed—and thinking along one of the two main lines planners a few years later would come to follow.

The July 4 letter—occupied in the main with speculation on his probable assignment to Wyoming and plans for Louise's visit there—ends with a wry note on changing attitudes toward the military as the country begins to accept the likelihood of war: "It amuses me now to see everybody getting friendly toward the army. Our troops from Fort Washington were spit upon by the good citizens on various occasions, and we were ever maligned and laughed at. But recently I took a convoy up to Camp Perry, Ohio, and people were offering the soldiers water." The conclusion strikes a more ominous note: "It's a damned good thing our forces are finally being strengthened. Right now we're not much better prepared than Belgium was."

In an earlier letter, written March 7, rumors of war remained in the background as Crawford offers an account of his work, an update about his moviegoing, and a confident musing on his social life and professional future. One page included an architecturally precise drawing of his quarters and a detailed listing of the tanks and trucks that are his responsibility, on the blithe assumption that his sister will share his fascination with engine displacement, muzzle velocity, carrying capacity, and four-wheel drive. It's all rather reminiscent of the drawing of his room and schedule of his days he posted from the academy—the fine detail can be a little dull. But one haphazard paragraph—his letters do tend to be disorganized—evokes the Hollywood theme that entranced him in boyhood and followed him to West Point. "I'm looking forward to seeing *Northwest Passage* eventually. Though our theatre is quite large, it rarely has good shows—mostly cowboy pictures. But Mary and I did see *Gone with the Wind*, which was grand, though very long; it even has an intermission."

For the rest, he seems less concerned with war news than usual, noting rather the social obligations his position entails and looking contentedly forward to the predestined unfolding of his career. "There are seventy-one officers in the regiment. Eventually they will all call upon us, and we will call upon them." Which will entail a new set of visiting cards, due to his jump in rank. "On June 12, I get promoted to First Lieutenant, then in seven more years I'm a captain." In fact, he is a lieutenant colonel by 1944. Rank comes swiftly in wartime.

In May, Crawford was still pressing the War Department for parachute training when orders arrived posting him to Puerto Rico. His feelings were mixed. Jump wings would virtually guarantee him an active role when the war began, and he's uncertain how well he would do with colonial troops. But an overseas post could be beneficial to an evolving career—and Mary would be able to join him. He decides not to contest the assignment though his hopes remain with the airborne, which seems to have replaced the Air Corps in his ambitions.

When he writes Louise about his orders on May 11, the infant parachute battalion is still an ugly duckling to the army's high command, which remains unsure of how such an unconventional force can best be employed. But the German Wehrmacht has been having some success with such units. Indeed, on May 20, nine days after Crawford wrote this letter, Germany undertook a brilliant airborne invasion of Crete, the largest such operation in military history and an inspiration to Allied planners compelled to recognize that this new kind of war was not a development they could afford to ignore.

"Parachutists are dropped from a low altitude and rarely killed while descending," Bill Crawford reassures his sister, before continuing:

At Waalhaven, Dutch farmers tried to snipe them with shotguns, but the German operation was completely successful. The Fallschirmjäger seized a landing field and held it until they could be supported by infantry, who in turn protected the armor that rolled in three days later. But things went less well for the Nazis in Norway, where half a parachute battalion was dragged through the fjords and killed on the hillsides where they landed.

He adds that American paratroopers in training drop into zones shielded by smoke screens and have so far had only one fatality and a few broken bones. "Of course what we can do in training and what the Germans actually have done in combat are two different things."

The differences cause him to brood about America's sluggish preparation for the coming war: "The public seems to think we're ready. They're anxious for us to get into it and get it over with. Hell, I *know* how few divisions we have, how incomplete their equipment is, how unfinished their training. We've made great strides. If we keep on at this rate, in six years we'll have an outfit that would be interesting to see in battle. But not now."

As on other occasions, he expresses disdain for pacifists who blocked rearmament a decade earlier and politicians eager for war in the present day. "However, we'll gladly go out and do anything we're told to do with the tools available—but I hope we can hold back for a year or so. In any case," he concludes sourly, "there's not likely to be much in the way of war in Puerto Rico."

BILL AND MARY CRAWFORD sailed from Charleston for San Juan on May 26, 1941. Neither much enjoyed the four-day journey. Lieutenant Crawford was drafted as "inspections officer," requiring him to confirm the orderly state of the passenger quarters every morning. Seasick the whole time, Mary missed the only drama of the voyage, which occurred when the USAT *Chateau Thierry* was shadowed for several hours by a sub running just below the surface with only its periscope exposed. The United States was not yet at war, but shipping was always in peril. The transport carried large American flags painted on each side to proclaim its neutrality, but it also sported deck guns, and Crawford, movie fan that he was, lingered by the rail composing in his mind a naval duel that seemed more appealing than his stuffy cabin below.

In San Juan, the couple settled into a spacious third-floor apartment in Santurce, a suburb eight miles from Fort Buchanan, where Crawford reported for duty the morning after his arrival. Promoted to captain, he was given command of Company F, 65th Infantry, and fell gladly into the familiar work. "Being with the soldiers did me a lot of good," he wrote in his journal. "I'd been away from troops too long. I was lucky to get this company—there's a high proportion of experienced noncoms and a good mess fund, particularly important to morale."

Infantry company commander. It was called the last good job in the army. You held something close to absolute authority over two hundred men, whose names you knew and whose lives you had sole responsibility to spend or save. Always, when you could, you saved them. But when you had to sacrifice them, you did so with an iron will and without a backward glance. You were aided in your work by an executive officer—a first lieutenant—and by a first sergeant, whose respect and allegiance sustained you. Your company was made up of four platoons, each commanded by a second or first lieutenant: three platoons of riflemen and one weapons platoon armed with mortars and machine guns. The battalion commander, a major, was in immediate authority above you, but he had no say in how you ran your company. You were happier than you ever had been in the army, and you would never be so happy again.

Almost immediately, the regiment left its garrison for maneuvers, to Captain Crawford the heart and soul of soldiering. "The best way to get to know an outfit is to go with it into the field. And I felt right at home with these men. Truth is, I think I'd feel the same way if I were plunked down into a German or British or Russian rifle company. Well, maybe not the Russians."

The maneuvers were challenging. "It's the rainy season on the eastern end of the island, so we marched and bivouacked in slashing torrents and many feet of mud." Still, he welcomed the experience, though he noted, "Truthfully, it seemed to weaken the men more than harden them."

His first impressions of Fort Buchanan were similarly mixed. "The place used to be little more than a target range and an ROTC camp, but with the build-up for the war there are a few thousand soldiers here, so there's a hell of a lot of mud and new construction." Crawford was entirely accustomed to the rapid tempo of army life and took the turbulent transformation of the old fort in stride.

Off duty, things were more problematic. Mary complained of domestic expenses. In their flat the water often goes off, the gas line fails, the wiring short-circuits. Accustomed to life in the field, her husband takes such things in stride, though he is impatient with the ruined roads—"all the cars seem to go to pieces here"—and a commute that throws him in with "the worst drivers in the world. I can curse fluently in Spanish, and often do when I'm behind the wheel." They begin the search for a small house closer to the post.

The island where the Crawfords found themselves in the spring of 1941 had come into the possession of the United States as one of the spoils of the war with Spain. As occupation of the Philippines had opened up the possibility of an American empire in the Pacific, so Puerto Rico pointed toward Caribbean plunder, and the relationship between the islanders and their northern masters was uneasy from the first. In the 1940s, encounters might be hostile or congenial. For Bill and Mary Crawford, they proved to be both.

"When we first got here it felt like half the people wanted to stick knives in our backs," he wrote,

> and while that has changed, the difficulties of daily life persist. Here the plumbing rarely works, and after a heavy rain water drips from the electrical outlets. If it doesn't rain, the city turns the water off to reduce shortages. If it does, your first floor sometimes floods. Tap water must be boiled and filtered before drinking. If you wash in a stream, you're at risk of deadly liver flukes. You can't walk barefoot in your house because God only knows what's crawling on the floor. People stop their cars and defecate in the traffic. Cops watch and do nothing.

Unhappy in the tropic heat and unaccustomed to the Spanish-speaking people, Bill and Mary at first responded to the natives with provincial suspicion and to the island with cautious dislike. But it took Bill Crawford only a week or two to start to feel at home, though Mary would prove less malleable. His language skills sharpened rapidly, and in his scant free time he began to rove the countryside, exploring the old colonial forts and meeting the new flora and fauna. He noted the crops—sugar cane, coffee—and seems awed by the array of fruit trees—almond, mango, breadfruit, banana, lemon, orange. The rainbow of exotic tastes and textures was a welcome addition to bland army chow. He interests himself in Puerto Rico's colonial past, and in its polyglot population even feels his racial tension easing. "Indian, Spanish, Negro—everybody mixed with everybody and now we have—whatever it is we have. Seems to work O.K." And it didn't take him long to grow past the parochial assumptions he'd arrived with, when he assumed English would be widely spoken since Puerto Rico was an American possession. "One still sees the Spanish flag quite often," he noted in his journal, "and I think the upper class still looks on Spain as its mother country. But the people are quite loyal to America, especially now. They rely on the power of the navy, and of course the Federal P. R. Reconstruction Administration is dishing out so much money it's bound to make friends."

The journal shows us a man prepared to fortify his character with an enlarged sense of the world. But his military duties left him little time for such study, even as they proved a source of some satisfaction and no small dismay. He scorned his regiment's blind emphasis on "hardening" at the expense of tactical training. "What good does it do to have a man make a forced march of fifteen miles if he can't serve his weapon at the end of it?" And he chafed against the budgetary limitations that crippled such useful maneuvers as he was able to impose. "I cannot get one single round of tracer ammunition for my machine guns."

A resourceful officer, he found ways around the problem, demanding simulated air strikes against fortified positions, cadging enough TNT to mimic ground bursts during company assaults, and arranging live fire exercises when possible. "I have become a real thorn in Headquarters' side down here. But I feel I am doing my duty, so I keep plugging." Even so, there are limits to what a junior officer can accomplish. "It's hard to work under people whose military thinking is based on ideas discredited ten years ago. But of course us young squirts can only follow the general trend of what the higher-ups desire."

Mary, meanwhile, was consigned to the army wife's round of ladies' lunches and bridge games, though she did enjoy time spent in her garden—like Bill, she exulted in the wild variety of fruits and flowers that flourished on the island. Unlike him, she could never quite reconcile herself to her fellow citizens and indeed would return to North Carolina before her husband completed his tour of duty. "I love Puerto Rico and could live here forever," Mary Crawford confided to her sister-in-law, "but first you'd have to kill all the people and replace them with Americans." This jaunty observation consigns her to the ranks of xenophobes, where—given his early history—we might expect to find her husband. But foreign travel and his work with soldiers have broadened Bill Crawford's horizons, and he is spared the idleness that permits such rootless scorn to grow.

The privates and NCOs of his company unfailingly elicited his admiration. Not so the American officers he has to work with—"Continentals," as they're called:

My Puerto Rican troops make damned good soldiers, but in the past this place has been a dumping ground for lousy officers who've used it as a country club. I serve under reservists getting "pay in grade" even though they know nothing about their jobs. Men who entered West

Point two and three years after I did and were kicked out for dumbness are now National Guard majors getting four hundred bucks a month.

He reached a bleak conclusion: "We make horrible long marches in the tropic sun but seldom have any combat exercises. This is a good place—but it's no place for a modern, thinking soldier."

THE UNITED STATES' entry into the war was only weeks away, and there was a steady drone of activity around the bases near San Juan, but no successful action followed from it. On November 2, Bill Crawford noted, "Last week Army bombers were sent out in flocks thick as seagulls but never found anything to bomb. The Navy hunted for a few days and then either got what it was after or gave up. The Coast Artillery batteries hauled up armor-piercing ammunition and got set to shoot something but nothing came near enough to get shot at." These actions followed reports at Fort Buchanan claiming a German Q-boat had sunk several British vessels further down the coast—presumably the Americans were hoping to draw the surface raider's fire in order to be free to fire back—but the incident faded without an engagement.

British ships were common in the region, and when two Royal Navy destroyers stopped to refuel at San Juan, Captain Crawford had a chance to talk with some of their officers, whose tales brought the shooting war closer to home. "On their way to Britain with survivors from Crete, they'd been strafed by German aircraft, made it through the Suez Canal, and were headed back to England the long way round. They had hundreds of wounded aboard. I talked to an engineer captain who'd also been caught in the debacle at Dunkirk, still angry at the absence of the RAF from the skies over the beaches." Crawford adds his own conjecture—that the Royal Air Force was in fact fighting the Luftwaffe further inland, and that without their efforts "no British would have escaped. But," he concludes, "criticisms of the high command are generally true. The British have a separate air arm that cannot co-operate with the ground troops. The Germans had the same trouble at first, but now they've more tightly integrated their commands." He can't help adding, "Poor old British. When they landed in Norway, I hear they took their golf clubs and fishing tackle with them."

It should be said that my uncle's disdain for Whitehall did not extend to the British rank and file, whose steadfast courage he greatly admired.

With no war of his own to fight, Crawford spent a fair amount of time assessing the one consuming Europe. He foresaw a German victory over Russia, then a new German front striking through the Middle East to assault British forces in North Africa. And he envisioned the end game very clearly:

> The war will drag on until Britain finally strikes Germany on land—
> with, in the end, American forces participating. I'm still not convinced
> we're ready, but I know we can turn the tide. Our state of training
> is intensifying, our industrial base is unequalled, and our potential
> reserves of manpower are huge. Given time, we can do the job. I
> don't think there's any doubt that ultimately we'll be in the war. And
> once we are, we'll finish it OK. But the longer we can wait, the fewer
> bloody blunders we'll make, I do believe.

By this time, he seems to have been largely resigned to his life at a prewar post in a tropical backwater. His days were spent in the field with his troops or at his desk handling the routine paperwork of his company, nights off quietly at home, weekends—when he had them free—dining with fellow officers and their wives at the club and exploring the countryside around San Juan with Mary. But he followed the war in Europe closely, finding it vaguely menacing if oddly remote. In his ordered life, little was happening and—though he was well aware of increasing tensions in East Asia—little seemed likely to. Such was the state of play on December 7, 1941, when the president of the United States informed the United States that it was now at war.

THE CHANCE OF IMMEDIATE ACTION in Puerto Rico seemed slim, but the Germans had submarine wolf packs in the Caribbean, and a small fleet of surface raiders—freighters fitted with deck guns and catapult-launched torpedo planes. Naval facilities at San Juan made obvious targets, and army units were swiftly put in place to defend them. F Company was one of those tasked with the job.

In a letter to his sister written a week after Pearl Harbor, Bill Crawford offered vivid details:

There was a lot to do right away. I had to find my lieutenants (they were at the movies), round up my company (mostly at the movies), and secure ammunition—entirely against regulations, I keep 6000 rounds in the company area so we don't go to war with empty guns. Within thirty minutes, we'd put a cordon defense around the dry dock and the radio station, set up checkpoints and sent out patrols. We sandbagged our anti-aircraft guns while the navy mined the harbor. We've been on guard for a week now but will soon be relieved by reservists—our mission in the 65th is to counterattack enemy units which gain toeholds in the islands.

Realistically, he saw almost no chance of such ground action developing in the near future, while being well aware that much of the Pacific was in flames—Wake Island, Midway, Guam, and the Philippines perhaps already lost to the Japanese. "But if the boys hold out on the various islands, we can build the Philippines into a monstrous base and then systematically destroy Japan. Once we get rid of their fleet," he adds, "we can knock those slant-eyed yellow bastards back a few centuries."

Only six days after the Japanese attack, little hard information had surfaced, and in its absence Captain Crawford gets a good deal wrong. He doubts the US fleet had been trapped in the harbor and suspects losses at Pearl were light. He doesn't hesitate to cite rumors, both dark ("the *West Virginia* was damaged terribly") and triumphant ("We got the Jap carrier and a number of subs"). And, while not buying into a conspiracy theory, he does believe the Roosevelt administration is playing up bad news to enlist public support for the war. Displaying a scorn for the enemy he would later abandon, he assumes the attack must have been orchestrated by the Germans as the Japanese surely lack the strategic skills to have managed it.

From a young officer whose occasional analysis of the European war has often been astute, this farrago of misreadings is surprising, but it doesn't foreclose his envisioning the probable end game in the Pacific with commendable accuracy.

Two months after Pearl Harbor, Captain William Crawford was sitting in his office going through the motions of dealing with the papers scattered across the surface of his scarred steel desk. The morning report, the revised duty roster, the new training schedule, a handful of memos from battalion HQ, a few personal letters—enough to keep him busy through the hollow hours of the day, enough to dull his ceaseless awareness that he was at war but the war was elsewhere. He has one man AWOL and two just back from leave, and a hard-working corporal due to be awarded sergeant's stripes . . . Crawford smiled. He relished the occasions when he was able to give well-earned promotion to his men. As to the rest, there were requisition forms from the mess hall, the motor pool, his request for additional ammunition for training kicked back to him for fuller justification, no surprises there.

The young captain squared the tangle of papers into a neat, pointless pile in the center of his desk, producing a thick white rectangle that threw a sharp shadow under the glare of the gooseneck lamp. He studied the pile without really seeing it as he sipped coffee slowly—there was excellent coffee on the island—from a heavy china mug.

Bill Crawford was not a deeply introspective man, but the events of recent days had opened new chambers in his thinking. He was a soldier under orders in a nation at war. Much that lay ahead was not within his control, but none of it needed to be altogether sealed away from his understanding. He had rarely pondered the fate that had led him to an army career, usually accepting his life's unfolding as predestined: from childhood, he had dreamed his father's dream for him. But now he was inclined to examine his journey's origins.

One element was real patriotism—elemental and unembarrassed. Like Louis, William was sustained by a deep love of country, but he would have been made uncomfortable by his father's sentimental way of proclaiming it. The shift in tone was cultural—Bill Crawford belonged to the *Casablanca* generation, which prized cynical speech countered by stoic behavior. He was entirely ready to fight for the flag but not much interested in waving it. Duty, honor, country. This trinity was one god. It required no comment.

No shame that a second motivation was more practical: if a career officer went through the war without a combat posting, even through no fault of his own, he could hardly expect preferment in peacetime. Promotions and decorations would come to those who fought. He had to be one of them.

The third motivation might have been the most important. It was also the hardest to grasp. In a class at West Point he had been introduced to an idea of Aristotle that had stayed with him in a somewhat muddled form. It had to do with virtue and human thriving. You succeeded as a man to the extent that you lived the full range of your powers, bringing your skills to bear on tasks that ennobled your society. You would at the same time become the best possible version of yourself. The idea made sense. If you were born with a gift, if you developed a talent, if through hard years of training you became proficient in an art, then to ensure your virtue you needed to practice it, to test who you thought you could be in a world that would tell you who you were.

Captain Crawford finishes his coffee. There it is, he thinks. My country is at war and I need to defend it. My profession is the army and I hope to advance in it. My skills are such as they are and I want to practice them.

On impulse, he rolled a sheet of onionskin into the ancient typewriter crouched on a narrow table beside his desk and began a letter to his sister. He was hardly past the opening pleasantries when the outburst came:

> Christ knows I feel like stowing away on a freighter or stealing a bomber and going to the Philippines. I can speak Spanish, I can fly a plane, I can drive a tank, a truck, a half-track, or anything else the army possesses. I can fire all our weapons, plan strategy or tactics, command any force up to the size of a battalion. I'm sure I could run a regiment in a pinch. Yet I have to sit here on a kind of glorified guard duty because that's where they sent me. *Because that's my job.*

Crawford underlined the last four words, realizing as he did so that he had turned the letter to his sister into a message to himself. Well, then, he should heed it. Buck up. And recognize, he ordered himself, recognize that the whole world was a theater of war. War had come to the Atlantic and Pacific. It would come to the Caribbean, too. The ocean already swarmed with U-boats and surface raiders. Oil refineries in Dutch Guiana processed Venezuelan crude. They would be prime targets. Above all, the islands gave access to the Panama Canal, whose defense was paramount. There would be plenty to do in Puerto Rico.

All true, but none of it offered much consolation. Whatever action came to the region would be by sea and air, and it might be years in coming. The Germans would have their hands full with the Russians. The Japanese were two oceans away. If the Axis could ever allot resources to the western Caribbean, they wouldn't send infantry. Bill Crawford had gotten it right the first time. While he was pushing papers in Puerto Rico, his classmates a world away would be leading men in battle.

While he was stuck in this fucking backwater, West Point had gone to war.

FOR THE UNITED STATES, 1942 was the first full year of war. Bill Crawford spent it at Fort Buchanan. He avidly followed the news from both fronts. From Europe, apart from a Russian counteroffensive that had crushed the German advance on Moscow, the news was mostly bad. From the Pacific, worse.

In January alone, Japanese forces, already potent in the Philippines, invaded Burma and the Solomons; in February, Singapore. April witnessed the Bataan death march, and with May came the surrender of Corregidor. But May also saw the Battle of the Coral Sea, where an American and Australian naval victory blunted the Japanese advance. For Crawford, the epic battle bore a personal cost—an old friend from Hertford, a navy lieutenant named Tom Nixon serving on the aircraft carrier *Lexington*, was gravely wounded in an aerial attack. Bill learned of this in a letter from Louise, to which he replied: "You said Tom was unconscious for two weeks after the battle and doesn't remember much of what happened. One night during the Coral Sea fighting I dreamed I saw him in a compartment on a carrier filled with smoke and debris, burning chunks of wood and metal falling. Tom was choking, gasping for air. I woke up choking and gasping and coughing."

This account is the more remarkable in that nothing like it appears anywhere else in his writing. William Crawford was a skeptical man, whose rare references to a spiritual realm tend to the comic or the faintly mocking. Quite unnecessarily, he points out the parallels for his sister, but beyond that doesn't trouble to ponder the dream at all.

Still, the combat wounding of a close friend renewed his sense of distance from the action. In a letter soon after, he writes:

I was so young during the First World War that I remember little of it. I do remember how eager Daddy was to fight in France and how disappointed he was when illness wouldn't let him.

I don't doubt I'll see action in the present war, which seems especially personal to me since I have so many classmates actively engaged in it. I get letters from many and learn the exploits of others in the *Army and Navy Journal.*

Of course, I also try to look past the personal. Having gone to West Point, and having studied and practiced tactics for the past nine years (not counting the wars with Daddy's old toy soldiers), I find it interesting to follow the grand strategy of the war as a whole, tracking the action as closely as possible, testing how well I can foretell outcomes and read their shadows for future events. I'd be first to grant that my successes are mixed. It's probably just as well I'm not a general.

This is false modesty. If the war lasts long enough, he may dare to dream of a brigadier's star. While still at West Point, he had written, "In peacetime, generals are made not by strategic brilliance but by length of service. War changes things."

Early in January 1942, William Crawford and a brother officer spend a weekend fishing for blue marlin off the Puerto Rico Trench, a vast oceanic fault near the coast. Returning to San Juan Sunday night, the two soldiers witnessed the collision of a pickup truck and a *publico*—an unofficial taxicab—followed by a brief firefight between the drivers, who pulled revolvers and began shooting at each other:

I couldn't see much of the fight except for the muzzle flashes, but when a stray bullet plowed into our fender, I cut the car lights, took cover, loaded my pistol, and sneaked in on one flank to investigate while Lieutenant Artman took the other. I figured it was time somebody disarmed the drunken fools. I hoped it wouldn't come to more than that, but I was ready to kill anybody who pointed a pistol in my direction.

When the American officers arrived on the scene, one man sat writhing with a bullet in his leg, while the other lay "damn near floating in his own blood." Crawford and Artman gave what aid they could and waited until the police and medics arrived. That took an hour. "My first firefight," Crawford muses, "and it was a couple of civilians in a scene out of a mystery movie."

In April, made regimental adjutant, he found his social life a little larger and registered some disappointment at one aspect of it. "Since the war

started, officers no longer really dress for dances, but the girls still do."
One occasion would require the formality he cherishes: on July 1, Captain
Crawford was promoted to major. Mary recorded the celebration. "We had
to have a party for the regiment, and Bill would have been chagrined by
anything less than full dress. Everyone had a good time, I think. Anyway,
they drank a lot."

In August, his sister sent news of a British commando raid recently under-
taken in Norway. The target was a hydroelectric plant the SAS successfully
destroyed. Secrecy naturally shrouded the details, so Major Crawford's pré-
cis is off target, though his conclusion doubtless is not: "That was probably
what we call a 'reconnaissance in force,' one that pressed the Germans to
commit reserves so the English could test their resources. The outcome will
have been carefully studied by Allied planners. It sounds like the kind of
classic operation destined to be modeled on a war college sand table."

On Christmas Day 1942, he typed four single-spaced pages of detailed
thanks for several boxes of Christmas presents. Carbons went to family and
friends:

> But the best present of all was good news from the fighting fronts—
> Wavell moving south to smash the Japs in Burma, Montgomery and
> our 9th Air Force tearing up the Germans in North Africa. Rommel's
> gang is beaten. The Russians are pressing south toward Rostov in
> what may turn out to be the most important campaign of the year.
> We're exterminating the Japs at Buna Airfield and the Aussies have
> joined us to help take back New Guinea. The end is nowhere near
> in sight, but a year that began so badly is signaling the prospects of
> Allied victory.

Christmas was shadowed not only by the war but by a rumor that female
dependents were to be evacuated from the island due to the fear of an Axis
attack. The threat kept Crawford on duty throughout the holiday, leaving
Mary to move alone to their new house, which for the first week was without power or water. But she exulted in the larger space and the new location,
and, as soon as their household goods were shipped down from Norfolk,
was content settling in. The threat of invasion passed.

An avid gardener, Mary took advantage of the island's year-round growing season to lay out beds of fruits and vegetables. Her husband helped

when he could but confessed in a letter to Louise that his duties left him little energy for domestic chores. "It's a beautiful night. The moon is shining through some royal palms—but I'm sleepy. The long hours of work in this stultifying climate enable me to give just so much, and it all goes to Fort Buchanan. I'm not a lot of use around the house, I guess."

In August, the tempo of training quickened, bringing weeks of field problems welcome after months in garrison. "Tent life is fine except that the canvas gets hotter than hell in the daytime and leaks like a sieve when it rains." His joke sounds like an old one: "The mosquitoes are smart here—they look at our dog tags to see if we're their blood type." But Bill Crawford understood the pleasantries were placeholders for the stories he can't tell. "As you know, there's very little in my work that I can write about so it's hard as hell to put together an intelligent letter. But I can tell you I still command a battalion here, and I'm also executive officer in charge of plans and training at the Replacement Center. That job takes most of my time. When I get a night free, we go to the movies."

His frustration returns:

It's a hell of a big war. I'm doing my part, I guess, but God knows I want to be in a more active phase of the fight. . . . Today is exactly three years from the date the German armies marched into Poland. On that day I was flying a T6 Texan over the Black Warrior River in Alabama. The following September I was stationed at Benning. Last September I was on maneuvers with the umpti-umpth infantry. And now I'm training a battalion of recruits. The Army's found different jobs for me to do, and I've learned a lot from all of them, but with the war raging on two fronts, the job I'm in now is not the one I want.

Weeks later, he answered a letter from his mother in which Kate had expressed her hopes for a lasting postwar peace and inquired cautiously about her son's marriage.

"You mentioned hoping that the day was not far away when love would replace hate," he writes. "I wish I could share that dream but I imagine that this war will end with greater hatreds alive in the world than ever before in history."

Don't worry, though, we'll have a little force behind us—an Army and Navy to back up your prayers. As to Mary, it has been particularly hard being separated from her, because our married life has been exceptionally smooth and happy and we both really love each other so much and in so many ways. In addition to the young romantic love we started with and still retain, our love has deepened and matured. I knew her well before I married, and I suppose that made me more certain I was right. I feel she is the proper wife for me of all the people I have ever known. But I shouldn't bore you.

He's not boring his mother—he's very nearly taunting her. To remember the defensive tone of his letter from West Point about Mary Shelburne, the urgency with which he assured Kate of his filial devotion, and the notes of doubt raised by both Kate and Louise before the wedding is to be reminded that Bill Crawford's marriage amounted to an assertion of will confirming him in his maturity as strongly as the army had. It's understandable that he should flaunt his happiness, though a little unattractive, as is his blunt reminder that the peaceful world his mother hopes for must be bought with blood.

BY SPRING 1943, Crawford had endured his exile long enough. He sensed the war sweeping rapidly past him. That winter, Allied forces had retaken New Guinea and Guadalcanal; Russia had crushed the Nazi armies at Stalingrad; and American heavy bombers were hitting German soil. At the Casablanca conference, Roosevelt had called for the unconditional surrender of the Axis powers. My uncle was determined not to sit at his desk or shepherd a company of trainees a moment longer than he had to. He put in for home leave and returned to North Carolina to reunite with Mary, who had returned earlier that year, and see family and friends. But he also took a trip to Washington, DC, where on March 30, he paid a call on classmates at Fort Belvoir, hoping they might be able to help him enter one of the theaters of war.

There was some risk in the move. He had left Fort Buchanan knowing he might have to return, and he had left behind a record of high achievement shadowed by struggles with his superiors. He had forwarded his records to the War Office, and there would doubtless have been some communication between Washington and the commanding general of Crawford's old outfit. If luck were with him, he could be in action by year's end. If not, he might languish in Puerto Rico for the duration. Awaiting the outcome in a hotel in Alexandria, he writes to Kate: "I'm awfully glad I came because I did get some things accomplished—subject to recall to P.R., I've got a good shot at an assignment where I'm certain to see action. Also I have permission to visit the War Department before leaving the United States and see if orders can be issued sending me to the combat post I want."

THE NEW PENTAGON building was now complete, and by April 1943 most military administration was already housed there. But there were still War Department offices scattered in federal buildings all around the city, and it was to one of those, a shabby warren somewhere in Foggy Bottom, that Bill Crawford reported on April 18. A tech sergeant admitted him to a dim room made large by its lack of furniture: there was only a wall of steel file cabinets and a wooden desk with a swivel chair behind it; a straight-backed chair for visitors; a flag; a presidential portrait; and a narrow, brightly polished window that sought, but failed to find, the river.

The man behind the desk is an assistant G1, a deputy chief of staff in charge of certain officer personnel assignments. He's a bird colonel, a retread, overage and overweight, but the Great War ribbons that bridge the left pocket of his blouse tell Major Crawford that this man hasn't spent his career behind a desk. The G1 is smoking a small black briar pipe whose foul perfume fills the room. He wears a West Point ring.

"Have a seat, Major. Tell me what I can do for you."

"I want to get in the war, sir. I've been in the Caribbean so long I'm growing gills."

"Important work down there," the elderly colonel says vaguely. "The canal . . . "

"That's a navy job, sir, an Air Corps job. I'm an infantryman."

The colonel rolls his chair back from his desk, tents his fingertips, and studies my uncle through a curtain of smoke. "You seem to have ruffled a few feathers down in Puerto Rico."

Bill Crawford is prepared for this loaded observation. He has rehearsed a reply that will—he hopes—combine tact with honesty.

"The 65th is a good outfit, colonel. First-rate soldiers and officers who for the most part know their jobs. But the army understandably doesn't allocate major resources to that, ah, theater. So I pushed pretty hard to get my people what they needed and in the process I guess I stepped on some toes."

"Go on."

"Well, I'm—I've been—a company commander, sir. I've trained men who may well be going into combat. It's been my task to get them as ready as I possibly can. I guess that's the best I can say."

The colonel with the Great War ribbons and the West Point ring—he has surely noticed the one this young man is wearing—lets a silence briefly linger; then, with a slight smile, he relents.

"Rest easy, Major. They've cut you loose at Fort Buchanan. You're mine now. The question is, what do I do with you?" The colonel nods toward the file folder centered on his desk. "You showed an interest in the airborne before they packed you off to Puerto Rico. That still the case?"

"Very much so, sir."

"Happens I have a place for a field-grade officer in a parachute class forming at Fort Benning next month. Any interest?"

"I'd welcome that assignment, colonel."

The senior officer's pipe has gone dead. He upends the bowl over an empty coffee mug and begins to dig at the ash with an unfolded paper clip. "It's a three-week course. Not sure what they'd do with you afterward. Truth is, the army's still sorting out the airborne. You might go to one of the battalions or on for more training—demolitions, sabotage, cloak-and-dagger stuff." There is a faint disdain in his tone, but Major Crawford decides to ignore it.

"I'll go where they send me, sir."

"We all do," the man behind the desk says sourly. He sighs. "Well, I'll have your orders cut. I hope this turns out to be what you're looking for. Jump school is pretty rough—physically, I mean."

Bill Crawford suppresses a smile that might be seen as mild insolence. Ever since his early teens, he has kept himself in shape, and since West Point he has understood physical fitness to be a fundamental duty. Nearing thirty, he prides himself on being able to count more push-ups than a nineteen-year-old recruit. On forced marches, he has sometimes run in place at the head of a passing column then lapped it as soon as it passed.

"That won't be a problem, Colonel."

"Well, we'll see."

CRAWFORD flunked the first week.

He had never flinched when faced with hard training, but jump school lifted the ordeal to a new level of intensity—the constant running, the exhausting calisthenics, the obstacle courses that can and do break bones, the hours of unarmed combat, the sleeplessness, the shouts—all carry him back to his plebe year at West Point. But he's older now, and the training is tougher. Yet there's a democracy to it that he finds appealing: a cadre sergeant can command a student officer of any rank to drop to the ground and give him twenty push-ups—"sir"—and the officer must promptly obey. Crawford also responds to the esprit of the program, the sense that the survivors will join an elite. So his initial failure stuns him, and—hardly a whiner—on May 4 he permits himself to bitch a little in a letter to Louise: "The first week of Airborne school was *very* rough. We had intensive physical training—five-mile runs, calisthenics to the point where a dozen men passed out, advanced jujitsu, tumbling, rope climbing. The judo is brutal. The object is to kill so it's difficult to practice. We injure a man or two a day by kicking each other in the stomach and sometimes accidentally in the skull." At which point, he has yet to lay eyes on a parachute.

There are aspects of the rest of the training I'm not supposed to write about—and of course nobody has laid eyes on a parachute yet. Out of sixty officers, a quarter have resigned from the course and another quarter were dropped for injuries, mostly broken bones and fractures.

The cadre are relentless. I don't think they're altogether opposed to killing a man here if it would save two others in the field.

All of which is to prepare a sorry confession: I have to repeat the week. The tropics evidently softened me. On the runs I would eventually pass out—get up and go on—pass out again. I fell when I fainted and hit the ground with my head half-a-dozen times. The truth is, I guess I was pretty badly hurt—but I kept on, hoping I'd be passed on determination.

I wasn't. I have to repeat the whole damned week, "A" stage, "hardening" as they call it, the kind of ferocious program I had my doubts about inflicting on the 65th in P.R.

In his second shot, Major Crawford drew on his soldier's heart to carry him past the limits of his body and was certified to stay in the course. He did not trumpet his victory, but he did permit himself to examine the odds. "Out of the 60 officers with whom I started, 33 are left. The course is tough. And it's especially made so for the commissioned ranks." Somewhat cockily, he announces that the next three weeks, culminating in five qualifying jumps, will be "easy sailing," though he recognizes that it will take some nerve to face the first tower. "Many refuse it," he muses. "You have to defy the law of self-preservation to do it."

The school is almost over before he has time to write again:

Week before last I took B Stage. We spent half of each day learning to pack parachutes, half practicing jumps from dummy planes and working on a landing trainer—an inclined I-beam down which we'd roll in harness to be cut loose without warning. The hardest task, as I'd expected, was the 33-foot tower jump. You fall 20 feet, then get caught—you hope—by a cable.

Last week we began practicing drops from the 250-foot towers, getting in some shock harness work and landing practice. We also learned to cope with being dragged along the ground by open chutes while we struggled to collapse them against the blast of an airplane propeller. Interestingly, these are the same machines used to create heavy winds for Hollywood movies.

I made six free descents from the tower, one at 11 pm—dark as hell; couldn't see the ground. It *was* spooky, but now I can take the stuff they throw at us in stride.

I made my first real jump a little while ago. The shock of the chute's opening bruised my shoulders but I think I managed an adequate landing. Style is important in the Airborne. They don't talk about it or teach it to you, but things must be done with panache.

We jumped from 1200 feet. The next jumps will be lower, and in four more I'll be qualified and Mary can pin on my wings. These final jumps will be easy, but I won't deny a touch of fear while I sat in the plane waiting to make the first. Then I remembered Daddy once saying fear is part of a soldier's life, that it doesn't matter if you have it, only how you handle it. When the order came to stand up and hook up, I didn't hesitate in the door. It does take some guts. It'll take more over Germany or France.

On June 21, 1943, Major Crawford graduated from the Airborne School and was assigned to the 511th Parachute Infantry Regiment at Camp Mackall, NC.

ON DECEMBER 13, 1943, my uncle signed a last will and testament, disposing of his goods and chattels in conventional fashion, but including an amusing bequest to his mother. "My refrigerator—isn't that touching? All she has is an icebox. Mine's full of food anyway and it would be an inconvenience to clean it out."

But he also included a deadly serious paragraph making absolutely clear his contempt for isolationist politicians:

> If I am killed in the service of my country, please realize that my death
> was the direct result of inadequate preparations by the United States
> and that my blood and that of thousands of others who died for our
> nation is on the stupid bastards who stripped America of her basic
> military requirements. Those people—Burton Wheeler, Gerald Nye,
> and men of like color—who caused the bulk of our fleet to be sunk
> in 1929, struck us a blow comparable to that which the Japs dealt us
> at Pearl Harbor and those well-meaning colossally stupid men should
> be hauled before a civilian tribunal, found guilty of high treason, and
> shot.

WRITING ABOUT HIS WORK, Major Crawford was usually terse. Wartime circumspection, exacting duties, and consequent exhaustion go far toward explaining this brevity, as does his modest assumption that his civilian readers may have limited patience with military lore. But in November 1943, he sent his ten-year-old nephew—my brother Arthur—a three-page, single-spaced report on a regimental exercise that's more vivid than anything he had written since leaving West Point. Nor would he offer such rich detail again until he is in a combat zone.

Beyond doubt, this generosity was prompted by Major Crawford's sympathetic understanding that a little boy, feverishly alert to the fervid culture of a world at war and proud to have a father and an uncle under arms, was the ideal recipient of a letter from the front, even if the front, for now, is still in North Carolina:

> The 511th had its first night jump last Friday morning at 2:30 AM—
> one hundred aircraft loaded with parachute infantry and all our gear.
> I served as supply officer for the regiment and jumpmaster on my
> plane. In the dim cabin light, I looked at the faces of the men. Some

were haggard, some anxious, some impassive, some feigned sleep. A number chewed gum or the stubs of cold cigars. Equipment bundles pressed against their knees. Faint moonlight glowed over the drop zone.

Not always such a vivid writer, here he takes the challenge of setting the scene, and kicking it into action.

When the red light flashed, I ordered my stick to stand up, hook up, and check each other's chutes and packs. Then I checked each man. At the crew chief's signal, I stood in the door, looking down on terrain I'd seen only on a sand table. We passed over a small lake, a power line, a scattering of buildings. The green light popped on. "Follow me!"—and I was through the door. We were 800 feet above the ground. After the chute cracked open, I looked around for planes close enough to pose a danger, ready to partially collapse the canopy so I could fall away quickly if I had to, but the sky around me was clear.

It doesn't take long to hit the ground from that altitude so right away I started scanning for obstacles to landing. The winds aloft were stronger than we'd expected. I was being swept across an open field toward dense woods. There wasn't time to slip the chute. I pressed my boots together and crashed down through the treetops, ending up hanging from the risers maybe thirty feet in the air—it was too dark to be sure. The limb I was hanging from snapped and I dropped again. I tossed my helmet down to see if could figure the distance from the sound of it hitting, and judged I was close enough to risk the fall without deploying my rope.

I was closer than I thought. Two passing troopers grabbed my boots and hauled me out of the tree. I had some cuts and bruises but it could have been much worse, and for a few of our people it was. We had a number of soldiers with broken legs and while making my way to the assembly point I stopped to help the medics give morphine to one man who'd slammed down straddling a high wooden fence. He died the next morning. Another jumper was killed when his chute wound around his legs and never opened.

Three of my stick ended up in the trees but none was badly injured, and the rest landed in the open field. As soon as the last man jumped, the crew chief on the C-47 tossed out our equipment bundles—350 pounds of communications gear and some of the heavier weapons like mortars and machine guns. We had our individual weapons lashed to us. Maybe you remember that I carry a folding stock carbine. Once we'd formed up at the assembly point we moved out to seize a bridge and establish a perimeter defense. Our mission was to prevent the enemy from sending reinforcements across the bridge to block an attack by friendly troops twenty miles away. Troopers from other battalions of the 511th continued to drop on both sides of the bridge as the fighting developed, some of them into the swamp it spanned.

I think you'd find night action pretty exciting. The imaginary combat is vivid—flares, illumination rounds, flashes simulating artillery fire. And the constant chug of mortars and the chatter and snap of blank rounds from machine guns and rifles.

We did our job. In a few minutes we had several thousand parachutists astride the ruins of the enemy's main line of communication. After bringing the exercise to a successful conclusion, we all marched home.

Now I must close because I have a lot of work to do. As big in scale as that night jump was, I'm preparing orders for my part of a *huge* exercise the 511th is going to be involved in very soon. Can't say much more about it now, but I think it will be the largest airborne maneuver the army has ever held.

In an undated letter from Camp Mackall, Bill Crawford announced his appointment as XO, 1st BN, 511th Parachute Infantry, "a part of the 11th Airborne Division." From this point on, he will wear the Angels' winged patch on his left shoulder. He had come to his last army home.

"I've made six jumps," he tells his sister proudly. "What's next we've not been told, but I'll be here a few more months at least. Please give Arthur my address and tell him we run 3.3 miles every morning before breakfast." Louise was living at Penney Farms, Florida, while her newly commissioned husband commanded an infantry training platoon at Camp Blanding.

ON MARCH 30, 1944, the author enters the story, an event he will not linger over long and one perhaps not worth mentioning at all, save for my uncle's ebullience at my appearance. Late in her pregnancy, my mother had written to ask if he would be my godfather, even in the lamentable event that I should prove to be a girl. Given the tenor of the times, his answer is perhaps a little surprising, especially as he reiterates it in subsequent exchanges. "Honored to be the baby's godfather, and I hope it *is* a girl—so there!" It's true that after I disappointed him, he at once began musing on the year 1962, when I would surely enter West Point, and he makes note of a fall his sister had taken, apparently without ill effect. Familiar as I am with the tone of their letters to each other, I'm quite sure my mother's apologies for her gender were made largely in jest, while her brother's reassurances were genuine. Whether, as Bill Crawford prepared to go to war, she was altogether happy to see him welcome a future warrior is another matter.

From HQ, 11th Airborne Division, Camp Polk, LA. Thursday, on April 6, 1944, Major Crawford wrote:

Dear Louise,

I am so proud of you and of my nephew I can hardly contain myself! Gee, Weez, I really am. I have never been so proud of anything in my life as to have a real nephew named for me. Naturally, he can never be any more loved than I love Arkie, who is my very close friend and in the future I hope close companion too, but this new model of yours quite takes my breath. Apparently the fall you took had no bad effects. I hope that whatever part of your anatomy you lit on is O.K. That's a fitting prenatal training for a paratrooper's namesake.

And he has his own big news:

I have been transferred to the General Staff Corps for Duty with Troops, and am now the G-4 of this Division. That is, I'm on the General's Staff and am in charge of supplying and equipping the division, and arranging its rail, water, and air movements. I'm still on jump status—but am no longer in the 511th Prcht. Inf. Incidentally—I've gotten in one jump here in Louisiana. Oh yes, I oversee all parachute maintenance, supply packing, etc. etc. That includes the Field Artillery parachute equipment, engineer equipment (rubber assault boats, etc. etc.).

If Crawford's own letters are a bit offhand about his appointment to the general staff, Mary is ready to exult for him:

The most wonderful thing has happened—Bill was made G-4 of the division. It was a great promotion in duty for him and should mean swift promotion in rank. I am so proud. He's been detailed to the General Staff Corps and instead of crossed rifles wears a star with the seal of the US in the center. He's awfully happy and has told me he would rather have this job than any other in the Army.

Her joy is clearly genuine, and I don't doubt his satisfaction was as well, but it has to have been a little shadowed by the fact that he's been promoted out of the infantry and into administration, no longer a troop commander but one of those higher-ups field officers often scorn. Having headed platoons, companies, and battalions, Crawford was eager to lead troops in battle, not help organize the fighting from behind the lines. Still, in jungle warfare, there sometimes were no lines. And he might remind himself that he would be G4 of an airborne infantry division, shock troops, a warrior elite.

His rise became dauntingly swift. He had entered the 11th as executive officer of a battalion; only months later he'd be helping shape the whole division's destiny and would soon wear a lieutenant colonel's leaves as a reward for doing so. And he was only twenty-nine years old. He hadn't expected to see captain's bars until 1947. All credit to the war! "War changes things."

Meanwhile, the social order also changed. Mary would become the colonel's lady. She had already watched the 511th pass in review to reward her for sewing the regiment's crest to its flag, earning a thank you letter from the commander, asking her to add the undoubted battle ribbons to come, after the war. More dismayingly, she and her husband had been invited to sit at General Swing's table at a division dinner dance.

"I was petrified," she tells her sister-in-law. "I even had to dance with him. I stepped all over his feet, I was so intimidated. Because he looks just like a storybook general—tall, commanding, white hair, blue piercing eyes. About the best-looking man I ever saw, except for Bill."

If my uncle had been casual in mentioning his success in a letter to his sister, to Kate he announced his new appointment with some fanfare, quoting in full the order appointing him—"by direction of the President"—and

sketching his new insignia in detail. He outlines the scope of his job, adding, "I'm amazed I was picked." But he still thinks of himself as an infantryman. "And I'm still a paratrooper—I wear the jump boots and the wings." And he's still a field soldier. In the same letter, he adds, "Last night I went through an infiltration course—crawling a hundred yards with tracer rounds kicking an inch above my head and TNT charges simulating shell bursts all around me. Now that my days will be crowded with paperwork, it was a useful reminder of what our job really *is*."

He finished with a note on the news from the fighting fronts—another reminder that his own war draws closer every day:

> I now believe that there's still a chance we may go to England. I
> believe that the Air Forces are going to be given more time to pound
> Germany before the invasion. Hence, we still may get in on that. Any-
> how—I'll find out eventually. I had felt sure that we'd invade by the
> end of March—but I'm not sure now. Meanwhile the Soviet armies

are in the north about 350 miles from Prussia, and in the southwest Pacific the allied forces are doing O.K.

BILL CRAWFORD'S CALL to the airborne would not have arisen from his career ambitions. Then as now, service in elite units training for unconventional warfare was not the surest path to a brigadier's star. Indeed, the twenty-first century is more hospitable to special operations than the 1940s were, and to the uncertainty of the airborne as a career path must be added indecision as to its employment as a force. Well into the Second World War, there was no established doctrine covering the most effective use of parachute troops. There was not even a shared conviction that the army should field such units. As with the debate over cavalry fifty years before, which asked whether horse soldiers should fight as regiments or raiding parties, the army high command was torn by the question of whether airborne units could be best deployed as heavy divisions or in lightly armed commandos.

That question would be settled at the Knollwood maneuvers,[8] in which Bill Crawford was to play an important part. But in 1940, when he first applied for paratroop duty, he was likely less motivated by tactical or strategic questions than by the sheer spirit of adventure that had led him to flying as a boy. Military culture celebrated the glamour of both pursuits, and a specific prompt was supplied by a popular magazine that served as the television of its day. The historian Gordon Rottman speculates that "the first time many heard about paratroopers was by reading a May 12, 1944 *Life* article whose exciting photographs inspired them to join."[9]

A dusty stack of old magazines adrift in the attic of the Hertford house quickly yielded a copy of this article. I eagerly leafed through it, as quite possibly Bill Crawford had done in the post library at Fort Benning. But, expecting a detailed discussion of the infant airborne project, I was a little disappointed by the back-of-the-book spread, finding only a short block of text and a handful of photographs. The article stressed the elite nature of the troops and the demands of their training, reaching a dramatic conclusion

8. Conducted in December 1943 and witnessed by the undersecretary of war and other high-ranking officials, this massive Tennessee exercise determined the future training and deployment of all American airborne forces.

9. Gordon Rottman, *US Airborne Units in the Pacific Theater, 1942–1945* (Oxford: Osprey, 2007).

about their probable use: "A parachutist landing in a strange country must be ready to read maps, operate a radio, seize an airfield, blow up a bridge."

Bill Crawford had already noted this in a letter to his sister almost a year before: "We have a parachute platoon here at Fort Benning, still in the planning stages. I tried my damnedest to get placed in command of it but didn't have enough pull. I put my name on the volunteer list anyway and may get in later." He expanded his ideas on airborne forces. "Parachute troops would be used in our Army to seize landing fields in South or Central America, or to chute down and roust any enemy outfit that had seized a base there. The parachutists would be followed by 'Air-Infantry' to be flown in and landed (not parachuted). Such units promptly placed would be worth many divisions later." We don't know why, in 1940, Bill Crawford was envisioning an invasion of Latin America, though he may have been giving thought to the "Banana Wars," a series of low-level conflicts waged by the United States early in the twentieth century in defense of its commercial interests in the region. Or he may have feared a Nazi victory there. But in any case his understanding of how airborne forces could be effectively used would be played out on many battlefields by the end of the war.

AIRBORNE TROOPERS were always willing to engage a foe, and they didn't have to wait for overseas deployment to find one. Straight leg infantry, encountered in the bars and brothels clustered around training camps, sometimes made the mistake of sporting jump boots they hadn't earned. These might be carved from the owner's ankle with a rigging knife. The little snap blades, issued to parachutists so they could cut themselves free from tangled lines, were strictly forbidden as part of a soldier's kit when in town, an order that was freely disregarded. And to bring increased firepower to a bar fight, men also sometimes sewed a silver dollar behind the pale blue badges on their garrison caps—a sort of concealed brass knuckle. But for the most part the troopers of the 11th could rely on their unarmed combat training, more extensive than that of conventional infantry, and all that they brought to a fight was fortified by their matchless élan.

As an officer, Bill Crawford would have steered clear of these brawls. Indeed, it would have been his job to punish men under his command who engaged in them. But except in the most egregious instances, like most airborne leaders, he was inclined to look the other way. Levels of aggression built into the training could not easily be set aside, and the bond between officers and men in elite units created loyalties larger than the rules.

Barroom battles were not the kind of experiences graduates of the Parachute School and veterans of the 11th Airborne could find recorded in three booklets prepared by the division's publications office.

I came across faded copies of each stacked in a corner of the silver trunk. The booklets have the feel of shabby high school yearbooks, center pages thick with thumbnail portraits of smiling men flanked by images of their exploits, mostly military but studded with civilian pleasures: dances, dinners, boxing, baseball games. Wartime censorship limits the detail with which training can be shown, and a certain sameness marks the parade of snapshots: we're given, again and again, panoramas of troopers swaying under silk; soldiers facing off in unarmed combat or horsing around in chow lines; riggers bent over long tables draped with parachutes; French generals on reviewing stands; jump-booted chaplains solemnly presiding over chapel services. A foreword provided by the NCO editors affirms that God is on our side: "To those who train hard, work hard, and pray, there is a day to come."

General Swing, in his introduction to a brief pictorial history of the 511th, contented himself with a secular note: "If the efforts you have made in training are applied in combat, our record there, soon to be written, will be one of which every man of us will be forever proud." One of those men appears in a picture on the next page, in a group portrait of the division's four assistant chiefs of staff—my uncle, second from left, with his garrison cap rakishly cocked, his trouser cuffs breaking precisely over his gleaming shoes, two ribbons under his parachutist's badge.

IN MAY 1944, advance elements of the 11th Airborne Division sailed for the South Pacific and their long-awaited entry into combat. Their destination was New Guinea.

The last of the division was ashore by June and joined its brothers in setting up operations in an area "completely clear of the enemy and safe as Camp Mackall." Gen. E. M. Flanagan, who served with the 11th in the Pacific and later wrote a major history of the division, may have overstated the case—sporadic fighting continued on the island until the end of the war—though apparently the 11th Airborne saw no action; even so, it was awarded battle honors for serving in reserve. MacArthur's intention was to ensure that the paratroopers had additional training in jungle warfare before he committed them, as well as time to become acclimated to the tropics. That alone would prove a considerable job. Edward J. Drea, in a study for the US Army Center of Military History, describes the dire conditions as "a commander's nightmare because it fragmented the deployment of large formations."

> On the north shore a tangled morass of dense mangrove swamps slowed overland movement. Monsoon rains of eight or ten inches a day turned torpid streams into impassable rivers. There were no roads or railways, and supply lines were often native tracks, usually a dirt trail a yard or so wide tramped out over the centuries through the jungle growth. Downpours quickly dissolved such footpaths into calf-deep mud that reduced soldiers to exhausted automatons stumbling over the glue-like ground. Fed by the frequent downpours, the lush rainforest jungle afforded excellent concealment to stubborn defenders and made coordinated overland envelopments nearly impossible. Infantrymen carrying sixty pounds of weapons, equipment, and pack staggered along in temperatures reaching the mid-90s with humidity levels to match.

"Thus," Drea concludes, "the US Army faced a determined Japanese foe on a battleground riddled with disease and whose terrain made a mockery of orthodox military deployments."

Acclimatizing took almost five months, during which General Swing established jump and glider schools to cross-train every member of the unit. (My mother remembered the scorn with which paratroopers viewed division members who didn't wear jump wings—"Whoops, glider troops!") He also assembled an elite recon team that had no official existence, as he wanted to be free to deploy it without accountability. The fierce tempo of the realistic training killed several soldiers, but it brought the 11th to a high state of readiness for the ordeal that awaited them.

Still, there was time for recreation. Carpenters and electricians built an amphitheater elaborate enough to host a Jack Benny show. There were old movies and pick-up baseball games, and General Swing made sure his troops were well supplied with ice cream, though it's not clear why he felt a nineteen-year-old paratrooper back from the bush would rather have an ice cream cone than an ice cold beer. These innocent entertainments were supplemented by the efforts of a few officers to produce raw brandy from a homemade still until the MPs shut them down.

ON MAY 8, V-mail makes its first appearance in Bill Crawford's letters— one typed page shrunk to a microfilmed scrap to save weight in the immense volume of correspondence travelling back and forth between the states and the worldwide theaters of war. Crawford gives one paragraph to his cross-country journey, remembering earlier trips through the Southwest with his parents, and one to the days on a troopship, where his chief pleasure is in old movies—*The Prisoner of Zenda* and *Under Two Flags* find favor. He can say nothing of his destination beyond confirming his safe arrival, but he does add, "Please tell Tom Nixon that I'm now working down in areas where he had some of his most interesting experiences."

Throughout the summer, he wrote his friends and family as often as he could. He was busy. Some letters are little more than phrases and fragments, but they compose his first set of sketches of his experience of the war: "There are thousands of Japs on the island, but they've mostly been pushed back into the hills where they're gradually starving or dying of disease. We are in a safe place but occasionally find a Jap Zero in the jungle—with the pilot rotting in the cockpit."

The division is inscribing its base camp onto a jungle "thronged with rats, bats, and natives—savage-looking but docile. Of course I studied maps and charts of the climate and terrain before we got here, but the reality—the heat and humidity, the mud and mire—is orders of magnitude beyond my expectation. The water supply alone is a challenge—we're making a tent city much bigger than Hertford."

The 11th Airborne celebrates the Fourth of July with green star clusters, parachute flares, incendiary grenades, flamethrowers.

On July 18, Bill Crawford was promoted to lieutenant colonel. He takes tea with a phalanx of Australian officers as they listened to Tokyo Rose, the silky voice of Japanese propaganda who hoped to demoralize Allied troops by discussing their operations and locations. Like his allies, Crawford chose amusement over alarm. He got in a good deal of flying, once soaring into the crater of an active volcano. He saw *The Wizard of Oz*.

But he was restless in a combat zone where his division was seeing little if any combat. He understood that General Swing—indeed, General MacArthur—wanted them acclimated to the islands before plunging them into the war, but he was irked by the home front assumption that the New Guinea campaign has been all but concluded. "Do folks know that the Japs here still fight like hell and kill lots of Americans? But they are getting licked—we kill a lot more of them. The war is certainly going better now," was his confident conclusion, "but it will take about two years out here to crush the Japs."

The base camp's tents shuddered through an earthquake. There were no casualties.

On July 11, a long letter to Mary—passed on to the Hertford crew—describes a flight to a supply depot three hundred miles south of division HQ to pick up "all sorts of odds and ends—light bulbs, wire, ¼ ton of nails." He sketches the countryside as seen from the air—"coconut groves, swamps, fern meadows, moss, rain forests on the slopes"—noting areas inhabited by pro-Japanese natives, as well as terrain so thick that an hour's flight would be the equivalent of a two-week hike with compass and machete. He prevails on the pilot to let him fly the C-47 for one hundred miles, his first time at the controls of a two-engine plane. "I did OK." Like his father at Kelly Field, he makes a detailed sketch of the cockpit. "A C-47 is a sluggish old thing. It's like flying a boxcar." The flight includes a dip into the caldera of a volcano, where clouds of gas and vapor inevitably remind him of the "Creation of Earth" scenes from *Fantasia*. Once more, his experience had taken him into the world of movies, where his imagination so often dwelled.

In a later letter, he returned to his observations on strategy, finishing with vivid details on jungle rot:

> We are all very pleased here with the good war news from Europe. Meanwhile, in the Pacific, our troops have gotten the part of the Morotai that we want—and the next step is to Mindanao and on up toward Luzon. We'll certainly be glad to get to the Philippines, because somehow that will seem the beginning of the end out here.
>
> Actually, it will take about a year or more to lick Japan—but when we get the Philippines at least we'll be back where we started. From there we can cut Jap supplies to Malaya. Then the British and the Aussies can clean up Malaya, Singapore, and the southern East Indies

while we strike for Formosa and the China Coast. Once we get Air Bases properly located in China we can pound Japan and reduce her air strength sufficiently to permit a landing on the Japanese Islands proper—then it will end.

"We have had some torrential rains lately," he continues.

I reckon we're approaching rainy season but it really isn't due until November . . . I got a case of jungle rot on one foot and have been having a hell of a time with it. It is quite painful—and the flesh just rots away—sort of a cross between athlete's foot and gangrene! But now I have it under control and am gradually ridding myself of it.

The affliction was nearly universal throughout the Pacific.

Jungle rot is a form of ulcer, a skin lesion that can be managed with antibiotics in its early stages but unless promptly treated invades deep tissue, causing great pain and leading in the most serious cases to amputation. At times, more soldiers in the Philippines were sidelined by decaying flesh than by combat wounds, and while the problem was well understood and treatment was available, the conditions of the battle zone made recurrence all but inevitable. My uncle mentions fighting the rot in several letters, but it seems not to have reduced his effectiveness or to have had lasting consequences.

September 15, 1944
We've advanced 3000 miles in the past year. It's Hertford to Frisco —the distances are staggering—and we're just getting out of New Guinea . . . I recently learned that Thad Dulin was killed at Cherbourg on July 22—shot through the heart by a sniper. He landed in the first wave 6 June, a battalion commander. We were second lieutenants together.

So Arthur's a supply officer, too! Tell him not to despair. He'll see combat yet, and probably with a company of his own.

There are comic details:

Yesterday I visited a friend recovering from an operation and saw a dog wander in and collapse under the hospital cot. Surgical outcomes are very good here, but there are few doors on the shacks we use for surgery. One doc mentioned seeing a wallaby hop over an operating table.

As for me, I'm still struggling with the damned jungle rot, but it seems to be clearing up. On the other hand, my new companion is dysentery. Half the regiment has it. To add to the misery, last night a Jap station did such a good job jamming our signals that we had no news all day.

I'll close for now, reassuring you of my safety. It's strange in a way. We're definitely in a combat zone but I haven't really seen any combat. Which doesn't mean our troopers don't find other ways to die.

Indeed, death was a constant presence. Training accidents, parachute fatalities, tropic diseases, vehicle collisions. One of the strangest accidental deaths took place when a team of engineers felling trees with explosives sent a splinter of wood through a soldier's heart. "And of course once in a while we have a suicide," my uncle notes blithely, "but the same is true in civil life."

In fact, much of his work resembles civilian life. As division G4, he is effectively a city manager, responsible for all infrastructure: streets and roads, power and water, housing, clothing, and food supplies. He also supervised building construction, aerial operations, parachute maintenance, and stockpiles of arms and ammunition. The warrior side of his work was not neglected; but his was not yet a city at war.

BILL CRAWFORD has often singled out a specific aspect of his work to describe, and in a letter of September 24 he focuses on the problem of caring for parachutes, made more difficult by the coming of the rainy season. His troops build a drying tower and deploy huge heaters "like those used by the Air Corps to warm up engines in Alaska." There are thousands of chutes that must be treated, inspected, and regularly repacked whether they've been used or not, equipment bundles with identifying colors to be prepared for combat drops—three hundred tons a day. Riggers work day and night with sewing machines "strong enough to sew sheets of plywood together."

All this gear and the men who use it are entrusted to the Troop Carrier

Wing, an outfit for which Crawford has unstinting admiration. "They are one of the biggest factors helping win this war."

> At Hollandia, for instance . . . a landslide took out the only bulldozer. They found another somewhere on the island and flew it in the next day. C-47s parachuted in all necessary supplies, under constant fire as they did so. On New Guinea, where distances are so vast and the last pockets of combat so scattered, Troop Carrier Wing hauls ammunition and rations everywhere.
>
> Just as important for morale, I'm able to send a plane once a week to Australia for beef, eggs, and milk, and another to a government farm two hundred miles from here for fresh vegetables. Given the constraints we operate under, the food here is fairly good.

As he does so often, Crawford concludes this letter with his thoughts on the progress of the war in Europe and his hopes that Russia will soon declare war on Japan. He despairs of China, where the struggle between the Communists and Chiang Kai-shek has paralyzed the effort against the common enemy, and ventures some predictions about the postwar world, seeing China locked in civil war for fifty years and Russia so badly bled as to be powerless. Meanwhile he is caught up in planning the attack on the Philippines while picturing American forces descending on China to begin the final invasion of Japan. As usual, his observations are a combination of clear insight and forgivable folly and his conclusion leaves off global thinking to evoke a more personal dream. "At the end of all this blood-soaked effort, I see most of us joyfully returning home. We fight for many reasons—but home is always uppermost in the heart."

New Guinea, October 6, 1944
> Glad young William put on such a nice show. I'm surprised that you want him to resemble me. Since that's what you want, I'm glad it's what you've got. It'll be interesting to me to see for the rest of my life how I used to look thirty years ago!

Then he gets down to business, and we begin to see the imperatives of logistics.

I've really been busy lately, planning planning planning. It is here in the office that the logistics are set up which win the battles. The office isn't much compared to the troops, I know; but down here tactics are secondary to supply because supply is so very damn difficult.

My "business trip" was made in a C-47, a plane I mentioned having flown one time, some time ago. It's a workhorse—cargo carrier, troop transport, pretty much whatever you need. We paratroopers train on it and generally jump from it in combat. Although twin-engine and of course a monoplane, in a way the C-47 is like Daddy's World War I Jenny, which also served many different roles (including being the first plane I ever flew or flew in). Anyway, I wrote Mary a rather detailed description of the trip which I asked her to forward to you and Mother. But here are a few highlights—

Now he will take us on that "business trip," and his imagery is animated.

The route went for times over hundreds of miles of jungle—with not a sign of life, no tracks, no huts, just a sickly green rolling hell below. Some places there were open plains with a muddy croc-filled river winding through. But jungles are usually very hilly. Only the swamp jungles are flat and they're really swamps. The normal jungle is straight up and down all mud.

We flew over one area where about 50,000 Japs are still holding out. They're well organized, and don't seem to realize that the New Guinea campaign is officially over. They are still fighting our men. We flew over numerous small no-count Jap garrisons. It wouldn't do to land or fly low. Also in the contiguous areas the natives turn forced-down Americans over to the Japs. In other areas the natives are canni-bals—and over 90% of where I flew no white man has ever been.

It's a big old place down here. As I left to return home, I saw planes taking off to go over the hill and strafe Jap airfields—no planes on 'em but supplies and Japs around 'em. Incidentally, I slept four nights less than 2,000 yards from the Jap lines. They stayed behind theirs and me behind ours.

Camped so close to the Japanese he could have seen their cooking fires, Crawford thinks about William Wallace and others in his clan who fought the Yankees. It never got this hot and humid in Virginia, but the same black magic would have prevailed: the sparks flying up, the hushed New England voices.

> Our forces patrol against them and keep them dominated and grad-
> ually kill and capture them. If we try to smash 'em they just fall back
> and to try to annihilate us. Their wild tactics take a hell of a lot of
> American lives, and they get headlines.
>   This is the Japanese way of war. It's not the American.
>   Down here we don't fight that way though. We've lost fewer men in
> the entire New Guinea campaign in which we've neutralized 300,000
> Japs, I reckon—with less loss than on Saipan. At Morotai we cut off
> 35,000 Japs, gained the key objective, and I think lost zero men, or
> maybe one or two. That's smart warfare for a civilized nation that
> should use its machinery to a maximum and spare its infantry for
> getting home and begetting more little infantry to keep us a civilized
> nation.

To a startling degree, the Japanese tactics resemble those of the Marine Corps.

> On New Guinea, we have many bad neighbors, but they are being
> killed off as economically as possible. The Army, anyway, is trying to
> fight a war that's sparing of American lives. Marines are a different
> story. I admire their guts but I'm sometimes baffled by their tactics,
> which involve chewing up an enemy island until every single Jap is
> dead and more than a few Americans also. The Army has learned
> to fight a more clever war out here, given the Japanese advantage
> in sheer numbers. I know the stateside papers give you continuing
> accounts of victory, but the fact is it's been nip and tuck, and but for
> good planning we'd have sustained some massacres.

Established on New Guinea, he wrote frequently, sending carbon copies to as many people as he could in an effort to keep in touch with as many correspondents as he could under conditions that made writing individual letters an impossible chore. This scattershot method enabled a flexible tone that displays close analysis of strategy: we're reading mostly sound thinking on the conduct, aims, and efforts of the war. My uncle knows his stuff.

My problem is that it doesn't always feel like *his* stuff. I don't want military theory, I want the details of his daily life. When this grit and gristle is crowded out by ruminations on the conduct of the global war, I can't help feeling he's letting his ideas overshadow his experience. But I remind myself that the division was not yet fully committed to combat. His own war smolders on the horizon; as he moves closer to it, his accounts will be ignited by the glow.

WAR, WE LEARN, IS WORK—it's sweat, an effort equal to digging a ditch with a shovel or climbing a twenty-foot shaky ladder with a cinder block in either hand. It is love and death as well, of course, but only those who have stood in the fire are free to speak with authority of that experience. The rest of us may at least notice that battle is cradled on a bed of mundane roles and occupations. It demands wheeled-vehicle drivers and pastry chefs, dental technicians, legal experts, watercolorists, specialists in the use of edged weapons, car mechanics, riflemen, priests, photographers, civil engineers. Combat support always outnumbers combat soldiers. In the Second World War, the ratio was at least four to one; in later years, much higher. Fighting relieves routine, but the further you are from the front—when there *is* a well-defined front—the more everyday your every day will likely be. In the Philippines, my uncle would work close to the action, but on New Guinea he had something like a civilian schedule to keep, ordered supplies to track, expended supplies to account for. Guns and butter, bullets and beans. The calculus is clear but the details can be daunting. Indeed, on New Guinea, all but overwhelming.

BY EARLY NOVEMBER 1944, General Swing considered the acclimatization and training period complete, and on MacArthur's command the 11th Airborne Division landed on Leyte in the Philippines. Attached to XXIV Corps, it was committed to combat, and the division faced hostile fire for the first time, under conditions spelled out by the historian Stanley Karnow:

> Leyte, a grim tropical battlefield, presaged Vietnam. . . . [The troops]
> were enduring agonies as they penetrated the island. Laden with
> equipment, they hacked through steamy jungles, the heat and humid-

ity soaking their clothes. They waded waist deep through swamps alive with leeches that sucked their blood, and they clawed up craggy cliffs whose sharp rocks slashed their boots and feet. Ambushes menaced them constantly, and they faced recurrent fire from tenacious Japanese concealed in trees, mountain caves, and holes in the ground. The going grew slower, tougher, and deadlier as enemy reinforcements poured in.[10]

The plight of the 11th was actually worse. Landing by sea, not in an airborne operation, the division found itself sent into battle as straight-leg infantry. Smaller than a regular infantry division and lacking heavy weapons, an airborne division committed to conventional ground combat has in effect already suffered catastrophic losses before the fighting even begins, which is why paratroopers are rarely fed into a sustained encounter across a vast battlefield, their style being closer to that of commandos. But the distinction is not always observed by higher command. Throughout its Philippine campaigns, the 11th Airborne—half strength at just over eight thousand—was given the same sort of missions usually assigned to sixteen thousand men, a circumstance that demanded boldness, flexibility, and sheer guts.

Transportation, supply, and logistics on Leyte presented a particular challenge, for which even the rigors of New Guinea were weak preparation. In the days that followed the landing, General Swing would call on Bill Crawford for a series of improvisations. They began with the beachhead itself, a narrow pocket on a crowded harbor connected by a long supply line to units scattered in the field—the opposite of Normandy, where broad beaches opened onto short paths to the action. Then there was the terrain—mud up to a truck's axles, narrow trails braided with thick roots. Where wheeled vehicles couldn't move, Crawford used foot soldiers, native bearers, even water buffalo. But his most daring improvisation was a plan to insert single parachutists and small bundles of food, ammunition, and medical supplies into deep pockets of jungle erupting in fierce firefights using the division's small fleet of L-4s, the Army's Piper Cubs. Resupply and reinforcements could have been carried out on a larger scale by C-47s, but 8th Army had a limited number of the transports, and they weren't always available to the

10. Stanley Karnow, *In Our Image: America's Empire in the Philippines* (New York: Random House, 1989).

11th Airborne, whose fights were scattered all through the mountains in tactical settings so fluid and rapidly changing that the darting little planes—unarmed, and often under fire—could sometimes do a better job.

It struck Crawford early on that mastering the logistics of an airborne infantry division in battle was not unlike managing a small city whose buildings were burning, whose water mains had burst, and whose power came on only two hours a day. Add gangsters shooting through the office windows and swarms of infected rats and you might get some notion of the scope of the job.

Walking to work one morning, Bill Crawford stepped past the wreckage of a Japanese Zero. The crash had sheared the plane's wings off at the roots—they lay a hundred yards back in the jungle, swarming with snakes and vines—but the fuselage had tunneled through the undergrowth until the propeller collided with a tall balete tree. There the relic rested, metal gone to rust, flesh to rot, for the pilot was still in the cockpit, hanging forward in his shoulder harness, face turned toward the trail, glaring at the passersby. His helmeted skull wore a mask of dried blood under his shattered goggles and the black gristle of the pilot's heart hung like a bell clapper behind its shield of bone.

But these were not the things that tended to spook soldiers using the trail—decaying corpses were the common coin of the island. Rather, it was the way the body, in its thriving ruin, seemed to take up a new position from day to day. Today, the colonel noticed, the dried arm reaching outside the open cockpit had curled up into a summoning gesture, as though its owner were imploring him to come closer and receive some dark confidence. He was minded to refuse. The first time he'd seen the pilot, Bill Crawford felt pity and revulsion. Now he felt nothing much except the vague sense that he would see that beckoning arm again.

In the tent that was now his office—the resort hotel that had once housed logistics had been strafed to rubble—he found his clerk, a gaunt tech sergeant from Indiana named Mainwaring, staring mournfully at a field telephone whose receiver he had just replaced. "Colonel, General Swing has the black ass this morning."

Bill Crawford sighed. He dropped his helmet on a canvas camp chair and laid his carbine carefully across the chair's thin arms. "Sergeant, I wonder if you could find a more decorous way to characterize the commanding general's concern."

"Sir?"

"Forget it. What is General Swing's problem?"

"A light bulb." The sergeant, aware he had suffered some sort of unmerited rebuke, was not inclined to be forthcoming. Crawford waited.

"He needs a light bulb for his map table. The one he's got is one hundred watts and he says it's not bright enough. He wants at least three hundred watts. I've been calling around. Sir," the sergeant said desperately, "I don't think there's a three-hundred-watt bulb on the island."

"Well, there might be one in the harbor. Get on the paperwork and let me think a little."

"Sir."

Colonel Crawford's first thought was that he was being asked to draw on his refined logistical skills and his twelve years in the army to hunt down a common household item that could be had for a dime in any hardware store in North Carolina. His second thought was that many peerless products could be found in the possession of the US Navy. He was a lieutenant colonel of infantry, assigned to the general staff, whose dream had been to lead men in battle, but whose present work involved placating inept supply sergeants and doing their jobs for them. So be it. As he had observed on more than one occasion, you go where they send you.

"See if you can find me a Jeep, Eddie."

Colonel Crawford's driver proved to be a taciturn sharecropper from south Georgia with a cud of tobacco draped behind one check and a very small fund of general conversation, so they rode in silence down to the bay where the ordinary chaos of unloading continued apace. Cranes, crates, bulldozers. Ships half-afloat. . . . While his driver parked the Jeep, Bill Crawford watched a kamikaze drill down through thin clouds to bury itself in the bridge of a Liberty ship. No one nearby paid much attention. The fireball was as commonplace as cargo on a crowded dock.

Crawford sought out the harbormaster, a US Navy lieutenant commander who listened without expression to his story, then nodded toward a hospital ship close offshore.

"See her?"

At first Crawford didn't—the red crosses painted on the bow were all but lost in the jumble of landing craft, tankers, transports, destroyers, and Liberty ships that crowded the harbor. Then he spotted the vessel and nodded.

"She boasts a fully equipped operating room, and they use the brightest goddam lights in the fleet," the sailor said thoughtfully. "I'm pretty tight with one of the surgeons. Find him a bottle of scotch from time to time."

"I don't have any scotch," Lieutenant Colonel Crawford said.

"I've heard the 11th has a still."

"MPs shut it down."

The lieutenant commander sighed. He was a short thick man in sweat-stained khakis, with fashionable green mold on the gold braid crusted on his cap. "Well, Colonel, I don't know how badly you want to make your general happy . . . West Pointer?"

"General Swing?"

"No, you."

"Class of '37."

"Annapolis man, myself. We've been giving you kaydets a fierce time the last few years."

Football. Of course. It was common knowledge throughout the 11th Airborne staff that Bill Crawford was in happy possession of two tickets to the 1946 Army-Navy game, wedged in his wallet like good luck talismans. There have been numerous attempts to buy them from him for truly remarkable sums of money. He had hardly expected his treasure to be known all over Leyte, but it's easy enough to imagine the harbormaster in a poker game with talkative army brass picking up a tidbit to tuck away for time of need. Ten minutes later, the tickets were in the navy officer's pocket and the two men were talking over the progress of the campaign as a launch sped out to the mercy ship bearing a gift from the harbor master to the thirsty surgeon. The three-hundred-watt bulb was the little boat's sole cargo when it returned. Riding back to the 11th Airborne base camp, Bill Crawford held the thing in his lap, swaddled in enough hospital gauze to protect the Christ child.

While the colonel was making his deal, the driver had been advised that their return route was suddenly unsafe. He mapped out another. My uncle nodded his consent. The trip took a little longer but there was no enemy fire. The only sign of the war was a tangle of blackened huts that had once been a village, and the bodies of its occupants. There were a few dead Japanese and Americans also.

Crawford huddles protectively over the precious bulb. For want of a light, he thinks. But not this time.

AN INTERLUDE. Bill Crawford stands, swaying with weariness, beside a private at a trench latrine. Both men lift their chins in a futile effort to avoid the stink. The enlisted man—gaunt, dark hair shaggy, dark eyes—is muttering to a buddy beside him about postwar plans. He wants to make shows for radio and television, suspense stuff, time travel, science fiction. Colonel Crawford can't resist interrupting.

"What's your name, troop?"

"PFC Serling, sir."

"Well, I overheard you. I'm interested in that kind of thing. I used to show movies on a sheet when I was a kid."

"See me after the war, sir," Private First Class Rod Serling says confidently. "I'll show you how to shoot 'em, not just show 'em."

Crawford grins. The grin—formed by cracked lips thick with dust and dried blood—is ghoulish. "I'm a lifer. I won't be looking for work. But I might try to knock out a script."

"I don't think it's that easy, Colonel."

"I guess not. But some ideas just come to me."

BURNING SHIPS AND FALLING PLANES, bombed villages, khaki corpses—Colonel Crawford bore witness to such scenes. Steadily and meticulously, he aided in their construction. The smiling boy who had sailed his first model planes over the rivers of coastal Carolina, the slim adolescent who had taken passage to New York to be beguiled by an aging adventurer, the stylish cadet on parade with cape and saber, the gallant young officer in dress blues who had danced through the night at a White House ball—all of these were folded into the calm professional, who faced the dark imperatives of his trade clear-eyed and wholly committed. *We will be killing here for years to come.*

IN EARLY DECEMBER 1944, Japanese commanders on Leyte—fearing American air power had grown strong enough to jeopardize the lines of communication between Tokyo and the South Pacific—launched an attack on the main American airfields, necessarily sweeping through the 11th Airborne positions that lay in their path. The assault was on a larger scale than the division had yet encountered. It involved enemy infantry brigades surging out of the mountains, demolition specialists tasked with destroying planes on the ground, and parachute raiders descending on headquarters and base camps.

Despite its epic sweep, the combined assault was a failure. Gordon Rottman allots it only a single paragraph in his brief history, though he does note that the attack of airborne on airborne was the only operation of its kind in the Pacific war. But E. M. Flanagan, whose longer book permits a larger story, devotes an entire chapter to the raid, which produced some of the most savage fighting of the Philippine campaign.[11] In these pitched battles, the division's rear echelon would be swept up along with the infantry.

Reading the historians' dry accounts, I found myself driven to imagine the scenes their limp official words concealed, though to do so was a kind of trespass. One story especially stayed with me: a platoon of Signal Corps soldiers, asleep in their tents, had been slain in their hammocks by the Japanese. I pictured the blades sinking through the mosquito netting that shrouded the sleeping figures, blood rising up to soak the gauze, as though the bodies below were one great wound. I thought perhaps some men passed from sleep to death without waking, moving from one dream to another, though probably most sprang alert as though a flare had gone off in their faces, doubled in pain or thrashing, entangled, in helpless rage. And I learned that the paratroopers who found the bodies said nothing, but numbly pursued the killers into the dense jungle, slaughtering them where they found them at a range so close that Japanese uniforms were scorched by the muzzle blasts.

Other instances of horror and valor abounded. One mangled American lay under the bodies of two Japanese he killed just as one held a grenade to the paratrooper's back and pulled the pin. Another rushed a Japanese machine gun single-handed, accounting for eight of the enemy before they cut him down; for this gallantry, Pvt. Ova Kelley was posthumously awarded the division's only Medal of Honor. History cannot say how many more deserved it. In the end, the long wave of blood rolled up to the tents and huts of the headquarters group, sweeping the staff—my uncle among them—into the maelstrom.

11. E. M. Flanagan, *The Angels: A History of the 11th Airborne Division* (Novato, CA: Presidio, 1989).

On December 7—the significance of the date is hardly lost on him—Bill Crawford begins a long letter to Mary about the attack. He can't give the details of specific operations or number the units engaged or even name the island where he's fighting. The result of the constraint is one of his most vivid letters, rich in detail, light on strategic speculation. Most important, he surrenders the fiction of his own safety. The account can hardly have made easy reading for an anxious spouse nine thousand miles away—who could say what happened an hour after it was posted?—but it survives as an eloquent document of the Pacific war:

> My darling wife,
>
> I've had a rather unusual day and I want to tell you something about it while it's still fresh in my mind. Yesterday I had to send all my service troops out to destroy about 150 Japs who had broken into our rear area. Apart from sporadic strafing and stray bombs, it's normally quiet back here, but for a while we had a small war on our hands.
>
> The fighting hadn't ended at suppertime so this area was just about devoid of troops except for us staff officers and a few clerks. I went in to eat supper and when I finished the meal walked back to my tent enjoying my first taste of ice cream in six months. I was still eating it when we heard the air alert. We never pay any attention to it because the Japs always pass over and go for the ships in the harbor, flying high to dodge the anti-aircraft. But this time the drone of the engines was heavy and low so I went outside to see them—18 twin-engine planes in tight formation. The sight was surprising as the only enemy air I'd seen before was scattered individual planes, usually fugitive Zeros skittering away from the beach. The formation sailed serenely above clouds of flak apparently helpless to knock it down. The left edge of the V actually passed directly over me. I wasn't worried be-cause Jap bombers always return from the harbor empty. But shortly after these planes flew by I saw the flash of explosions as they unloaded their bombs.

We are about to bear witness to an epic moment in Colonel Crawford's war.

I was standing outside my tent still eating the ice cream 'cause I didn't want it to melt. Then I saw some more planes, coming in very low—less than 700 feet. Couldn't understand why bombers would be returning at that altitude so I decided they were transport planes, ours. They had their navigation lights on and their exhausts were flaring white and unsteadily as the pilots adjusted their throttles. As they descended, lights atop the fuselages began to blink. By now I'd figured the planes were C-47s, arriving late and somehow sort of lost. The sun had set but there was still twilight. A lot of people were hollering "Don't shoot, they're ours!"

But they weren't. And they weren't C-47s. Turned out they were American DC-3s that had been sold to Japan years before the war and refitted as troop carriers.

I realized that a chunk of wing from one of those planes had returned to me in the form of the silver trunk.

There was a kind of shocked stillness as we realized what was happening. Then everybody opened up with machine guns, carbines, rifles, pistols if that was all you had. The planes came steadily on—a V, another, another—flying through the hail of bullets. Bright flashes would occasionally play along one of the planes where the rounds were splattering. The transports sailed over us and faded from sight—in their wake, a solid mass of yellow puffs. I figured a distant AA battery had finally registered and that the action was about to die down. Then, by God, I saw another squadron of comparable size approaching in a similar formation. It gave one a sort of eerie feeling to see so much Jap air force flying unscathed overhead—and so damn low. I reckoned for an instant they were some bomber of a type I wasn't familiar with. Then I looked back at what I'd thought were drifting ack-ack puffs and, by the light of the blazing gasoline the bombs had ignited, I saw that they were parachutes.

I was watching a Japanese airborne invasion.

I was watching a Japanese airborne invasion. Colonel Crawford's view is entirely professional.

It was very pretty. The light made all the chutes look orange. And it was a beautiful jump. They must all have gotten the "go" signal together, for all the sticks started at the same imaginary line through the sky. The men were well spaced. They'd made smooth fast exits. The air was filled with them. It felt strange to be on the receiving end of a tactic I'd practiced so often, stranger still to be a ground soldier at the time. From a technical point of view, I couldn't help watching the swaying figures with real admiration—they were brother parachutists. But they were also enemy soldiers. I felt fifteen seconds of fear. Then I ran to my section to start assembling my men.

Meanwhile the second squadron started discharging its troopers. One chute showed prematurely. Everybody shot at it but fortunately didn't hit it for it turned out to be an equipment bundle full of grenades.

He has not felt fear before. If we may trust his report, he will not feel it again. There is simply too much work to do.

FIVE LINES CENSORED

At daybreak today (Dec. 7th) with a handful of local soldiers gathered together we attacked and have driven the little bastards away and killed about half, I guess.

Some Japs attacked an isolated switchboard and a bunch of our cooks went to the rescue, killed 54 Japs and didn't lose a man. There are one hell of a lot of dead Japs around here. But we've suffered some losses, too. Most of last night I hugged the ground because there was too much lead flying around about waist high. It went through our map boards and tents and through a few people. I had my men in foxholes in two-man teams with one awake at all times. No Japs got in to us but they did attack troops a hundred yards away.

The raid caught us at nightfall—hundreds of Jap paratroopers—just a handful of us staff officers and clerks—so we couldn't do a hell of a lot in those first hours but this morning things are very different.

It seems that if you just stay in there and slug it out with the Nips you can kill a whale of a lot of them and keep them disorganized. Then a good counterattack does the trick. Of course, there are people who don't stick it out and that makes it harder on the well-disciplined troops who do.

It's funny how the papers say we have the Japs in a pocket and are about to wipe them out. Well, soon we will, but not today.

THREE LINES CENSORED

After the damn planes all flew away we sweated out the thought that this might be just the first of many waves to come—but no more have come so far. Any that do will receive their deaths much more quickly than did the lads who landed last night. The only time I was afraid was for about fifteen seconds. That was just about the time the second wave jumped.

THREE LINES CENSORED

I was part of a damn small group there. But then I went to my men, and started coordinating things, getting 'em ready. I'll close for now. I saw Walter Oakey yesterday. Good to see him. He looked fine.

Crawford picks up the letter again the following day:

Well, as I sit here writing there's a regular fusillade of small arms fire buzzing around and the sound of grenades exploding. I seem to be in the middle of a small battle. It is gradually moving away from here but a little while ago there was shooting going on all sides of me.

It's sort of hard to write because it's very busy and there are a lot of people around here. I can see wounded being brought in to a little tumbled-down wooden-floored thatched warehouse the medics are using as an aid station. The roof supports have been blown sideways so that the roof half covers the floor and half covers the mud outside. The medics move swiftly among the stretchers, giving blood plasma to the wounded. I just saw a Negro soldier brought in on a canvas stretcher dark with blood. The colored troops out here are mostly in service and support battalions but I have seen some fighting with the tenacity of straight-leg infantry.

It seems silly as hell to be writing you now, on the fringes of a firefight. But the truth is I got all my work done last night, setting up the flow of arms and ammo out to the field, fitting logistics to the operational plan. Obviously it's all *ad hoc*. We're responding to a rapidly changing situation while in close contact with the enemy. But our plans seem to be working. Don't know how long I'll be able to continue writing. The bombs cut most of our communication wires so I've got calls in to the parties I need and I'll interrupt this letter when I can transact my business.

One lieutenant here just died. The medics couldn't save him. He had severe pulmonary wounds.

There's an interruption—I'll go see what's up and resume this later.

* *

Interruption gone. A few of the little rascals sneaked around behind us but they have been eliminated now.

The asterisks sprawl across the page like tiny black explosions, filling the white space. I can see my uncle ducking through the canvas flap of the tent, as he locks and loads his carbine or pulls his .45, alert for a raiding party that might be fifty yards, or fifty feet, away. Hoarse cries, running figures, muzzle flashes, the crack of rifle fire, and the curt stutter of machine guns. Maybe he stands outside the tent a moment, calmly shooting Japanese like a secretary taking a smoke break before returning to his desk. Maybe— reassured by a passing officer that the situation is under control, the enemy scattered and retreating—he never has to pull the trigger, but turns back and retrieves his train of thought: "they have been eliminated now." To me, the broken letter is a magnet. I look again and again at the white space, the asterisks, drawn to the dark enchantment of all that they conceal.

IN THE ATTACKS of early December, Bill Crawford had come to know his enemy at close quarters. He was not unimpressed.

"I've learned a little about Japs," he wrote on December 13:

They are not supermen, but they *are* super fanatics—and they have plenty of courage. From the air they are horribly efficient machines of death. In the harbor time and again I've seen them circle patiently through terrific anti-aircraft fire, then choose their moment and dive straight into the hold of a ship. There's a huge explosion—a spout of flame and billows of black smoke. The ship may burn for hours before it sinks.

In the margin of the letter he sketched in color such a kamikaze attack. The neatly drawn explosion looks like a bright red crown.

Moving to the enemy's performance as infantry, Crawford picked out weaknesses and strengths.

They are not particularly good marksmen but they have fine weapons. Their equipment is in general very good and well designed. It's surprising to find that they have plenty that isn't copied from American or European sources.

Contrary to what many Americans think, some Jap units are made up of big men, largely from their northern islands. They run over six feet tall and well over 200 lbs.—but they are definitely the exception.

Their tactics are poorly executed—they don't utilize concealment very well when attacking. But when defending they never know when they're licked.

A defeated Jap company will not surrender. The men hide—lie in swamps up to their noses—conceal themselves in trees—disguise themselves in native clothes—then they rush out and try to kill somebody in a suicide attack.

Patrols of Japs habitually shoot and bayonet civilians. That's no propaganda, either—it's true.

Their lunatic fanaticism and their genuine courage have made this a hard campaign. The war here hasn't been quite as the papers have reported it. At one time things were awfully critical—the Japs were getting troops in faster than we. But finally we seem to be getting the upper hand, and now we have them in a sort of trap. They can still supply themselves and put in reinforcements—we'll just leave them bottled up, the same as we have tens of thousands in New Guinea. But isn't over yet. They are determined to exterminate us on this island, and there is still plenty of fighting. ~~I've heard that in Germany~~

Bill Crawford breaks off and decides to strike out that sentence. He had heard that, in Germany, American officers ordered their soldiers to feed German prisoners from their own scant rations or go hungry. That was interesting, but perhaps not something to write the folks at home about.

Still, it seems to me the war is ahead of schedule—at least we've reached the northern hemisphere! But I'm no longer confident I can predict the end—only the victory. "I'll Be Home for Christmas," as the song says. Though maybe not next year. But it surely will be nice to get home. I don't like the Philippines particularly.

Realizing a vivid account of the airborne attack can hardly have set his readers' minds at ease, Bill Crawford will post an update before the end of December, assuring them of his relative safety.

It was announced in one of the GHQ communiqués that the 11th Abn Div. had been engaged in heavy fighting on Leyte. That's true. The fighting continues even though the main resistance is broken and Jap annihilation is inevitable. Things are much better here. We don't see so many Jap planes. They bomb only about once a night now. The American seizure of an airstrip on Mindoro gives us a forward base to prepare for early blows elsewhere.

Where I am now any chance of being wounded is practically nil. I did get caught in the middle of a Jap parachute attack but that's all over with. I wrote Mary a bit about it and asked her to forward the letter to you.

At several times in this campaign things were awfully damn critical —more so than people at home will ever know I suppose but it has turned out OK with a very complete victory and a loss to Japan of over 100,000 good troops.

It's safe where I am . . . Our strategy in the Pacific is sparing of American lives. These claims appear more than once in the letters and ask for inquiry. Is he whistling in the dark? As a staff officer, he *was* relatively safe—until he wasn't. And the 11th Airborne did suffer fewer casualties than some brother divisions (620 KIA, 1800 WIA). But an overall Pacific campaign that cost one hundred thousand American lives and a quarter million wounded can hardly be called "sparing," and Crawford was never far from the sound of the guns. I think he was balancing two imperatives here—the wish to share as much as he could of the drama with friends and family at home and the intent to allay their fears by minimizing his danger. This makes the truth of his experience harder to locate except at the moments when his war glows so hot there's no concealing the intensity.

EARLY IN DECEMBER Bill Crawford ran into an old friend from Hertford, a Marine Corps artillery officer named Walter Oakey, whose howitzer battalion had been firing missions in support of the 11th Airborne's final operations on Leyte, and invited him for lunch. The meeting was a thousand to one chance, Major Oakey noted in a letter to Louise Woods, adding a wry comment on my grandmother's fervent piety, "Kate will no doubt say it had nothing to do with chance at all."

The officers' rendezvous was not uneventful. The road Oakey planned to use to my uncle's headquarters had been recaptured by the Japanese just as he began his trip, so the major and his driver zigzagged around it, taking fire from time to time. Bill Crawford scrounged a good combat meal: potable water, shots of medicinal brandy, dried beef, canned peaches, coffee, and cake. After lunch, Bill asked Walter if he would like to take a Grasshopper flight to drop supplies to a platoon isolated in the mountains, and also have a look at the area impacted by Marine artillery to observe the effect of the fire. "The Japs," Oakey notes, "shot at us for looking." The men had hoped to find time for a second visit, but the intensified fighting made that impossible. They never met again.

"Bill seems very well," Walter Oakey concluded his letter, "and he's doing an excellent job. But combat has worn him, as it has worn us all. You mustn't expect him to look quite so youthful after years in the tropics and months in the war."

Dated January 12, 1944, and postmarked the sixteenth, Walter Oakey's letter doesn't give the actual date of his visit to my uncle, but one paragraph places it at the time of the Japanese attack of December 6—which may have come within moments of Major Oakey's departure: "A few minutes after I left the rascals came over with 24 bombers and about as many transports, dropped parachutists and took the airfield just like that. The bombers strafed us and damn near got us, too. They killed several hundred natives and soldiers and held the field for over a week, destroying all the planes."

In the midst of combat, Oakey has a thought to spare for those at home. "All the troubles are not at the front and wives who have to sit out the wars have their own anxieties. In fact, in war it's the woman who pays, rearing and preparing to lose the next generation. I hope people will have sense enough to skip a generation after this one."

As a member of the generation he hoped might be spared, I'm grateful for the sentiment, however patriarchal. And I remember Colonel—as he would become—Oakey very well as one of the more interesting adults to people my childhood. A gaunt, taciturn figure, he had apprenticed himself to a local attorney and passed the bar years before the war—no need for law school. He was a well-read man who lived with his strikingly beautiful wife, Marjorie, in the house next to my family's; years later, he built a house by the river where he kenneled a pack of blue tick hounds he took by train every year to Canada for the fall hunting. Like most Marines, he was proud of his service, but he kept few mementos in his study, and I never heard him talk about the war.

IF MY UNCLE still sometimes regretted his elevation to the general staff, he had been involved in division logistics long enough to develop respect for their complexity, and he was intrigued by the way one day's work could entail the planning of a battle and the next be taken up with a single item of supply. Once his chief clerk signed for a shipment of M3 trench knives, whose registration and distribution throughout the division consumed most of an afternoon. This short, brutal blade was soon to be replaced by a shorter bayonet, but since 1943 it had been issued to shock troops like the airborne, an analogue to the Marines' dreaded KA-Bar. At one time the knife had struck the young colonel as an anomaly, a medieval weapon in a modern war. But he had been trained in its employment in hand-to-hand combat, and he had seen men come in from patrol offhandedly wiping blood from their blades. Six inches of steel might still be as useful to a soldier as a hand grenade. Indeed, an order had recently come down from headquarters telling the troops how to conceal their positions in night attacks. *Don't give yourselves away with rifle fire. If the Japs are outside your perimeter, throw grenades. If they're inside, use your knives.*

AS THE CAMPAIGN ON LEYTE ground toward its close, Bill Crawford received a letter from a classmate fighting in France. This officer, slightly wounded, had been granted a week's R & R in a recaptured village where life had taken on, as he wrote, an "uncanny normality"—bistros and bars were open, the women were friendly, you slept under sheets. Of course, there was always the war to go back to, the gods of carnage of the battlefield. But for a time an Allied soldier could enjoy something like the lost world of peace.

Then too, the war in Europe offered cultural touchstones absent from the Pacific. Two lines by Randall Jarrell capture the difference:

> In bombers named for girls, we burned
> The cities we had learned about in school

Combat in the Pacific may have had an especially savage quality because of the region's remoteness, both geographical and cultural. Few American soldiers knew much of Japan beyond "banzai!" and American popular images of the Japanese didn't scruple to caricature them as savage little yellow buck-toothed rats. As to the indigenous cultures of the islands the war consumed, they were simply swept away in the firestorm.

Individual encounters were sometimes barbarous, and the isolation in which they were enacted severe. Americans in the Pacific fought with trench knives and flamethrowers against an enemy ready to mutilate the wounded and desecrate the dead—which American soldiers and Marines did also. The land offered no background of farms and villages you might feel you were defending, no foe with features like your own, nowhere to retreat if your spirit broke, no mercy if you were captured, nothing to do but endure.

ON JANUARY 22, 1945, the 11th Airborne was put on alert for redeployment. On the twenty-seventh, advance elements embarked for Luzon, landing by amphibious assault on the thirty-first. Five days later, Bill Crawford updated his wife on the action in a letter postmarked February 4, written aboard the troopship.

> I can't say much more than this: we're at sea again. The division has wrapped up its work on the last island successfully and we're embarked for a new one in what is going to be one of the biggest operations in this sector of the war.
> The last few days before we sailed were hectic and made harder for

me by what the Army calls an FUO (Fever Unknown Origin) and a broken tooth. I was sleepless and very busy for several days. But I'm getting some rest aboard ship though I'm still taking a lot of atabrine since the medics think I may have a touch of malaria.

The affliction was as common in the islands as jungle rot, so it seems very likely that he did.

We're facing some hard fighting but I'm glad we're on our way. The place we've left had many disadvantages for my work—the mud and mire, the heavy rains, the swollen rivers that seemed to wash away bridges as soon as we built them. Of course, there's no reason to think where we're going will be much better. But I'll get to see things I've wanted for a long time to see.

What lies ahead of us is going to be most interesting. The war in a form that I've not encountered yet—I can say that much, I guess. All the planning and organizing, the co-ordination of resources, the thinking through of endless contingencies—it's all been on a much larger scale than I've ever had to do before. Soon I'll see how it all works out. Things are moving quickly.

The faster the war goes the happier I become. The European situation looks very promising—we may see victory over Germany before the end of 1945. Out here 6th Army continues steadily in its drive on Manila. Soon we'll be back where we started from three years ago. But now we're the ones with the power to strike—and the blows will fall.

He concludes with a rare romantic reverie, musing on how much he misses Mary, on how long they have been parted, on his dreams of seeing her again. His tone touches a rare chord of the erotic—"when I get home I expect to see you in a pair of very high-heeled shoes"—before concluding cheerfully: "I'm hoping that my landing in the States will be at a dock that doesn't require climbing down a cargo net and wading through bullet-soaked surf."

AT THE END of the Leyte operation, General Swing expressed his pride in the division in a letter to his father-in-law, Gen. Peyton March—the same Peyton March whose favor Kate Crawford had sought in 1918 in the matter of her husband Louis's career.

"Wish you could see these young men of mine fight," the division commander exulted. "It would do your heart good to see the calm joyful manner in which they kill the rats." Praising the troopers' ardor, he singles out a dawn attack that "caught 300 Japs sleeping outside their foxholes . . . we slaughtered them there with bayonet, knife, and hand grenades."

Brutal as the action on Leyte had been, Joe Swing knew Luzon would be even worse. In another letter to his father-in-law, he noted that the earlier strategy of bypassing pockets of isolated Japanese would no longer serve. "That is all over now. The Japs are reinforcing their garrisons on Luzon to an extent that makes almost every attack a frontal one. The chances of seizing an undefended beachhead from which an assault can be launched are nil. We're going to have to fight for every inch."

Swing's fight would not only be with the Japanese. MacArthur's original plans for the invasion of Luzon had called for dropping the 11th Airborne in small, scattered groups all over the southern part of the island. Swing's response was coldly furious. "If you want to take my division from me, general, relieve me of command. But give my men a fighting chance." He prevailed.

No one was more relieved than my uncle, who was apparently present at another battle of wills between Swing and Eichelberger, 8th Army CG. E. M. Flanagan enlists John Conable, the division's assistant quartermaster, to recount the episode: "I think on January 21 Bill Crawford came back with General Swing. He woke me up in an excited state about four in the morning. Everything had changed. He told me the new plan."

We need not linger over the details in order to understand the men's ebullience. The original plan would have sundered the 11th into small units that could be reduced by the enemy piecemeal, that would be hard to reassemble into full strength, and that would present problems of resupply even more daunting than the chaos of Leyte. To invade Luzon with the division intact, whether by air or sea, would concentrate its firepower and simplify the problem of supply.

The sea approach was chosen. Planners of the division's amphibious landing on Luzon were convinced it would be largely unopposed.

WHEN THE ASSAULT BOAT dropped its landing ramp into the surf at Nasugbu, Bill Crawford stepped into hip-deep water warm as flesh, holding his carbine just above his head. The low jungle that fringed the beach offered a mocking silence until he and the rest of the staff officers were out of the ocean and struggling onto the shore. Then a machine gun opened fire, shredding a trooper twenty yards to Crawford's right and making the sand writhe as it traversed toward him. General Swing and his contingent went to cover in a gully as bullets and explosive rounds kicked up the sand around them. The brief ordeal, in Flanagan's account, produced a moment of light comedy when Colonel Schimelpennick, the chief of staff, idly picked up a scrap of shrapnel and proclaimed, "Ow, it's *hot*." Swing glanced at him coldly. "What did you expect?" he said.

One bullet chipped a rock and sent a stone fragment the size of a dime spinning. My uncle felt a sting on his cheek and touched it, retrieving a fingertip of blood.

BILL CRAWFORD was growing impatient at the failure of the navy gunner on his group's landing craft to lay down suppressive fire. He announced that he would run back down the beach and take over the boat's fifty-caliber himself. Crawford was halfway out of the gully, ignoring the bullets popping around him, when Swing grabbed him by a boot and dragged him back behind cover. "Goddamn it, get back here, colonel—I need my G4."

Crawford obeyed but watched for a chance to return fire. It came when the Japanese gunner sent up a shower of sand between him and the rest of the contingent. He sprinted toward a hummock and took cover behind it. "Every time I'd stick my head up to try to locate the bastard," he wrote, "that gun cut loose. It seemed sort of amusing and didn't bother me at all."

This tranquil observation is one of the most provocative in all the letters. It's hard to know how to parse it, but the effort seems worthwhile—the offhand words might be a minor key to character. Was it an attempt to allay Mary's fears by camouflaging his own? Was it mere bravado? Or were my uncle's words the truthful record of a dissociative mood, suggesting he was refusing the experience? Here is one of the places where my own innocence of combat poorly serves the story. I'm allowed conjecture but finally must relinquish the mystery. Even so, I'm drawn back to the night of the Japanese airborne assault on Leyte, when he parted the flaps of his tent either to engage in personal slaughter or to shrug and return to his desk to finish his letter. There's much Mary cannot know, beginning with all he has decided not to tell her.

He reports being pinned down by the gun for nearly twenty minutes before a pause in the firing gave him a chance to break from cover and lead the men with him off the beach. "During a lull we ran like hell and got across a big clearing and made our way to the little town."

A little *town*? It springs like magic from his page, and he pauses on Main Street long enough to praise its beauty—"so unlike Leyte." The town has a green courthouse lawn and asphalt streets—we might be back in Hertford. For a moment, Bill Crawford seems almost to have stepped out of the war, though not for long. In the next paragraph, he has made his way through heavy fighting to another beach, tasked with determining its suitability for off-loading cargo. And in the next, the bleeding gash on his cheek has been noticed by a medic.

"What happened to you, Colonel?"

"Don't you have wounded to attend to, Doc?" His tone was dismissive.

"Let me have a look, sir."

Crawford relented. Medics were enlisted men, but they carried the authority of their profession. When this corporal, sheathed in blood, was satisfied as to the minor nature of the wound, he let his quarry go.

"You'll get the Purple Heart anyway, sir."

Crawford absently shook his head, his thoughts already back to the job at hand. He needs soundings of water depth and an assessment of the quality of the inshore sand. Accompanied by an engineer he shortly orders into the water, Crawford "cautiously skittered out onto the open beach" to see if he would draw fire from the cliff above. Getting no reaction, he waved his arms and shouted into a silence that seemed to promise safety, so he sent the man into the lapping water. Still no fire from the Japanese.

It's hard not to be drawn to this image of foolhardy bravery: the young colonel seeking to draw fire even as he ponders the mathematics of amphibious supply. The behavior feels of a piece with the uncanny calm he'd brought an hour earlier to the landing. Maybe he had sunk into one of those states of grace where a soldier feels invulnerable. Maybe he was unwilling to order the trooper to take a risk he wouldn't first test himself. Maybe he was just acting crazy. At all events, the silence didn't last.

With the man in the water, I retired toward cover and as I did a Jap rifle opened up on me. There was a dugout ten or fifteen yards to my left, so I ran toward it, drawing my pistol and fumbling for my last grenade but I'd somehow dropped it while running, so all I had was the .45, which would have to do at close quarters. Anyway I had to get some cover from that rifle, so I jumped into the dugout. Thank God, it was empty.

Before nightfall, my uncle had been back and forth between the beach and the town, confirming the viability of offshore supply, inspecting bridges for mines, and laying track for a narrow-gauge railroad. He knew the task he would be facing. "The logistics problem is terrific. The better the troops fight, the harder is my job," he writes. "They use more and more ammo and they get further and further away from the sources of supply."

Close to the end of the letter time has collapsed on itself. If the first few pages covered the first few hours of the landing, we are now some days into the campaign, and Lieutenant Colonel Crawford has moved his G-4 office from a tent to the rubble of a school and finally to an abandoned resort hotel, which affords him a "soul-satisfying view." He likes Luzon, finding it much like California. "The weather is beautiful." Still, his work keeps him sleepless, his fever is constant, and the jungle rot that plagued him on Leyte has flared up again. But the campaign is progressing.

We have got the Japs licked so far. We've been fighting day and night, which confuses them. They always say Americans stay inside their perimeter after dark and generally that's true. So we've been surprising them with our continued and unceasing night attacks. This swift advance looked impossible when we landed, but we've kept the pressure on with a very rapid pace. And we've done our old trick of bypassing pockets of resistance and leaving the Japs to starve, which of course compounds the question of supply. In effect, there's no rear area. But this method confuses the Japs. And it defeats them.

We've been on Luzon for four days now, and we're going to try to smash into Manila before 6th Army gets there. We—a little diversionary unit—hope to surprise people.

PLANS FOR THE BATTLE OF MANILA had been in development for some time before the invasion, perhaps as far back as the Japanese occupation of the islands, which had come under attack within hours of the Pearl

Harbor raid. Douglas MacArthur, ordered to Australia in March 1942, made his famous vow to return and soon began his struggle with the War Department to redeem it. Outweighed by navy strategists who found the idea of a Philippines campaign premature, he had to wait until 1944 to begin operations on Leyte and until January 1945 to attack Luzon. The ultimate goal had always been Manila. By the third of February, the city would be under siege. By the third of March, it would be very nearly obliterated.

Few historians question the necessity of wresting the capitol from its captors, but for more than seventy years there has been a debate over whether the battle had to be conducted with such savagery. The trapped Japanese fought to the death and accompanied their desperate defense with a program of rape and murder of civilians as vile as any they had ever conducted. The relentless Americans held back at first but ultimately released air and artillery barrages that destroyed entire neighborhoods, not sparing hospitals, schools, churches, and government buildings. In the sharpest urban fighting of the Pacific War, countless cultural treasures vanished and as many as 140,000 civilians died. The Japanese lost two hundred thousand men, the allies far fewer (eighty-three hundred dead, nearly thirty thousand wounded). The fighting lasted for a month. In those thirty days, the city suffered the damnation of Hiroshima or Stalingrad.

Bill Crawford did not live to see the end of the battle he had some part in planning, but—even granting the bloody chaos of its outcome—he would have had reason to be proud of the role his division played. He would also have had reason for anger at the way his division was used. Three British historians who have analyzed the action hour by hour concluded as much:

> Eleventh Airborne was not well suited to a deep advance—it was small and not equipped with armor, heavy artillery, or sufficient vehicles—and should have been devoted to securing Tagaytay Ridge (its stated objective) until reinforced or relieved. Eichelberger chose to ignore this restriction. . . . [The division] predictably bogged down as soon as it encountered determined enemy resistance around Nichols Field and began to take heavy casualties. . . . In the end the only tangible result was to ensure that the Japanese had no escape route out of Manila to the south, although it should be added that the airborne troops themselves fought with incredible bravery and undoubtedly

diverted enemy resources that could have been devoted to the defense of Manila.[12]

In the end, MacArthur had his victory—and his victory parade. And the Angels went on to a mission, very nearly their last of the war, that has given them an abiding glory: the raid on the Los Baños prison camp that killed the Japanese garrison and freed over two thousand internees with few losses to the raiding party. Gen. Colin Powell has remarked, "I doubt that any airborne unit in the world will ever be able to rival the Los Baños prison raid. It is the textbook airborne operation for all ages and all armies."

Had he survived the Battle of Manila, Bill Crawford would have pondered the aftermath. That would have enlarged his understanding of his war, and I suspect would have prompted him to an account surpassing his reflections on the Japanese airborne assault on Leyte. I can't help regretting the loss of a mature perspective we will never see.

WE MIGHT PAUSE here a moment to consider just how much the 11th Airborne had undergone since its deployment. The division absorbed weeks of punishing in-country training, received its baptism of fire by plunging into jungle warfare of unsurpassed intensity, and reached some dark zenith when tasked with a leading role in urban combat widely held to be unequalled in ferocity in the annals of the Pacific war. This, in a period of five months. American boys, twelve years old in 1939, playing with Red Ryder BB guns and Lincoln Logs, losing themselves in *Superman* comics and Flash Gordon serials, were six years later killing Japanese soldiers in a fetid jungle and then helping reduce a city once known as the Pearl of the Orient to fifteen square miles of smoldering rubble.

ON THE AFTERNOON of February 5, Lieutenant Colonel Crawford was summoned into the august presence of the commanding general. Joe Swing looked tired, and too finely drawn. The stony features that had so awed

12. Richard Connaughton, John Pimlott, and Duncan Anderson, *The Battle for Manila* (Novato, CA: Presidio, 2002).

Mary at the division's dinner dance were more sharply chiseled than ever, but the general's corvine glare was dulled, and his skin had a touch of saffron. Malaria? The tropics were draining them all. Crawford saluted, Swing returned it, then started in without preamble.

"Eichelberger's attaching himself to us for the drive on Manila."

Lt. Gen. Robert Eichelberger, commanding 8th Army, was Joe Swing's immediate superior.

The young colonel assembled a tactful reply. "I guess that's an honor, sir?"

"Yeah, an honor that may cost me operational control. He's going to want to shape the tactics and he doesn't know a goddam thing about airborne."

"Maybe the staff can, uh, ride herd on him, general."

"Maybe. But there are other aspects of this show that give me pause." Swing drummed thick pale fingertips on the topographic map under his right hand. "MacArthur's already planning his victory dance. He's encircling the city. The Japs'll have no way out. They'll have to fight to the death."

"They generally do," my uncle observed.

"Yeah, but you always leave the enemy an escape route. Sun Tzu." Swing smiled suddenly. "Whom you read at West Point, I expect."

"We did, sir."

"Anyway, grand strategy is not why I called you in, although I know you have a taste for it. Sit down, colonel." Swing indicated the canvas chair beside his own, and slid the map under his fist across the table so Bill Crawford could study it in the strong glow of the general's splendid new three-hundred-watt bulb. "I think that's our path into Palenque, but I want to be sure. There's room to maneuver, though no doubt the approach is thick with Japs."

My uncle was intent on the map. "You have photo reconnaissance, sir?"

"Yeah, and intel from local guerillas, though I'm not sure how good it is. I need somebody to take a closer look." He turned his fierce—there, the old power was back—gaze on the younger officer. "Properly, this is a job for the G2 shop, but I've got all of them on another project. Besides, you've more than once worn two hats for me."

"I'll fly up that valley for you, general."

"You'll ride—if you go. I want you in the observer's seat, eyes on the ground. I want sketches of what you see. If you go," Swing repeated.

"Low-level photos?"

"Sketches. Pen and ink. I want a different feel for the terrain."

"Sir."

A pause. The mood changed. Now in Swing's voice was some of the paternal affection he was usually careful to conceal. "This is strictly voluntary, Bill. I mean that. A treetop flight could lock in the pieces of the puzzle, but I can move without it and still be 90 percent sure."

"Let's shoot for a hundred, sir."

"It's not a milk run and this is *not* an order. But I won't say that again."

Nor did Crawford repeat his consent. No need—he'd given it. Swing nodded briskly. "Tomorrow morning, then, soon as you've got good light. Take any plane and pilot you want."

"Is Lieutenant Lanier available?"

"He will be. Report to me as soon as you're back on the ground." Swing stood, signaling the end of the interview. Crawford stood, saluted crisply, and took his leave. Decisiveness. That's why Joe Swing wore two stars. One of the reasons.

The colonel worked in his bullet-shredded office through the rest of the afternoon, flushed with a low fever in the tropical damp. At the end of the day he began a letter to Mary, but lost focus and left it unfinished. He ate his dinner early—freshly baked pork loaf, biscuits, baked carrots, a thin slice of chocolate cake. In the field, he would have eaten C-rats like any other soldier, but at base camp there was a full kitchen and the food was accordingly better. Shortly after his meal, Bill Crawford retired to his tent and slept well.

IN THE MORNING, Lieutenant Colonel Crawford walks out to the airstrip, where his pilot is already waiting.

And it seems I'm waiting, too—a phantom of longing that can cross ocean and jungle to hover over the battleground. In Hertford, of course, I'm an infant asleep in a Civil War crib. But in the sky above Luzon I am an older child, closer to my brother's age perhaps—I can't be certain. But I'm there. My uncle hesitates, stops in mid-stride, and glances up. There's nothing to see, of course. But I can speak to him. And he can hear me.

On that day, I am not quite one year old. I live in a world of women, not a world of war. I am carried along on a current of love and warm attention, I reach out greedily for food and drink, my cries are comforted, with mute delight I watch the walls to see the dancing shadows of the river. I float to sleep on the singsong of soft voices. I have all I need.

In a few years, that will not be true. I will still want the women's love and care, but I will need something else as well. I'll play zestfully with my older brother and take a cautious pleasure in my father, who like many men has perhaps returned from the war with a diminished capacity for ordinary life. He is kind to me but a little remote and when I'm ten or twelve years old I won't be much moved to confide in him.

I will need my uncle. I'll need the company and council of a man still young, cheerful but battle-hardened. A man of strength who wears it lightly. A man who loves and teases his big sister, who feeds my hunger for war toys and war tales, who tells me easy versions of his exploits, celebrating the gallantry of others with little mention of his own, delivering the battles without the blood. He will know how to do this, how to soften the truths of Leyte and Luzon into tales to tell a child. He will tell about the landings he made under fire, about the Japanese parachutes blossoming like flowers in the twilight.

He will hold me rapt.

But though I love to see him in his summer khakis, his shirt sometimes rumpled even with its brigadier's star, soldiering is not our only theme. He's amused by my schoolyard antics, indifferent to my academic shortcomings, quick with praise when I succeed. He passes lightly over my boredom with sports, but he *is* puzzled that mathematics and the sciences don't speak to me. I don't tinker together radios the way he did as a child, don't build worlds of the future with Erector sets.

But I do love airplanes. I work hard on the balsawood and plastic models he brings me, fighters and bombers, B-25s and B-17s, Zeros, Corsairs, Spads, and Sabre jets. I even essay a copy of my uncle's own L-4, though his father's Jenny, with its intricate web of wings and wires, is entirely beyond me. Always I work in haste, smearing the glue, daubing the paint, pasting decals outside their outlines. My bedroom fills with these totemic toys.

And the first time Brigadier General Crawford takes me, aged five, up in his Piper Cub, lifting off a field in Elizabeth City and following the river until the shadow of the wings brushes my grandmother's house, I have the sense of an exile's return.

I can tell my uncle anything.

So now, on that February day in 1945, I tell him to come home. To come back. Cancel the flight, hangar the plane. End the mission—it won't change the war. *I need you.* I'll need you in the years ahead. You have given your youth to your country. You've stood in the fire, risked all, accomplished much. *Come home.* We'll sit on the back porch of the old house in the summertime, watching the fireflies, drinking (as one does in the South) sweetened iced tea. Your brother-in-law, my father, will join us and switch the tea for bourbon as you and he share anecdotes about Korea, a war he saw coming, a war you survived. The twilight will deepen and I'll remain motionless, listening to the stories, hoping to remain unnoticed until long after time for bed.

So come back. Come home. I need you more than your division does.

Until that moment, my uncle has been listening. His hand is hesitating on the aircraft door as he looks into a different future, half-convinced. But I've made a fatal plea: *I need you more than your division does.* Saddened, he turns away and climbs into the cockpit, nodding to the pilot as he straps himself into the observer's chair. The prop ticks over. The engine coughs and catches. The pilot works the rudder, guiding the little plane to the edge of the ragged field.

THE L-4 IS SPOTTED from the moment it enters the valley. Sporadic rifle shots pass through the fuselage, leaving narrow tracks of light. One bullet splinters the Plexiglas of the observer's window. Another shatters the radio. The pilot and his passenger look on the damage with a shared disdain. Rank separates them, but both are young men, both airborne infantry. It will take more than a few stray rounds to challenge their poise.

Bill Crawford, easygoing with junior officers, ventures a casual conversation. "Where're you from, lieutenant?"

"Alabama, sir."

"That so? I learned to fly in Alabama. Well, I learned the army way."

The pilot grins. "They have been known to take the fun out of it."

"But I started as a kid. I was in the cockpit of a surplus Jenny before I ever drove a car."

Lanier nods and glances at his passenger. "But you didn't want the Air Corps?"

"They didn't want me. Eyes." Crawford wonders idly whether the lieutenant had seen himself as a fighter pilot before having to settle for slower, smaller ships. His dream as well. And his father's.

A bullet skids across the windshield the way a thrown clamshell skips across the surface of a lake.

"Might be time to vary the altitude," the colonel offers mildly.

His tone is nonchalant but the pilot responds so swiftly that Crawford knows he feels rebuked and regrets the unnecessary remark. Lanier is a brave man and a good aviator.

The pace of the ground fire picks up a little. It's as though the trees were angry. But the snarl of the motor is steady and only a few rounds discover the plane.

My uncle has a clipboard balanced on the knee of his olive drab trousers—faded herringbone. He's sketching certain features of the narrow valley. Reconnaissance flights have photographed much of it, but the Grasshopper can fly lower and slower and the G4 shares with the division commander the sense that a map hand-drawn by a close observer may capture a different truth of the terrain. That the eye may sometimes see more than the camera.

The end of the valley is closing in. Scattered houses begin to announce the outskirts of Paranaque. The pilot gains altitude and banks steeply into his return, but Crawford taps him on the shoulder and points down.

"One more pass."

"Sir?"

"Take us back through the valley. I want another look."

"Getting pretty warm in there, Colonel."

My uncle doesn't answer, and the pilot doesn't argue. His remark is no more than the next line of a script for a scene both men see themselves as fated to play out. Neither can quite believe the flight may well end in ruin, though a return journey through the valley will be many times more dangerous than the approach to it was.

Treetop level. Lower. Bill Crawford sketches rapidly. The pilot hums a Tin Pan Alley tune. The Grasshopper trudges faithfully between the trees, hardly higher than a crop-duster. The Japanese gunner catches it with the precision of a trout fisherman dropping a caddis fly. The little plane shudders and slows politely to receive the fire. The 7.7 mm rounds from the Nambu, a Type 99 designed for anti-aircraft work, slam into the cowling, crawl along the cabin, and stitch an even pattern of craters the length of the fuselage before turning the rudder into a ragged sail.

Somehow the remnants of the pilot bring the remnants of the plane to earth. The Grasshopper skitters across a grassy slope and comes to rest less than one hundred yards from the patch of jungle that had lashed it. Sound of fabric tearing, metal rending, the motionless propeller stabbing into the earth, then silence, sudden and absolute. The death of the plane has been the work of a moment. The death of the pilot, too. Crawford sees that at a glance—the torn body slumped over the instrument panel, the shower of blood clinging to the shattered windshield. Good man. God knows how he had managed the crash landing. *If I get out of here . . .* Hardly likely. Anyway, this is no time . . .

My uncle looks to his own wounds. There are cuts on his forearms that amount to nothing and a gash on his forehead bleeding freely, but the chief danger is that he could be blinded by the flooding blood. More serious: a wound in his left thigh turning the herringbone fabric of his trousers dark. He rips the cloth away and studies the ragged furrow, six inches long but shallow, nowhere near the femoral artery. He'll need to dust it with sulfa powder but there's not yet much pain. If that comes, there's a morphine syrette in his first aid kit and another in the pilot's. For now, he must have his wits about him.

A 30-cal. carbine rests on a rack in the cabin within reach, extra clips stored in a musette bag beside it. Crawford pulls the weapon free. A Nambu bullet has turned part of the stock to splinters but the action looks undamaged.

With his good leg, the colonel kicks open the passenger door. He drops through the opening, keeping his body loose and letting his shoulder hit the ground in a paratrooper's roll, then crawls under the fuselage to put the wreckage between himself and the tree line. He knows it would be best to crawl away from the Grasshopper altogether to the shelter of some other cover, but he finds a strange comfort under the drooping wings of the familiar plane.

Crawford waits.

From the jungle, silence.

TIME IS FIXED, time is flowing. Bill Crawford has fallen into the first phase, has heard the deadly drum of ordinary hours sink toward a loaded silence. The blood-soaked world sparkles fresh around him.

THINK. He must think like his enemy. The Japs have seen the Grasshoppers many times. They know that the little planes are unarmed, that they carry a crew of only two. The wreck in the clearing presents almost no danger. The pilot and his passenger are no doubt wounded; one or both may be dead. If alive, they will have only sidearms. But it wouldn't matter if the Americans were equipped with a Buck Rogers death ray. They're within rifle range, a sniper with a scope could kill survivors from a treetop, a mortar round could blow apart the ruins of the plane.

And yet the Japanese hold fire. There can be only one reason. They mean to rush the wreck, to take him prisoner. They have no way of knowing he's a staff officer but they'll recognize a lieutenant colonel's silver leaves, and they'll be curious and they have well-known ways of satisfying their curiosity. It doesn't really matter. Every American soldier in the Pacific is aware that the Japs treat any prisoner they take alive with unsurpassed savagery.

So Bill Crawford isn't going to let that happen. He has a full clip and several more stacked on the wing beside him. He remembers a fragment of Kipling, a poet much favored by his father, advice to a wounded trooper facing an implacable foe: *Jest roll to your rifle and blow out your brains, and go to your Gawd like a soldier.* Soldier of the queen. Of the king these days. King George. King Franklin. King Farouk. King Kong. King bloody cobra . . . He had seen a king cobra in the jungle once, a huge snake raised up like a tower of venom, hood flaring, long body dancing . . . *I am death.* Kipling again.

Steady on.

He wonders why they are waiting. He wonders why they don't howl "GI you die!" or "Fuck Babe Ruth!" or any of their usual taunts. The silence argues the presence of a serious commander, a man facing him across the clearing who can maintain fire discipline, keep his troops in line, and bide his time. Crawford studies the edge of the kunai grass, looking for the point that lies closest to the plane. The Japs will come toward him from there, covering the shortest distance. And they may wait until dark, though it isn't yet mid-morning, and the hours could cost them their exhausted prey or open them to attack from the American patrols that will soon filter into the valley. Not soon enough. Certainly nowhere soon enough for him.

He sips warm water from a canteen. There are several within reach in the wreckage, only one of them pierced and drained by a bullet. Water will not be a problem. Neither will ammunition. There's food, too, a box of K rations somewhere in the shattered fuselage. Bullets can only have improved it. And the shallow furrow on his left thigh, crusting up already, has hardly started to throb. He may not need morphine. Christ, he's actually in pretty good shape. If only he weren't crouched in the wreckage of an observation plane commanded by a corpse and surrounded by a thousand rabid Japanese, the day would be turning out damned well. Crawford glances ruefully up toward the pilot. So. I finally got my combat command. One soldier. And he's dead.

The impact of the rapid action of the last few minutes sinks in suddenly. He feels himself shudder. Not fear: shock. For a moment he rests against a collapsed landing gear strut, bringing his rough breathing under control. Slowly. Slowly. More slowly still. That's it. Time to tend his wounds. He mops the blood from his forehead, opens his first aid kit, and fishes out a small gauze compress bandage to press against the cut. Then he tears open an envelope of sulfa powder and sprinkles it over the long gash on his thigh, like salt on meat. He makes a sloppy job of the bandage.

HE SUCCUMBS to a cascade of images.

Cy Caldwell on the dock to greet him as the Norfolk steamer rocks against its stanchions in the harbor in New York. Somehow his father is on the dock as well, in his leather aviator's coat, helmet, and goggles. Hertford, with its streets that end at the river, its old houses shaded by oak and magnolia, sweetgum and cypress. His sister Louise, short golden hair in a bob, laughing, leaning on a railing of the new drawbridge that spans the Perquimans. The old churchyard behind Holy Trinity, with its crumbling Confederate graves. The parade ground at West Point, where you stood at attention for hours under a July sun with your rifle sinking like an iron bar into your shoulder. Dress blues, a flashing sword, the music of a military band. Dancing at the White House. Learning your trade, from the engraved letters on a calling card to the blood on a bayonet. Black coffee, fresh oranges, Pearl Harbor. Stepping into empty space for the very first time.

And Mary.

I think images like these drifted through my uncle's mind in his final hour. But I don't think he lingered over them. A self-described pragmatic Scot,

Bill Crawford was drawn to problem-solving and he would have stated this problem plainly to himself: not to be taken prisoner and to make the enemy's attempt to do so as costly as he can.

He sets reverie aside, slides a loaded magazine slowly into the belly of the carbine until he hears it lock in place. He works the bolt, seating a round securely in the chamber. Snaps the safety off. He rests the barrel of the weapon softly on a mound of earth scraped from the valley by the falling plane. He brings the muzzle to bear on a thicket of palms at the edge of the jungle closest to his position. Aligns the sights on the spot where a target must presently appear. The morning sun lights up the killing zone. There is little breeze. The range is short—almost no deflection. He knows what is going to happen. He will kill the first Japanese who steps out from cover. He will kill the second. He will very possibly kill or wound the third. After that, the fight will begin to pass out of his control. He is content for that to happen, content with the pattern of a life designed to bring him to this moment. His father pays a final call, this time in boots and spurs, a cavalryman of another age. Louis Crawford salutes his son—his superior officer. Bill Crawford returns it. And I think he may be smiling as he raises his rifle, a strong man armed, wounded in the wreckage, waiting for the Japanese.

WILLIAM CRAWFORD was a soldier of note in a division swiftly writing itself into legend, so it's possible that the army would have managed to send an elegant duet of casualty officers—a fellow infantryman, and a chaplain—to knock on Mary Crawford's door, standing in silence in their dress blues and composing their features to meet the look they would see on the new widow's face when she saw them. But in a war that had already claimed a small city's worth of American dead, such ceremony wasn't always possible. So it may be that word reached her on a scrap of yellow paper—"The War Department deeply regrets . . . "—a Western Union flimsy handed over by a boy who cannot meet her eyes. Mary knows what the telegram will say before she opens the envelope, and when she does the words seem to come from another world. Standing numbly in the hallway, folding and unfolding the page as though a tenth look at the terse words could change them, she may have entered that silent space known to many who must accommodate the sudden news of the death of a loved one, a space in which time shuts down.

Moments before, the room in which she stands bore a certain aspect that hasn't actually changed: a jacket hangs just so on a coat hook, a newspaper lies tossed on the hall table with its headline proclaiming a victory and its classified ads a sale, flowers crowd a vase where the maid has placed too many blossoms, dust motes bob in a beam of light pouring over the transom. None of that has changed since the arrival of the telegram, but none of it has meaning any longer. The world is emptied out.

You don't reach your seventies without encountering loss and grief. But I cannot know—and I find myself reluctant to imagine—the hours Mary Crawford had to live through on that day, the way time changed from a river to a rock as she absorbed the news that her husband had joined in death some half-million of his brothers and sisters and countless millions of his friends and foes on a planet more soaked in blood than any dark god could ever have conceived.

By early evening, she has composed herself. She reaches slowly for the telephone to make the first of the calls that must be made.

Of course, it may not have happened that way at all.

THE PERIOD immediately after William Crawford's death lets us encounter for the first time the voices of those who had lived in his light. There are letters of condolence from friends. There is a letter, the only one I have, from Louise Woods to Kate Crawford. There is a thoughtful letter from the Rev. Edmund Jillson, gently urging my mother not to lose her faith in her bitterness over her loss: "All's well with Bill now. He's safe with God at the end of the road we all must travel." There is a letter from an Episcopal bishop so lifeless and formal that it's not worth quoting. Above all, there are several letters from sister to brother, written days after his fatal mission, and returned to her unopened, marked *Deceased*.

I opened them, the first person to read her words in more than sixty years.

Louise had been haunted by foreboding for some weeks. Unable to completely master her fears, she wrote Bill on February 4, a short note that confessed her worry, which she had usually been scrupulous to hide. But she followed it soon after with a long message in a more sanguine tone:

How you write such wonderful letters from out there I can't imagine. I don't see how you remember who *you* are, let alone who your loving sister is. I'm going to make you a medal: The Golden Heart for Sending a Laugh from the Midst of Battle to a Sister Who Misses You Like Hell.

I hope you're at the base camp, bleary-eyed from movies and sated with beer. Only a temporary respite from blood and mud, I know, but maybe it'll be enough to cure your jungle rot.

I'm glad you've discovered beer. I like the stuff but I have to think about my figure. *You've* never had to worry about your weight. And besides your eyes are bluer than mine and your hair is blonder and you don't have freckles. And you're so much sweeter that Ab Abernathy said he didn't see how we were born in the same family. What I don't see is, why is the good child in jeopardy and the bad child safe at home? I asked Mamma that once, when she was giving me a religious talk, and she told me a whole lot of stuff about you being so good that God protects you, but he wouldn't take a chance on a stinker like me.

She tells her brother of her mixed feelings about her plans to settle for a time with her in-laws in Iowa, where my grandfather was working at a VA hospital, "but I do need a rest from Mamma." She mentions Walter Oakey, who "is where you thought he was." The conclusion is not that easy to read: "Goodnight, good-looking, and all the love in the world. Some fine day— and oh, won't it be a fine day!—I'll see you again."

It will take ten days for news of Bill Crawford's death to reach his family. On February 8, Louise, now in Iowa, writes to Kate:

I hope you're not worrying too much about Bill, but that's an empty sort of thing to say. . . . I listen to the news broadcasts and hold my breath and say my prayers. I feel that he is all right, I honestly do, from the bottom of my heart. I don't think he's even wounded and I know he's glad and proud to be such an important part of this epic liberation of the Philippines. We've learned a little from his letters, but won't it be wonderful when he's *telling* us the stories in person? Nothing matters now but his coming safely home.

But instead there was a telegram. And the soft knock on the door.

WE HAVE NO WAY of knowing what Joe Swing felt. Bill Crawford was a protégé, in some ways a son. Swing would have grieved. His staff might have with silent accord left the office to give him ten minutes alone. Then the commander of the 11th Airborne would have gotten back to work, back to the war.

ONE WEEK LATER, my mother dispatches a V-Mail, which will be returned to her:

Dearest Bill,

I used to wish the papers would print things about your outfit while action was going on and now they do and it's hell. Every night I read something, though nothing very conclusive, about the 11th and the fighting in Manila, and I go crazy trying to fill in the gaps. I'm proud as I can be that you're part of this business, but I *wish* you were stuck behind a desk in Washington. Awake and asleep I think of you.

Young William was introduced to baked custard tonight and was so enthusiastic he practically fell in it.

On February 18, Tom Nixon—the Hertford friend and navy officer injured aboard the *Lexington* in the Battle of the Coral Sea—writes Kate Crawford:

Call it telepathy or what you will but Bill was on my mind constantly all day yesterday and when I heard the news last night I was subconsciously almost expecting it.

What I have to say now is horribly trite but it comes from the heart: we are going to win this war because of men like Bill—men of courage, imagination, and kindness, to name only three of the virtues he possessed. These same qualities, I know, make your loss greater, but they have also given many others a greater share in it.

Louise Crawford Woods to Kate Russell Crawford, Knoxville, Iowa, February 24, 1945:

You said on the telephone "This had to be."

I don't feel that way. It was wanton murder—all their deaths are wanton murder. The blood is on the heads of the dollar merchants in all the lands. The Japs and the Germans, with their horrible lust for power, could have been beaten before they started if the democracies had banded together and looked to the future while there was still time.

When Italy went into Ethiopia, when Franco was nursed by the Nazis, when Japan began the rape of China. But I'm speaking in clichés and perhaps I'm wrong. Perhaps you're right—it "had to be."

If so, I wish my sons had never been born.

The last line might come from a Greek tragedy, and history supports the larger argument. But Bill Crawford's sister doesn't fail to acknowledge his role:

None of which changes my pride in the fact that my brother gave his life in defense of an ideal and that he struck many telling blows for that ideal before he died. To me he was integrity, and the soul of it; he was a hill to lift up my eyes to; and he was something else—he was so damned much *fun*. We never, never had to explain our jokes to each other. I've taken out a million memories of him in the past week, and I'm grateful that I have so rich a store, because it must last me as long as I live.

THE ARMY HAS TACTFULLY ADVISED the widow of three ways Bill Crawford's posthumous medals may be presented: in a public ceremony, a private ritual, or by mail. She agrees to the first, feeling she'll regret it later if she doesn't. "But after this, I don't want to see soldiers marching. I don't want to see the flags flying or hear the music of a military band. I don't want to be on an Army post ever again," Mary writes to Louise on August 17, 1945, enclosing a copy of an official communiqué from HQ Army Air Base Seymour Johnson Field requesting her presence at a ceremony with full military honors to accept her husband's medals. One of them is the Silver Star, third highest award for valor in the annals of American arms.

The citation for the medal reads as follows:

For gallantry in action at ___ on 6 February 1945. During a division attack on the outskirts of ___, Lieutenant Colonel Crawford volunteered to personally perform a special mission for the Division Commander. Knowing full well the hazards involved, this intrepid officer proceeded on the mission in a liaison plane under heavy sniper fire. Lieutenant Colonel Crawford was killed in the performance of his duty. His courage and devotion to duty set an inspiring example for the command and reflect the highest traditions of the armed forces.

This was written while the Pacific war still convulsed the region. Operational security dictated the opaque tone. The two blanks are now easily filled in—Paranaque and Manila—but the full nature of the "special mission" will probably remain unknown; anyway, I could not find it detailed in any history. A division newsletter published more than fifty years later notes Crawford's death under fire in a plane crash, nothing more. Then I chanced on a website called US Militaria Forum, where in August 2012 a series of posts identified his pilot and speculated that the fatal flight may have been a reconnaissance mission to check the results of the combat drop on Tagaytay Ridge. The scene as I envision it stays close to that version but draws on the meeting I've already imagined between Bill Crawford and Joe Swing.

I'm proud to bear my uncle's name and happy to serve as a kind of belated secretary to his story, but I can no longer see him only as the warrior prince whose ghost hovered over my childhood. There's more gain than loss in this. In fuller possession of his short life, I start to feel some of the warmth I felt toward his colorful father. The sullen notes he sometimes stuck in childhood and the disquieting values he embraced as a youth became faded shadows of the resolute and cheerful man. His army career rose like a rainbow with a pot of blood at the end. His marriage opens a question: Why no children? But I can't even answer that about myself. His relationship with his sister was luminous; with his mother, perhaps more than ordinarily vexed by her compelling need. As for his father, death ended the connection before time could show how good a mentor Louis might have been. But the outcome may have been a deeper link—Bill Crawford carrying on to his last hour a dialogue with his father's ghost that often sustained him.

MY UNCLE'S LETTERS are usually typed, and his typing is accurate. When handwritten, they're in ink. His cursive is sprawling but clear, and he employs flourishes that display a strong ego—the downstroke on the capital "B" in "Bill" is doubled, he circles the dot on the "i." Small sketches are fitted into the margins of some letters, cartoonish but technically accurate, like his father's. I'm reminded of the illustrated journal Billy Crawford kept in New York in 1930.

For security reasons, combat soldiers could be forbidden to keep journals or diaries, and letters were censored, though officers were ordinarily trusted to censor their own. William Crawford was scrupulous on this point, so his correspondence from the Pacific is silent as to locations, troop movements, and specific operations. But the blanks he had to leave are easy to fill in from postwar histories and the letters themselves form a tapestry of his experience amounting to the journal he was not allowed to keep. In that sense, the multiple carbons serve a general readership by governing his tone, which, while maintaining an awareness of his destined reader, doesn't vary greatly, though the most humor can be found in the letters to his sister, with whom his candid and affectionate relationship made possible a detailed and jaunty narrative of his days. Letters to his mother show more reserve while still managing to supply a sense of the importance of her son's memories of Hertford and home. And the handful to his wife are irreplaceable for their accounts of combat.

But while the letters are a rich resource, working my way through them I encountered a silence that puzzled me—they often seemed oddly unpeopled. My uncle was vivid in descriptions of the jungle, astute in his commentary on the war, comprehensive in his account of the perils of his work, and compelling when he offered images of combat. But the reader rarely meets other soldiers. As a member of the general staff, Colonel Crawford would have been in daily consultation with his peers. He was one step away from the division commander. He would have had files of junior officers and senior sergeants scurrying to do his bidding. But we don't often encounter any of them. It is as though Crawford lived in a world of his own construction, noting West Point classmates killed in action, or inquiring into the lives of family and friends at home. But in his own sphere he appears isolated.

It's strange—because there's evidence outside his correspondence that he was a convivial, sympathetic, and even witty man. Indeed, the letters themselves bear repeated marks of humor and high spirits. But in the Pacific, he sometimes seems to deliver monologues from an empty stage. (This made me wonder whether Cy Caldwell, in his turgid attempt at reading the boy's character, hadn't intuited at least one aspect of the man William would become.)

Yet that isolated nature—in which D. H. Lawrence saw a fundamental aspect of American character—seems to have been at least sometimes bridged. Mary Crawford speaks of her husband as being "the most loved officer in the division," and a colleague long after the war wrote to my mother, "I'm one of those characters who loved Col. Crawford." Maybe my uncle compartmentalized his relationships or met each circumstance with some different aspect of his character. Military service set him apart from civilians. Combat set him apart from noncombatant soldiers. Rank fenced off friendships. His mother and his marriage made their own demands. And increasingly I have the sense that something elemental and isolated in his character—good nature, social flair, and professional aplomb aside—made him walk alone.

WARRIOR RENOWN travels on parallel paths. There is the official reputation, written in shorthand above a soldier's pocket in ribbons that stand for the medals, awards, honors, and decorations granted over the course of a long or short career. These may be merited, and more. They may in fact fall short of celebrating the full scope of an achievement. But some honors may be given too quickly to those who may have done too little to earn them.

Thus that first fame is shadowed by a second: the opinion actually held of a soldier by his or her peers, the bubble reputation in the cannon's mouth granted by those who have served with the trooper in the field. This unofficial reputation, even if rarely spoken, is perhaps most to be trusted.

In 1960, fifteen years after Bill Crawford's death, his sister Louise opened a letter from an advertising executive in Greensboro, North Carolina, a veteran of the 11th Airborne Division's South Pacific campaigns. This fellow officer had known the young lieutenant colonel well, in garrison and in the field, and was moved to share his memories. The letter is short, but one line lingers. After expressing condolences for Louise's loss, it remembers William Crawford's courage under fire and competence in his work before concluding: *He was the officer many of us wished we could be.*

This, I think, was my uncle's highest accolade.

That said, there is merit in the tangible emblems of a soldier's life, and good reason they should be passed down to those dearest to him. But Mary

Crawford, numb with grief and hardly hoping to be reminded every day thenceforward that she'd once been married to the army, gracefully relinquished to her sister-in-law three emblems of her husband's journey, which my mother in turn left to me: his father's sword, his Silver Star, his West Point ring.

WAITING FOR THE STORM
Major A. R. Woods and the World of the Secret War

Uncle Sam ain't no woman
But he sure can take your man
—Old Song

COMING IN FROM THE FIELD long after dark, my father went directly to his bedroom, took off his khaki jacket, loosened his tie, unbuckled the straps of his shoulder holster, and slid the snub-nosed Colt revolver gently onto the nightstand where it rested between a depleted pint of Suntory whiskey—"bottled especially for the American forces"—and a crumpled pack of Camels, aware and amused as he did so that he was creating a tableau that might have illustrated the dust jacket of a Raymond Chandler novel.

But the little pistol was not a prop. Arthur Roy Woods, Jr.—more usually simply A. R. Woods—had been obliged to deal with two intruders in the last three weeks, and while the first likelihood was that these were ordinary burglars, the nature of his work was such that he had to consider other possibilities.

Woods poured a short drink from the bottle of Suntory. Then he sat down on the bed, lit his twenty-seventh cigarette of the day, and pulled a small notebook from his shirt pocket. He added some brief comments to the notes he had made earlier, mostly writing in plain text but now and then calling on a substitution cipher that would have been opaque to all but one intended reader.

He had spent the afternoon debriefing two field agents. The first was a local national who had passed the previous week above the thirty-eighth parallel observing certain maneuvers of the North Korean People's Army. The man had been in the north twice before and returned with aplomb but this time he seemed shaken. The second was an American who had been working to establish the identity of a German national, resident in Korea throughout the war. The German had almost certainly been a Nazi advisor to the Kempeitai, but his cover story was nearly flawless and the agent—a highly skilled professional—had been repeatedly frustrated in his attempts to penetrate it. "If I could just shoot the son of bitch," he said helplessly.

"I'm not altogether opposed," my father said, "but right now I think that would cause us more problems than it would solve. Be patient. There's no hurry. He'll come to you."

A routine day. Tomorrow would not be routine. A. R. Woods had awakened that morning in a new nation, the Republic of Korea, and the next morning he was to have an hour's private conversation with its new president, Syngman Rhee. Woods would brief Rhee on some of the work American intelligence officers were undertaking on behalf of his new democracy. Some of it. And he would answer Rhee's questions. Some of them. He was a little surprised that a higher-ranking officer hadn't been given the assignment, but when he made the point to General Hodge, Hodge had laughed. "You know as much about all this as anybody, Hank," the commander of US forces in Korea said, "and you've got that affable nature that will make Rhee think he's a step ahead of you and that chess player's mind that assures me he won't be. You've got the job unless you really want to refuse it."

Woods took a swallow of his drink, feeling the warmth of the cheap whiskey widen through his chest. He let his eyes drift about the room, absorbing its spare graces: the *tatami* mat crisp and soft under his slippered feet, the hanging scroll—mist, mountains—that was the only decoration, the sliding *shoji* screens whose translucent paper walls released a soft fall of moonlight. The narrow bed, oak table, and gooseneck lamp were the room's only concessions to Western ease, and they were plain enough to preserve the austere aesthetic.

He made a final entry in his notebook concerning the agent who had been in the north. The man was a good agent but Woods saw early signs that he might be starting to unravel. The instructors at Holabird had been right: field operatives were always needy, baby birds with their beaks open—more money, better quarters, a medal, a pension, a job for the wife, above all a way out, some promised route to safety when the fire burned too brightly, got too close. The man had taken an extraordinary risk to bring back several pieces of new information. They might prove priceless or worthless. Context would tell. Either way he should not be sent north again.

The phone rang as Woods was finishing his drink.

"Hank? How'd things go?" Jay Vanderpool never spent time on small talk, and both men made it a rule to keep telephone conversations as brief as possible. Vanderpool was an army colonel with an Agency connection.

"The fellow you met last week?" Woods said carefully. "His business is thriving, though I think it may be time to find him a new assignment. The other guy has run into some roadblocks, probably temporary."

"Good, good." Vanderpool paused. "I've heard a little more about that paperwork we were promised, but I still think it's a myth."

Woods's silence told his colleague even so indirect a remark might be a little careless. The colonel said swiftly, "Let's get together for a drink at the club tomorrow."

"Sixish?"

"See you then."

Vanderpool rang off.

Woods went to bed. He slept lightly, under a silk sheet soon filmy with sweat. August lay thick in the little room. There wasn't much relief to be had from a crippled electric fan trawling for air at the foot of the bed. In this quarter of the city, the night was quiet. Once a pariah dog barked out in the alley, whose funk of wet charcoal, *kimchi*, and human shit seeped into the house with special vengeance on humid nights.

An hour before dawn, Woods felt himself tugged from a shallow sleep by the sense that someone was standing motionless in the hallway. There had been no sound—rather, a deepening of the silence. He freed himself from the tangle of sheets, armed himself with a flashlight and the revolver, and moved slowly to the bedroom door. Ten minutes later he was satisfied there was no one there. But it was hard to shake the feeling that someone had been.

He went back to bed and slept well for several more hours, waking pleasantly to the trilling of a songbird in the garden and the sound of shuffling feet moving about the room as his houseboy laid out breakfast on the low lacquered table under the window. When the servant saw that the *gaijin* was stirring, he nodded good morning and wordlessly withdrew. Woods lit a cigarette. He thought of mentioning the suspected intruder but decided against it. The servant had been of little help on the other two occasions. He slipped from his bed and sat down to his meal in a rustle of silk pajamas.

The breakfast was simple: a plate of steamed rice with a raw egg stirred into it (which cooked the egg somewhat), a small bowl of miso soup, a dish of pickled vegetables. Hot black coffee.

He ate slowly. There were times when he still felt nostalgia for a traditional American breakfast, but the sparse Korean diet suited him. A Japanese diet, really. As with the architecture of his little house and the design of his garden, much of the country lay under a palimpsest of *Dai Nippon*, whose colonizers had deformed the local culture of this hapless land starting in 1910. The surrender had stripped the Japs of their power, but not of their presence. Korean hatred of the vanquished overlord was something my father occasionally found useful in his work.

When he had finished his breakfast, he dressed for the day—seersucker suit, no shoulder holster—and carried his coffee and a thin leather briefcase into the garden, whose dwarf pines bristled in the August sun. The azaleas and peonies were past their prime, but the walled space still possessed the charm of its little pond, on whose dark surface a single lotus swam, and of the polished stones placed artfully beside the bamboo gate.

Woods glanced at his watch. The staff car that was coming for him would arrive in twenty minutes. Time enough to review the handful of notes, files, and official documents with their seals and stamps and imposing signatures that he would be carrying to the meeting. He spread them out on a table under the pines and lit the day's second cigarette, then glanced briefly at a one-page profile of the new South Korean president. In the past week he'd read it through many times.

Syngman Rhee was an unusual figure for an Asian politician, a Princeton PhD who had spent the war years in Washington lobbying for Korean independence, which he assumed would naturally follow an Allied victory. His claim to the presidency was strongly supported by American policy makers, yet aspects of Rhee's rise were concerning. The man was a polished thug who might well have a corpse or two on his list of vanquished foes. But he was the best of a bad set of choices. Syngman Rhee was a rabid anti-communist, which would play well in Washington, and a devout Methodist, which would gratify the rest of the country. That he was a patriot there could be no doubt. But his nature was intensely authoritarian. Something closer to dictatorship than democracy might not be too far off in his thinking.

"Mister Wood—sir." The houseboy was standing in the doorway. "You driver here, sir."

The quondam US Army major nodded, sank his cigarette in the coffee cup, reloaded the briefcase, and went through the garden gate to the driveway, where a black Buick waited. It bore no official markings and when the driver dismounted he was in civilian clothes, but Woods recognized an elderly staff sergeant with whom he had worked before. Indeed, the man sketched a brief salute and Woods—after a moment's hesitation—returned it.

"Morning, sir."

"Good morning, Sergeant. That's okay, I'll sit in front." The driver closed the door smartly behind him.

"Where to, sir?"

"The Blue House."

The Blue House was the compound of executive offices and residences that had been the citadel of Korea's rulers and their retinues for nearly a thousand years. The NCO permitted himself an arch glance at the man beside him. "No shit. *El jefe* himself, Major?"

"That would come under the heading of 'need to know.' And it's 'mister' now."

"Yessir." The driver put the car in gear. "That still takes some getting used to."

"For me as well," my father said.

The staff car wound its way through the streets of Seoul, which seemed at that hour to be a city of women: women pounding laundry on stone slabs, women spinning silk or weaving linen, women laughing and talking together on street corners as they balanced huge clay crocks on their heads, or sorting through produce at an open market with babies slung on their backs, women cooking meals in iron ovens within walled courtyards, their daughters in middy blouses dancing attendance. Of course there were men as well—they just seemed less visible. As the car bounced bone-breakingly along broken roads and rutted mud alleys, Major—now Mister—Woods saw artisans through the doorways of little shops engraving small bowls of brass and bronze, old men with thin beards and long mustaches bent over games of Go, astrologers with their charts laid out before them doing good business in the markets.

Scenes like this had formed ritual tableaux in city and countryside for a thousand years, but their tranquility could always be broken. At one corner, the staff car crept past the struggling figures of a snarling policeman and a ragged beggar whose white robe was already spattered with blood. The cop, towering over the cringing man, was raising his baton for a second stroke when the car passed beyond the picture.

"I hate to see that shit," the driver muttered.

My father said nothing. Violence ran like red wine through Korea. He had encountered it in person, once when he was slightly wounded helping American MPs quell a riot, another time when he was shown the mutilated corpses of fifty South Korean cops laid side by side like dead fish on a dock. He had lost field agents. He'd read the constant news of border clashes and assassinations. In small villages, he had been present at encounters with the opposition when weapons had been drawn. Violence was the language of the land. You had to be able to read it.

The staff car turned onto the long avenue that swept gracefully toward the Blue House, the presidential palace of all Korea until 1945. Now the country was cleaved in two as though by a sword. In the north, Russians and Chinese vied for control. In the south, Americans had established a protectorate. To call the peninsula a powder keg tethered to a slow fuse was to announce the obvious, and to say that the fate of South Korea rested in any large measure on the meeting that lay ahead would have inflated its importance. But to suppose that the coming hour might move the needle on the dial between peace and war strongly in one direction or another was not an illusion. This then was a heavy load to carry, and for a moment my father was tempted to pull out his notes for a final quick review lest he'd let some small crucial point evade him. But he resisted the temptation. He left the briefcase closed. He was ready.

A. R. WOODS would seem to have been an unlikely warrior. When Germany invaded Poland in September 1939, he was an attorney with a private practice in the seacoast town of Southport, North Carolina, living with his wife and son, my older brother, Arthur. He was a cerebral and largely sedentary man, gone a little soft since his college days when he had worked summers as a railroad laborer. He spent his leisure time with pipe and book in an armchair. His only exercise was walking his dog.

The legal practice was reasonably successful, but his clients were often impoverished. He was once paid a bushel of shrimp for gaining the acquittal of a fisherman accused of murder in a knife fight. He considered his future

largely open, and—in 1939—he was not overly concerned about American involvement in what was still a European war.

Not so my mother, whose beloved brother William was a professional soldier eager for action, and whose beloved France would fall to the Germans on June 14, 1940. On that day Louise Crawford Woods was devastated. She had never been to Paris—she had never been out of the country—but as an art student in Philadelphia she had lived in the world of the Post-Impressionists and it was an article of faith with her that the City of Light was the soul of civilization. Now it would be trampled under the jackboots of gangsters with murder in their hearts and no more culture in their souls than could be crammed into the Horst Wessel song. The news came over the radio early in the morning. In tears, she woke my father, who mumbled that it was no skin off his ass before he rolled over and went back to sleep. I don't think she ever forgave him.

A. R. Woods (far right), as railroad laborer, summer 1930

He was similarly offhand about Pearl Harbor. Hearing that news, he paused thoughtfully, and then said: "I give little brown brother about six months." (He was less casual a year later when more became known about the failure of American plans: "There should have been some hangings by now.") The casual racism hardly merits comment; the phrase had been common coin since it was first used by Americans in the Philippines forty years before. But the timetable is noteworthy—Did my father, a well-read man who stayed current with world events, really believe that the United States, radically unarmed and unprepared, could vanquish the empire of Japan and its Axis allies swiftly? My guess is that he intended to reassure my mother. His immediate task was to determine where his own path lay.

The answer given by his ancestors back to the time of King Philip's War was spoken with one voice: when battle came, you went to meet it. But there was no need to rush. War work of all kinds would swiftly open. As a man past thirty and the sole support of a wife and child, he might have been spared the draft. As a lawyer, he was eligible for a direct commission. I don't know what conversations he may have had with his wife about the

matter, but I do know that his brother-in-law—now railing against a fate that had consigned him to the Caribbean while war raged on elsewhere in the world—had been quick to offer suggestions. On February 18, 1942, Bill Crawford wrote his sister, "If Arthur hasn't settled on some defense work already, tell him to try that Judge Advocate General's job I wrote you about. He's well-qualified and the chance for action is greater than he might suspect. The FBI makes sense, too, given Arthur's fluent German. But I have a hunch he might really find a home in military intelligence. Anyway, keep me posted."

I have no details of how my father spent the six months after Pearl Harbor. He seems to have explored the possibility of a direct commission in the Judge Advocate General Corps, and to have looked into the idea of the service in the US Navy. But neither thought bore fruit. Meanwhile he continued his legal practice and lived his life as though the world had not taken on a strange new shape around him. But he watched the progress of the war in those fateful early months when the possibility of Allied defeat seemed very real—the months when, though he'd asserted his confidence in a swift Japanese collapse, the Axis scored victory after victory. And in due time he came to his decision. He may have discussed it with his wife, though I think it more likely he would have announced his resolution as a fait accompli. Like other spouses in the dark summer of 1942, she would have mastered her fears and supported his action. I remember her once saying, "The Second World War wasn't something you got to sit out."

And so, in June, Woods traveled to Camp Wheeler, an army post near Macon, Georgia, which—abandoned after the First World War—had been reactivated in 1940 as an Infantry Replacement Training Center. He wore a good summer suit and carried a small suitcase filled with shirts and books. It would be months before he saw either again. On a red dirt parade ground before the low barracks building that was to be his home for weeks to come, he stood with a hundred other men and raised his right hand to swear the old oath his father had taken many years before, the same oath both his sons would take, many years apart, many years later.

MY FATHER'S LETTERS from basic training open onto a world that would be largely familiar to any man—and in his day and mine it was mostly men—who soldiered in any Western army over the past three hundred years. Some elements of the ritual change—the ordeal may be now longer, now shorter, it may embrace new doctrines in weapons or tactics, adapt to geography or the developing protocols of a given generation's war—but the fundamentals seem timeless: the bayonet field and the rifle range, drill and ceremony, first aid and field sanitation, hand-to-hand combat, the obstacle course. Perhaps not every recruit feels himself part of the rear guard of the long march of history, but so many experiences are held in common with the foot soldiers of Wellington or Washington that you sometimes recognize a brother in unexpected places or unfamiliar ways. I remember a visit, many years after I was out of the army, to the Castillo de San Marcos in St. Augustine, Florida, built by the Spanish in 1672, walking along a parapet that ended in a guardroom—a visceral reminder of walking guard on such

A. R. Woods with the author, Hertford, North Carolina, 1945

a path at Fort Dix, New Jersey, nearly three hundred years later and ending my watch in just such a small room. My Spanish counterpart and I would have found a common language in which to bitch through the long dull hours about the weight of our weapons and the pestilential nature of the sergeant of the guard.

But one mustn't grow too nostalgic about this stuff. A great deal of basic training has little to do with the evocation of a storied past. Much of it is hurry-up-and-wait, classes cancelled and orders countermanded, empty hours, futile duties, exhaustion undercut by tedium. And this is never more true than at the beginning of the process, when the new recruit endures idle days while waiting for his company to form.

Of all the passages in my father's letters, none speaks to me more eloquently than this brief line: "Our main difficulty is that the training cycle hasn't started." He has been at Camp Wheeler a week or so. His cohort has been issued leggings and denims—"I look like an old-fashioned Zouave"—and settled into a routine of sorts: dawn formation, calisthenics, chow, scrubbing the barracks, then "odd jobs until evening."

There is probably no other point in our military experience so precisely parallel, and none that sheds more light on the legerdemain that turns civilian into soldier. My own week of limbo was spent much as his was, with the added burden that my little group still wore its rank civilian clothes. We were torn from our bunks at dawn, put through the daily dozen (army exercises), stuffed with powdered eggs, then led away in ones and twos by vicious corporals who needed somebody to dig post holes, move file cabinets, or paint walls. I don't think we even got to do anything as military as the dread KP. We were civilians, herded through civilian jobs, and the worst part of our burden was the sight of men no more than ten days our seniors in the service, wearing the uniform, marching in formation, and counting cadence as they swept past our laboring little groups, awarding us looks of scorn if they bothered to look at us at all.

Intended or not, the psychology of delay is brilliantly successful. It makes men less nostalgic for the lives they've left than eager to begin the life before them. No military spirit is required, just the normal human impulse to get on with things. Neither soldier nor civilian, the recruit feels adrift in the system, unclaimed by a destiny he knows he must covet as his own. It's a week that seems to last forever, but finally the company forms. You've been issued your uniforms, class A's and fatigues, your boots, your dog tags, the OD blouses, the strips of cloth sewn above the shirt pockets designed to tell you as well as others who you are: WOODS. US ARMY.

FROM THIS POINT, Private Woods wrote few letters. Basic training doesn't admit of much free time, and such as there is tends to be colonized

Author and his father, 1966

by enervation. "Sleep every chance you get, and there won't be many," my father advised me when I went off to the army in 1966, and I'm sure that in 1942 he followed his own advice. But now and then he did find time to capture his Camp Wheeler experience:

July 14
Today a seven-mile hike with full field pack and rifle. I don't know how much it all weighs together but I'm sure the SPCA wouldn't let it be put on a Missouri mule. One hundred degrees in the shade if there were any shade, and humidity to match. Twenty men dropped out but I stayed on my feet. It's all that clean living.
Thank Christ it rained on the way back. We survivors hit the company area cocky as hell and feeling fine. But before the rain the heat was appalling. The general notion is that we're being trained to fight in Libya, which I suppose means most of us will go to Alaska.

He is already acquiring the language of the foot soldier, that persistent irony with which absurd situations can best be tamed. And he is alert to other occasions for humor, an element surprisingly common in one's early days in the army, when the mismatch between military protocol and apprentice ignorance is at its most confounding:

July 27
Funny story came my way today. A lot of the boys pulling guard around here are proving a little slow to learn. One properly stopped a major the other night with a "Halt, who's there?" The officer identified himself and waited for the next command. Silence. Finally the major snapped, "Boy, isn't there something else you should say to me?" To which our hero answered, "There sure is, and you'd damned well better stand there until I think of it." It's even better than the tale of the recruit who got the chain of command backwards and asked the captain's permission to speak to the first sergeant. Actually, given where immediate power lies, that might not be a bad approach sometimes.

And again:

July 30
Had training films on the Army's various vehicles today. Fairly rudimentary. I learned that you put gas in the tank to make the motor start, turn the wheel left to go left, and so on. I'm fairly sure most of us could approach the subject at a more advanced level but the Army has its ways.

Nevertheless, thirteen weeks of basic training played out against the background of the war, which ensured a rapid tempo and a swift immersion in the necessary arts. Tasks and classes spun past in bewildering succession, often appearing to be unrelated to one another. In a single day, Woods would follow seventeen straight hours of KP with gas instruction and a session of small arms.

August 5
Tear gas with masks on—and off. Trained (outside) to recognize odors. "Chloropicrin smells like flypaper, mustard gas smells like garlic, lewisite smells like geraniums, and phosgene like fresh corn shucks." At the revolver range, I was plenty nervous because it's easy

for some damn fool to make a mistake with a revolver—much easier than with a rifle—and I was glad when it was over. The range safety officer, a major, said it was the most dangerous day we'd spend in the Army 'till we got to the war.

Another time what looked like a week's worth of training was packed into a single day:

September 11
    In the morning, we ran the obstacle course—twice. Six hundred yards of hills, hurdles, walls, traps, tunnels, ropes and bridges. This reduced everybody to racking sobs. We recovered with calisthenics.
    In the afternoon, there was a three-mile hike with full field packs and weapons in 100-degree heat followed by repeated attacks on a high, cactus-studded hill. After evening chow, a night reconnaissance patrol. My platoon never did find the enemy, so we were spared some barbed wire and a few fixed explosions. Got back to the company area around 4:00 pm having been on the go for twenty-two hours without pause. They *did* have the decency to give us today off.

Reading these accounts I feel a degree of awe. My own stint of basic training was not only five weeks shorter, it was somewhat less stringent, but it took all the energy I had—and I was twenty-two years old to my father's thirty-five. And I, too, trained in a time of war. But it was not a war that enlisted the whole nation's dedication. Taking up arms against Hitler and Hirohito doubtless stiffened the will of A. R. Woods and his cohort. One of his letters reflects as much:

September 15
    The war seems comparatively far away here, but I get the same feeling you do when reading *Time* and *Life*. I see it from the sidelines with everybody else but I can't help feeling we need offensive action not six months or a year from now but *now*. If we don't gamble soon we may not get a chance to gamble at all. My gang here is ready to take our chances—but we want to *get going*. I can't help feeling there's too much boondoggling in Washington and too little will to get in and slug it out.

There's no saber rattling here, just the grim determination I found in my uncle's letters as well. But the passage stands out because it's the one place where Woods as a private meditates on strategy. For the most part, he's content to note the details of the day, most of which record the immemorial arts of preparation for an infantryman's war:

September 19

Today's class in hand-to-hand combat was more informal: we gathered in a crowd with 2x4s and attempted to beat the hell out of each other. I got a little banged up but I had a good time.

Shot well with the M1 on the range today but with the BAR two rounds got jammed in the breech so I said the hell with it. Spent the rest of the day cleaning the machine guns. The damned things are so perverse, they seem almost human.

We gather in squads on the bayonet range, where straw dummies swing like hanged men in wooden frames. Comes the order "Fix . . . *bayonets*!" We do. Comes the question, "What is the spirit of the bayonet?" "TO KILL!" we roar, and spring forward one at a time to enact the dummy's doom. Most of us see the silly side to this—it's more a war movie than a war. But we take the work seriously. I don't think many bayonets get thrust in modern combat. But it does happen, and we must know how.

I learned how, too, and with the same slight sense of unreality. My squad talked about the ancient art a little. There was general agreement that we could probably pull the trigger on an enemy soldier trapped in our sights a respectable distance away, but it was hard not to feel queasy about the idea of shoving a foot of black steel into a human belly. These nice distinctions are not raised in training. Indeed, the only observation I recall about the ultimate aim of our work was shouted by a noncom addressing our loose formation: "Men, we do not want you to die for your country, we want you to make the other sonofabitch die for his!" The line is pure Hollywood but they actually say it. I'm sure my father heard the same cheerful admonition.

And so the days piled atop one another, reassuring in their uniformity. But during September, there was a change in emphasis. "Almost all our work is tactical from here on in," he notes. "Theoretically, at least, we have a working knowledge of our weapons by now and have had sufficient physical conditioning. Now we plan and execute attacks and defenses of all kinds—night raids, ambushes, perimeter defense." And by October, he knew what his next post would be:

> I read one Ellery Queen and two *New Yorkers* last night. Cleaned shoes and shined gear the next morning. They gave us a good lunch today: Spam and peas and mashed potatoes and ice cream. As you will gather, there's not much now happening, but I'm not unhappy or particularly bored, merely marking time 'till I go to Fort Benning and doing as little as possible, along with the rest of the boys. My whole gang is stale from overtraining and impatient for the cycle to end.

Before it did, he was able to secure a three-day pass and his wife eagerly took the train from Norfolk to Macon to join him. But the weekend was not an entire success. She must have reflected her disappointment in a letter to her brother, who offered a tactful reply. "Glad you got to visit Arthur in Macon," Bill Crawford wrote from his Puerto Rican redoubt:

> And you're right—infantry basic training is not exactly a picnic. But if Arthur's been on the rifle range, he's close to the end of it. And Louise, don't fool yourself—he was damn glad to see you, even if his letters afterward were, as you say, "phlegmatic." I can promise you that what might have seemed like indifference was no more than exhaustion. Believe me, some of the things he's undergoing would make anybody want to bite Jesus on the leg.

It's not hard to imagine that Louise Crawford Woods, for many weeks a lonely wife and single mother, had headed south seeking a romantic interlude that yielded rather less romance than she'd hoped for. "Phlegmatic"—sluggish, apathetic—the word may have been well chosen. But the passing state will surprise no one who has made his way into the final weeks of basic training, when a soldier's primary lust is likely to be for sleep.

Even so, her complaint may have had less to do with listless passion than emotional unavailability. Certainly my father was not a demonstrative man. He always closed his letters with "love," but in reading fifty of them, I don't recall once seeing the phrase *I love you* or *I miss you*. I remind myself he was a man of his times, bound to a model of machismo that made it hard to find a language for feelings and would have forbidden its use even if he had. Still, the failure leaves a silence in the letters—in most instances, they read as though written less to a lover than to a friend, perhaps indeed to a friend who doesn't know him very well. As their son, I'm content to be spared the written record of my parents' love life, but as a writer I feel I'm being deprived of part of the story.

It is, in any case, not the part that most interests Bill Crawford, who passes swiftly on to military matters.

> Tell Little Arthur hello for me. He'll miss this war, but he *just* will. Six
> years should finish it up, though it may take a year or two longer." He
> concludes: "I'm anxious to hear that Arthur has gone to Fort Benning.
> I admire him one hell of a lot for taking all this on when he could
> have honorably found an easier path to service. I know the training
> has been hard. OCS should be less physically demanding and he may
> find it a lot more interesting.

Confident that his brother-in-law would gain admission to Officer Candidate School, Major Crawford—always capable of a beau geste—had mailed Private Woods the gold bars pinned on his shoulders when he graduated from West Point. But though my father had planned on becoming an officer from the day he entered the army, there were no guarantees; there were some odd hoops to jump through, including an interview with the selection board, whose questions were not confined to the art of war. In late October, he noted: "Among other things, I was asked whether I thought Scarlett O'Hara was the heroine of *Gone with the Wind*. Just as well I'd been cautioned that some questions 'may sound foolish, but we're just trying to get you to talk.' Extraordinary."

Woods had hidden the second lieutenant's gold bars in the few inches of his footlocker reserved for personal belongings, less from fear of censure should they be discovered than from the same superstition that will prevent him from trying them on a day before he's commissioned. But he has been told unofficially by his platoon leader that he did well before the selection board, whose primary interest was assessing his aptitude for command. For the rest, his basic military skills were more than adequate and his body no longer resembled that of the easy-living lawyer he'd been only a few months before. He stood just over six feet tall. His weight had dropped to 175 pounds, he had a thirty-two-inch waist, and a supple new strength that had carried him past every obstacle. "It'll take a year of hard drinking once I'm out of the Army to get myself in shape again," he noted dryly, but it's evident that his new vigor is a source of justifiable pride.

At the end of October, he received his orders for OCS, and with them an immediate promotion to corporal. The two stripes will be his until he pins on Bill Crawford's gold bars, and they show up on the sleeves of all his future classmates save one, an event that provokes Camp Wheeler to the last bit of comedy basic training will provide:

October 26
Everybody in the barracks got this promotion, except Silverberg, whose stripes for some reason don't come through until tomorrow. Be sure that twenty-eight corporals have had great fun giving orders to one miserable private, who swears he'll turn the tables on us when the time comes. We pointed out that we will always be his superiors by 24 hours and he'd damned well better not wake the senior NCOs.

OVER THE YEARS, there have been a number of paths to an army commission. West Point supplies the core of career professionals. College ROTC programs, obligatory at land grant universities, produce large numbers of reservists. Direct appointment is afforded doctors, lawyers, clergy, and certain specialists. Battlefield commissions are not unknown. But, especially in time of war, when manpower needs accelerate with nearly unmanageable speed, Officer Candidate Schools have proven essential. As demand dictates, these sometimes multiply, one school for almost every branch. But the combat arms—infantry, armor, and artillery—are always key to the enterprise, and during the Second World War the Infantry OCS at Fort Benning, Georgia, lay at the heart of them all.

When Corporal A. R. Woods reported there in November, the school was new. It had graduated its first class less than three months before Pearl Harbor, but it drew on the resources of the long-established infantry program at Fort Benning and it profited from the thinking of its primary architect, Gen. Omar Bradley. The students called it Benning School for Boys. They were called ninety-day wonders, for the swiftness with which they earned their commissions. The term could be mocking or respectful. Graduates themselves cherished the story of a conversation between two old soldiers, a colonel and a master sergeant. "Hell, Sarge," the colonel growls, "we both know junior officers are worthless." "Yes, sir," comes the reply, "until that five minutes when they're not."

As was true of his weeks of basic training, Officer Candidate Woods's letters from Fort Benning were few in number, but most reflected his satisfaction with the course—"the instruction varies between excellent and superb"—as well as his abiding sense of the comedy that lives persistently at the heart of army life:

November 12

Every morning after breakfast we have fifteen minutes of what makes my friend Stephen call this place a cross between a monastery and an insane asylum—voice exercises where everyone shouts "Hong Kong, sing song, ding dong!" at top volume followed by shouted mass commands—"Left face!" "About face!"—that collide with each other to produce an intentional chaos. We also hear mysterious shouted commands coming out of the deep woods every night. The purpose of all this is a mystery.

In some ways, the program recapitulated the weeks of basic training, but with much more attention to minutiae and with an entirely different focus.

November 14

Today we started work with the M-1—back over all the ground I covered in basic but with much more thoroughness and in much greater detail. The emphasis, as in all our work, is not only upon the acquisition of knowledge and skills but the ability to teach them. As we've been told time and again, we have to be able to do anything better than any of our men but it's not as vital to actually be a crack shot as to make sure your soldiers are.

In the field, he took pleasure in the sheer spectacle of massed firepower, and in the demands of combat exercises more elaborate than any he had encountered at Camp Wheeler:

December 14

A bit of fun this week—they trooped us out to the bleachers to watch an artillery barrage. Howitzers—75s, 105s, 155s—from way down the valley dropped rounds in front of us, close as 500 yards. HE, ricochet, twined fused shells, indicatory fire, full salvos. It made a very pleasant noise and kicked up a hell of a lot of dirt.

We also ran the blitz course. You start at a dog trot, armed with a variety of weapons, and encounter an array of tactical problems: snipers, machine gun nests, enemies firing from shacks and ditches. The idea is to check reaction times and choice of weapons in each situation. I enjoyed it.

Meanwhile, Bill Crawford, still languishing at Fort Buchanan was following from afar the exploits of his brother-in-law, writing Louise at the end of the month:

I'm sure Arthur is in this thing 100% and getting all he can out of it. Of course it's not like studying Anglo-Saxon at Penn or crimes and misdemeanors in law school—Army instruction can seem dull until you realize that the mastery of some small detail might mean the difference between victory and death. Still, this is new territory for him, and I think he's shown a lot of guts in heading straight for the infantry. I know you're worried, but you should also be damned proud.

Louise Woods *was* proud, as well as pleased to have found a more buoyant version of her husband when she visited Fort Benning before Christmas than she had encountered during the exhausting final weeks at Camp Wheeler. She may not even have minded his teasing:

December 28
Just in case your morale needs a little building, several of my classmates are still coming up with flattering comments about you—"a girl with not only beauty but brains." I merely say "The best is none too good for Arthur." To you I'll say I think you're even better looking than you were when I met you. And you *do* have more sense.

"They're throwing the book at us this week," he wrote on January 17, 1943, "but I'm confident I can take whatever's coming. We mounted a dawn attack on Tuesday—much wandering all over the muddy hills and muddier valleys of Georgia. Well, it's drawing to a close." With fewer than four weeks to go, buoyed by the high marks and stellar reviews he'd received from the beginning—capped now by the rumor that the school wants to retain him on the teaching staff—he exults, "The bars are in the bag."

Still, when he gets his new uniform fitted in preparation for the graduation ceremony, he doesn't pin them on his shoulders. "Being slightly superstitious, I haven't put the rank on yet." Almost from the beginning of the course, members of his class have been falling by the wayside, and now, with only days to go, the weak are still being sent to the wall. "I'm sorry for them," Woods writes. "I know a few boys who ship out tomorrow and they're looking pretty grim. But honestly, after eight month's work, better them than me."

In the end, the work wasn't wasted and his confidence wasn't misplaced. By late January, he had signed his discharge as a corporal and taken his oath as a second lieutenant in the Army of the United States—a clumsy neologism used to distinguish temporary soldiers from regulars, who belong to the United States Army. No matter. The gold bars on his shoulders confer equal authority on all who wear them. And no one is more exultant over the new lieutenant's commission than Maj. William Crawford, who on January 13, 1943, again writes his sister from his forlorn Caribbean post:

I'm so proud of Arthur! The Army has gained a damn fine officer, one with book learning and common sense as well as a fine body— essential to us infantrymen. Men like him demonstrate the strength of OCS. West Point can give our Army its professional core, but a war like this one demands one hell of a lot of citizen soldiers fit to wear gold bars. I'm glad he and I are in the same business. We're separated by an ocean, and I've never even seen him in uniform, but there's a feeling in my heart that goes past brother-in-law to brother-in-arms. I reckon you know what I mean.

He adds:

Arthur's age and education will give him better judgment than the younger men's and might earn him an immediate commission as a first lieutenant. Whatever happens, the training he's been going through is the toughest thing he'll face in the Army outside the war itself. And I have a hunch he'll find the next phase of his life in uniform a lot more interesting.

Bill Crawford's generous welcome cements my father's role as a bridge between two warrior families, and it carries no hint of the envy Crawford may well have felt over the probability that his brother-in-law was closer to combat than he. For Woods was determined to find his way to the fighting. He had set aside the idea of joining the infantry OCS staff. He was no longer interested in being an army lawyer. And he could not relish the prospect of a desk job. He had come too far and worked too hard for that. In the space of eight months, he had gone from sedentary seaside attorney to highly trained infantry officer. He had mastered small-unit strategy and tactics. He had qualified with every weapon used by an infantry company, from a handgun to a trench mortar, often rated expert. He had developed command presence. His body was honed and supple, his mind focused and free. He was primed to lead forty men into hellfire without a backward glance. He was ready for war.

But war was not ready for him.

Five possible explanations present themselves, in no special order. One was that he was considered overage for an immediate combat assignment; another, that his status as husband and father might have delayed it; a third was that his legal training, always visible in the background, would have recommended him to the Judge Advocate General's office—indeed, a friend lurking in the orderly room had heard the CO mutter, "JAG gets first crack at Woods—if they don't want him, the infantry can have him." A fourth is that his declining an apparent offer to remain at the school as training cadre had made his masters indifferent to his fate. But finally it may simply have been the Brownian motion of the army in action that gave my father his first assignment: as CO of a recruit platoon in a basic training company. He took on the job with stoic resolve, well aware that you go where they send you, ready to make the most of it until something closer to battle comes along.

SECOND LIEUTENANT WOODS reported in at Fort McClellan, Alabama, on February 2, 1943, to take up his first command. Conscious he would be as new at his job as his men were at theirs, he was well aware he would need to rely on an experienced platoon sergeant to help with the heavy lifting, and that he would have to balance the air of effortless command that had impressed his superiors at Benning with a degree of sympathy that would earn the trust of his troops. Only a few months away from standing where they now stood, he felt confident of making a success.

Established in 1917 near Anniston, Alabama, Fort McClellan, like so many army posts, found itself placed on caretaker status after the First World War, then vastly expanded in the months following Pearl Harbor. By 1943, the fort was primarily an Infantry Replacement Training Center where recruits focused for nine weeks on the techniques of urban warfare many of them would face in France and Germany.

IRTCs, constructed across the country throughout the war to teach new soldiers the basics of their unfamiliar trade, had graduated more than 2.5 million men by the spring of 1945. My father's posting to the center at Fort McClellan was the kind of first assignment often given to new officers on the theory that commanding a few cycles of trainees would enlarge their experience of leadership and so serve them well in combat. But from the point of view of the troops, the centers themselves suffered a flaw confessed by their names: *replacement*. Paul Fussell has pointed out that a new soldier couldn't fail to ask himself, replacement for what? To which the only answer would have to be the wounded or the dead. And as these men were fed into combat one at a time, the experienced companies they joined were indifferent to their presence and might not even learn their names before they died. *Yank* magazine, an official US Army publication, ran a story in April 1945 thick with interviews with veterans of the war in Europe who groused that IRTC training was neither long, realistic, nor thorough enough to prepare new soldiers for the realities of combat. But it does seem to me from my father's stories that he trained his own platoon hard and well, perhaps reasoning that he might one day find himself in action beside them. One of his first letters from McClellan gives a picture of how he went about the job:

February 5, 1943

The new recruits came in yesterday, teenagers most of them. I drew the fourth platoon. I wonder if I looked that awkward—it's unbelievable. I've got a good platoon sergeant and good corporals and we've been harrying them unmercifully in true Army fashion. I bellow at the group and the non-coms bellow at the individuals. They're coming along all right—don't seem to resent a thing.

After the first two weeks we'll let up a little, but the company commander insists we keep after them for now and that we'll have to do. The kids run the obstacle course within a half-hour of their arrival; I run it with them. It's a lot easier than the ones I've seen so far. After that it's "Left, right, watch your intervals, pick up the step, suck in your gut, hup toop threep four, eyes front, there's nothing on the ground in Alabama," and all those other kindly words so often thrown at me.

A few weeks later:

As to my platoon—they're working hard and so am I. They're rounding into surprisingly good shape. We get along fine together and both they and I are lucky to have a good platoon sergeant who knows his business. It's no myth that NCOs are the backbone of the Army.

Not every NCO. Within three weeks of his arrival, the gold bars still fresh on his shoulders, Woods was feeling pretty salty as he sorted out an issue with the company's top sergeant (having already complained that Fort Mc-Clellan "isn't 'Army' enough—but I'll straighten 'em out").

At one point I had a small run-in with our first sergeant and now he ain't first sergeant no mo'. The CO dropkicked him down to tech and if he doesn't soon change his opinion of second lieutenants I'll personally guarantee him a buck private's empty sleeve or a court martial for insubordination. This damn place is enough like a Boy Scout camp as it is. I don't feel too bad about it—our present company commander, who's all right for my money, fell heir to said sergeant when he took over the company. The man was not very efficient and was slated to get smacked down anyway. My difficulty was fairly small but I'd gone three quarters of the way with this jerk before and I'd had enough, so the CO used that to do what he wanted to do.

Woods enjoyed his work. He rejoiced in the relative luxury of his quarters, a tarpaper shack heated by a coal stove and shared with two other men, but cared for by a striker, an enlisted servant who "tidies up, makes fires and beds, and shines our shoes. Did I mention that it's better being an officer?"
Still greater splendor was provided by the officers' club:

February 12
I have to say the peacetime Army did itself proud—great high ceil-inged rooms with hewn timbers handsomely trimmed in scarlet and gold, heavy rugs on waxed hardwood floors, leather armchairs strewn

about, huge stone fireplaces with massive andirons—very Union Leaguish only more so.

In this elegant setting, the drinks flow freely, the wine is vintage, and the food rarely fails to please. "Lobster for lunch and steak for dinner," he blithely informs his wife, who presumably is subsisting on ration points. "I have to eat the damn stuff—it's all they have."

Training his platoon was his primary duty, but Woods shared with other junior officers the post's administrative tasks, including a twenty-four-hour tour as regimental OD—officer of the day—which he calls "a brief moment of glory." He seems to have enjoyed the ceremonial aspects of the job, parading before the flags and guidons, responding to the bugle calls, snapping out salutes to officers and noncoms bringing squads, platoons, and companies to attention before him, describing it all in four pages of fine detail fit for a field manual before recalling the fraying patience of his civilian readers and concluding sheepishly, "Hadn't meant to write all that gibberish but got started and didn't know where to quit." I'm reminded of Bill Crawford's dutiful description of his cadet quarters—two enthusiastic soldiers letting the incidentals of their stories crowd out the core.

Ceremony apart, his duties involved shepherding two lost tourists off the post at the behest of an irate colonel, summoning a plumber to fix a broken toilet, citing offenders for unlocked doors and unsecured rifle racks, and reviewing the guard just before being relieved of duty. "At which point a large brushfire was reported somewhere on the post which, thank God, I didn't have to deal with."

By now a first lieutenant, A. R. Woods was stationed at Fort McClellan for just over a year, long enough for him to shepherd half a dozen platoons of new recruits through their training cycles and more than long enough—in his view—to confirm him in the role *he* has trained for, that of a combat commander. But the army moves in mysterious ways. Confidently expecting orders to Europe or the Pacific, in March 1944 my father found himself packed off to Camp Blanding, Florida, yet another IRTC, though this time as officer in charge of the rifle range. The assignment was only the first of a bewildering variety of tasks he would be given, each one of which seemed to take him further from the fighting. He was in much the same position as Bill Crawford when Crawford began rattling the chains at the War Department to get a combat assignment. But Woods was a first lieutenant, not a major;

an OCS grad, not a West Pointer. The only pull he could have in the army would be his brother-in-law himself, and he was reluctant to tug on family ties to secure personal advantage. For now, he must wait.

At Camp Blanding, Woods found the rifle range in chaos. "I've got 800 men cycling through, we can't locate their records, and some of them haven't been paid in four months." Under the circumstances, the birth of a second son in far-off Philadelphia would seem to be the least of his concerns, which may explain why he responds to a telegram from my brother announcing my arrival, "For God's sake tell me what hospital your mother is in!" He recovers nicely from this gaffe, writing the family that the proud papa has been passing out cigars—"Robert Burns, no less—no nickel stogies"—to celebrate the advent of "William Louis Woods." (I had never known this early version of my name until I came across this letter.)

In due course, Woods sorted out the problems of the rifle range. His reward was to be made officer in charge of the regimental mess. As OIC he certainly never put his hands in a sink, but he did have to reconcile himself to the fact that his dreams of glory had become a nightmare of slops, and certainly found (not to his surprise) that in the deluge of paperwork was couched a jargon of supply as recondite as that of any bureaucracy in the army:

> Right now I'm taking a complete inventory of stuff on hand and it promises to be one of those far into the night jobs. It's hard to catch up with the kitchens until they're through for the day and even harder to remember that a Marmite can is a "Container, rd. incl. M41 with inserts" or to recall the distinction between a "pot, stock, with cover, fifteen gallons" and a "pot, stock, with cover, fifteen gallons, S and S."

He was able to find some amusement in the job. When the amount of china broken daily by careless troops became unacceptable, he posted a large sergeant with a thick neck and huge arms holding a coffee can labeled CHINA RELIEF by the mess hall door. Most diners considered it prudent to contribute.

There were certain perks as well. "I had quail on toast for breakfast this morning. One committed suicide by flying into a power line. So I took him to my top chef, a Frenchman from Louisiana, who broiled him with butter and bacon. You may well suppose this meal was the envy of all onlookers."

A final note from the consolidated mess reminds us of the burdens laid by the Lord on an officer of a democratic army:

April 15, 1944
We make sandwiches for about 500 men daily and do a decent job, I think. But one unhappy soldier wasn't pleased with his and he complained to the chaplain. Not enough egg in the egg salad—I believe that was the problem. So the sky pilot took out after me. I pacified him politely. But I wouldn't mind having a word with the soldier.

Complaining troops are common in a conscript army—during the Second World War, just over 60 percent were draftees—and the qualities of the men my father saw in the ranks was sometimes a source of frustration to him. During his first command at Fort McClellan, Woods had written that "My platoon is mostly low IQs from Pennsylvania and Rhode Island but they try hard and are at least learning to keep in step. One or two of them give me nightmares but they'll be all right—and now I must leave you to see if the proper number of windows are open in each hut." And now at Camp Blanding the product looked no better:

May 1
I don't know if I ever made clear the kind of troops I've been worrying about. The first great mystery is how they got past the induction station—psychoneurotics, neurasthenics, gripes, goldbricks, pie-eyed, and just plain bats—and we have about 1,200 of them. I stood by sick call one day and all I heard was "Oh, Doc, my back!" We had one joker repeatedly passed fit for duty who insisted on marching with a rifle over his shoulder and a cane in his hand.

But these bleak (and funny) characterizations were countered by his admiration for the NCOs he worked with and his sense that even the most hapless of the young soldiers under his command were willing and, ultimately, mostly able. "They're rounding into pretty good shape"—"They're coming along"—"They try hard." Lines like these crop up in the letters more often than the notes of resignation, and they do some justice to a grousing rabble of citizen soldiers who would ultimately take their share in the defeat of two of the most powerful armies in the world.

BY THE SUMMER OF 1944, the war had begun to favor the Allies. The Japanese had lost India and the Germans the Crimea. There had been a breakout at Anzio and a breakthrough in Rome. Intensified bombing throughout Europe predicted the epic battle to come. We have arrived at the sixth of June.

Two days after the Normandy invasion Woods took note of the event with a lighthearted tone that nevertheless reflects his chagrin at having missed it:

June 8
   Looks as though they managed to pull off an invasion without me, while I still fight the Battle of Blanding.
   In other news, I've been transferred from the IRTC School to the Battle Courses, where I'm busily engaged in teaching house-to-house fighting. Just at present I'm in charge of demolitions. I wired up and detonated sixty charges of TNT yesterday. Takes a steady hand but there's little danger if you know what you're doing and damned if I don't enjoy it.

His new job afforded him an honor he was unaware of at the time. June 10: "We ran a Jap battalion through the Battle Courses yesterday. I'm sure they're all right, certainly they work hard. Still, you can't help wondering."

Lieutenant Woods's doubts were widely shared. Deployment of Nisei soldiers had been controversial since the beginning of the war, when those already on active duty were dismissed from service even as their relatives were forced into "relocation" camps. But by early 1943, the Roosevelt administration had accepted a War Department recommendation that Japanese-Americans be allowed to serve in segregated regiments. Some of the men my father trained would form the nucleus of the 442nd Regimental Combat Team, which was to become the most decorated unit in American military history. I like to think that in later years he had the grace to regret his misgivings.

In any event, he would have had no time to dwell on them. His duties kept enlarging. On June 16, he reported:

Right now I'm busy playing landlord to five full colonels and a smattering of small fry who clutter up the place. They know nothing about the camp so I'm a constant source of information and a general

errand boy. In addition, of course, the court keeps functioning twice
a week and the ranges go on. I'm now the disarming and demolitions expert, assigned to check all theoretically inert shells, mines,
and booby traps used in training. They keep calling me up like mad
to take a look at a chunk of harmless-looking metal and say "OK,"
which usually I do, but the other day I found a couple of theoretically
disarmed anti-tank grenades which were lousy with TNT so I scraped
it out. That's not as dangerous as it sounds since TNT will detonate
only when given a special kind of shock. Otherwise you can put it on
an anvil and hit it with a sledge and nothing happens.

While his wife may have found his sangfroid reassuring, the placid behavior of one sort of explosive didn't guarantee the safety of another sort, or
account for the variety of charges my father had to dismantle on a routine
basis, all the while serving on courts-martial, playing majordomo to field-
grade officers, and waiting forlornly for assignment to some fading theater
of the war. It doesn't surprise me that this flurry of unfocussed activities had
him pondering escape from a service that overvalued him on the one hand
and underused him on other. But his time was soon to come.

BY JANUARY 1945, Lieutenant Woods had held a wide variety of assignments at Camp Blanding: platoon leader; regimental mess, postal, supply,
and legal officer; regimental S-2, acting school commandant—the bewildering mix hardly exhausts the list. (I'm reminded of the parade of jobs
weighing down Louis Crawford as he worked to win his pilot's wings.) Did
his superiors find him such an adaptable figure that they could move him
swiftly from place to place, confident he would thrive in any capacity? Or
were they constantly testing him, looking to find the one job for which he
was suited above all others? The duller probability is that Woods was simply
led at random through a host of administrative functions in a fort the size
of a city (at one point during the war, Camp Blanding was the fourth largest
metropolis in Florida). But the outcome in any case was to make him lose
hope in the likelihood of a combat posting.

Still, one way or another, he yearned to be overseas before the end of the
war. He arrived at the notion of serving in Civil Affairs in the Far East and put
in an application for reassignment to that branch. The request was warmly

endorsed by his CO, who rated him as superior in every area and confirmed Lieutenant Woods's self-evaluation, which stressed his language skills, administrative experience, and background in teaching and law. Woods would seem well suited for Civil Affairs, a branch that mediates between the army and the civilian population in a war zone. But his request was denied by Gen. "Vinegar Joe" Stillwell himself with the terse observation "Too much time in the Infantry." It seems an odd charge to lay against a soldier.

In a letter to his wife dated March 28, 1945, Arthur mentions having offered legal advice to Kate Crawford and Mary Shelburne, who had sought his help in clarifying the deed to the Hertford house, a matter apparently left uncertain at the time of Bill Crawford's death. Mary, with much grace, was eager to have her mother-in-law retain unquestioned full possession. "Strictly speaking, it's no affair of mine," my father writes, "but they asked me. I've recommended that Mary execute a quit-claim deed, and I think you and I should take out a loan to satisfy any other entailments on the property." The short passage is noteworthy because the affairs of the Crawfords have never been mentioned in his letters before, and especially because it constitutes the only written reference (and that, indirect) to his brother-in-law's death. It also gives a sense of what my father thought life might be like in the town that had been a trap for Louis Crawford and a haven for his son: "Given Mary's wishes, it appears the house will eventually come to you. For what it's worth, I could imagine retirement there. There's room for a garden, we'd be on the river, and close to the sea. Not a lot of mental stimulation, I expect, but there are a thousand books I want to read before I die, and that old back porch wouldn't be a bad place for it."

But the letter as a whole commands attention for altogether other reasons, especially its bleak final paragraph:

The news from Europe sounds good. Maybe they'll turn some of us old men loose after that mess is cleaned up. I haven't heard anything specific yet but it seems reasonable. Frankly, I hope so, I'm getting worn out with the Battle of Blanding. If they want me to soldier, I'd be glad to do so, but this Boy Scout business is getting me down, and it looks as if I'm tagged for the duration. They keep opening new centers, though, and after I've given them a chance to promote me and they do or don't, I'm going to try at least to get posted to another camp. Maybe a change of scenery is what I need.

This letter marks a low point. His dejection is evident. He had entered the army in good faith in 1943 and—surmounting the barriers of age, overeducation, and a sedentary nature—trained hard to become a combat infantry officer. The army found jobs for him, but never that one. And by the spring of 1945, with the end of the war in Europe approaching and the likelihood of his gaining a command in the Pacific fading fast, he begins to consider finding a route out of the service and a return to civilian life. There would be every reason to suppose that his next letter, written from a separation center, would have contained melancholy reflections on his curtailed career in the army and his hopes of finding legal work in Washington or Philadelphia as he charts an uncertain return. Instead, it is thick with intrigue and postmarked from Tokyo, where he is commencing nearly five more years in uniform—years that will prove the most challenging and rewarding of his military career.

OBLIGED TO BRIDGE THE GAP between these letters with a fable, I turn to one of the ways a secret agent may be recruited, familiar in the annals of Anglo-American espionage: an Oxford don or a Yale professor invites a promising youth to his digs for sherry and floats the vague notion of government work—"might amuse you, a bit out of the ordinary." For better or worse, social class is often the avenue; had he gone to Penn State instead of Penn, my father might not have been placed on the path to military intelligence. (The thought has its origins in the wartime office of the OSS, whose initials were widely said to stand for "Oh So Social." It would be much the same in the early days of the CIA.)

By October 1945, Lieutenant Woods had made no headway in improving his position. He was still shuttling back and forth between several unrewarding jobs, unable to secure either a new assignment or an early release. His despondency increased. He wrote to Louise:

> This place gets more and more unsettled with each passing day, but I think I'm the forgotten man. Of our original cadre with the school, by next week there'll be only one remaining, and they've been shipping officers—including average officers—right and left. Col. Willis got his orders for Meade two days ago and he was one of the few officers left in this camp from the original contingent. But me—no. I'm invaluable or something.

I see him one evening on his way, alone, to the officers club for a drink. At the bar, he falls into conversation with a young colonel wearing a well-cut civilian suit. They buy each other rounds of scotch. Conversation flows easily. Of course, it touches on the war. The colonel, as a major, had commanded a battalion in France and been slightly wounded; hence his present desk job, about which he is a little vague. He listens sympathetically to my father's story, asking occasional questions that seem neither inappropriate nor intrusive. He's a well-read man with whom Woods turns out to have much in common, including an alma mater. The lieutenant confesses his frustration at his haphazard career; the colonel listens without offering false consolation. The drinking is light and the evening ends early. In the morning, Lieutenant Woods ponders the encounter, feeling a certain forlorn pleasure. Then he puts it out of his mind.

One week later he is sitting at his desk, signing or countersigning reports, dispatches, manifests, dockets, indents, communiqués, and proclamations. War is paperwork. The rat's nest of cigarette ash in the ashtray at his elbow deepens. His coffee has grown cold. He slides the next flimsy free of the stack and signs it without really looking at it. His mind is still mostly on a letter from Louise, whose chipper tone can't quite conceal the despondency that has gripped her since her brother's death. The phone rings, a welcome distraction.

"Lieutenant Woods."

"Arthur? How are you, my boy?"

"Well, I'll be damned." My father hasn't heard the voice twice in ten years—the dry Oxbridge whisper, the cadence that always seemed to confess doubt even while expressing confidence. Dr. Elliot Hastings, from whom Woods had learned his Old English and Middle High German at Penn. "How the hell did you find me?"

"With some difficulty. I trust I'm not calling at an inopportune time?"

"Not at all. It's good to hear your voice—just unexpected."

"To be sure, to be sure. But tell me, Lieutenant, how have you been?"

The conversation meanders for several moments—reminiscences, absent friends, the prospects for the postwar world. Woods gives the easy chatter some small part of his attention while pondering the still-unspoken reason for the elderly professor's call—it can't just be for old times' sake? But the talk remains vague. Even the weather is mentioned. Thoughts turn to their respective families. How is Louise? Hastings had always thought highly of her. And the boy? Two boys now, my father says. Two boys? Good show! And more such. And more such.

There seems to be a slight shift in tone when Elliot Hastings abruptly commiserates with my father about his stateside war. "I expect you wanted to get overseas."

"I did. Now I just want to get back into ordinary life. But the army seems to be in no hurry about that."

"Well, you serve at the pleasure of the president as I recall, my boy." A pause. "Arthur, let me perhaps surprise you. A week or so ago you had drinks at the club with a lieutenant colonel who identified himself as Tompkins. He wore civilian clothes. He took something of an interest in your story—the war years, the years before. It turned out you and he had in common college years at the University of Pennsylvania."

Jesus Christ. Another pause. Lieutenant Woods lights a cigarette in order to outwait it.

"Arthur? You still there?"

"Yes, sir."

"Your conversation was quite informal—insubstantial—but I believe Colonel Tompkins left you with the idea that your military career might still offer a more rewarding trajectory."

"Professor Hastings, I think I just want to get out."

"Well, don't make up your mind too quickly. I have a number for you to call. The chap you talk to will arrange a meeting and take things from there. You're under no obligation to make the call, of course, but I hope you will. I suggest you do. I think I can promise you a much more interesting war."

"The war is over."

Dry laughter rattles the wire. "Well, we'll see. Whatever you decide, please don't mention *my* call to anyone. Sorry to be so hush-hush, but there it is." A final pause. "It was good to talk to you, Arthur. You were one of my best students. Please give my regards to your family. Good-bye."

My father hangs up the phone slowly. Old Hastings—I'll be damned. But he is not altogether surprised. Among the students at Penn, even before the war, it had been rumored that Professor Hastings enjoyed the confidence of certain shadowy figures in the federal government.

Woods needs no further urging to make the call. He will never know for certain the identity of the voice at the other end of the wire but the conversation is brief and surprisingly straightforward. Within days, he was enrolled as a student in the basic counterintelligence course at Fort Holabird, Maryland, and within weeks was writing exultantly to his wife, "I think I've found the job I was made for."

I think he had, too. The army had already let him develop a side of himself that had slumbered before the war. In basic training, he had discovered an appetite for soldiering and at OCS an aptitude for command. His work at Penn had established his strengths as a scholar, and his years of legal practice had given him experience in the analysis of evidence, the conduct of interrogations, and the presentation of arguments before a dispassionate judge. He was skeptical by nature, and alert to nuance. Disappointed in his quest for combat, he was now entering a branch of the military where a risk of violence followed the flag even in peacetime, and he was virtually guaranteed a foreign assignment whose romance he was still young enough to appreciate at a historical moment when the end of one war might well prove the overture to another.

His new life in those years will be like a tale by Joseph Conrad or Graham Greene. The American officer—part soldier, part scholar, part spy—on the frontiers of empire in the middle of what was already being called the American century.

HIS LETTERS DO NOT GIVE the details of his training, but it seems safe to suppose that the weeks at Fort Holabird would have acquainted Lieutenant Woods with the basics of his new trade—with the roles of case officer and field agent, techniques of agent handling, surveillance and disguise, false flag operations, cutouts and dead-drops, and some of the subtleties of the webs he will be called upon to weave. And he would have refreshed his skills with a handgun, on a close-combat course that offered cardboard targets shaped like men instead of bull's-eyes. But much of his work would have taken place in a classroom, a setting where he had always been at home.

Toward the conclusion of the course would have come the question of his first assignment. He hoped for Germany, where the occupation had already created administrative zones that would be fertile environments for intelligence work. His college education had been centered on the cultures of Europe, and his knowledge of German was good. A year earlier, he might have fought his way into the fatherland at the head of a platoon. Now his duties would be of a different kind, but they could be equally rewarding.

He got his orders early in December. The army can always surprise you.

CAPTAIN A. R. WOODS, newly promoted, arrives in Japan on December 15, 1945.

He makes landfall at Atsugi after dark in a C-54 whose crew is unfamiliar with the battle-damaged airfield and whose pilot seems determined to kill everybody aboard. With the radio out, the plane spends two hours looking for the landing strip as the last of the fuel drains from the tanks. The pilot locates a beacon that proves to mark a mountain peak and pulls up just in time. Then he comes in downwind with a faulty altimeter, thinking the plane is on the ground when it's two hundred feet above it. Gunning the engines to circle back for a second try, the airplane driver ends up hitting the runway at twice the normal landing speed, at which point he steps on the brakes and corkscrews all over the strip trying to miss the shell holes that pit the tarmac. "I was glad to get out," Captain Woods noted mildly. "Thank God we've got a navy."

The newly arrived officers convoy through Yokohama on their way to Tokyo. Both cities have been bombed into suburbs of hell, block after block as flat as playing fields. Four months after the end of the war, a certain deathly faint miasma still haunts the ruins.

On his first morning in the capital, Woods snaps a picture of a charcoal seller bent under his burden, trudging with bowed head down an alley of ghost factories dressed in skirts of broken brick and shattered glass. Perhaps memories of Pearl Harbor and Bataan fuel this remark:

> These people are destitute and I am not one whit perturbed—except for the kids. They're another matter. And I don't believe any of them will go hungry if there's one GI in the neighborhood with a candy bar or a K-ration. This afternoon, returning from a staff meeting at GHQ I gave our ten-year-old doorman a little candy and gum whereupon two more urchins appeared from the shadows and now I have three eager assistants swarming around my legs anytime I enter or depart my quarters.

For the first few days, his quarters are in the Women's Pharmaceutical College, Spartan and often unheated. But the food is good and offered with some ceremony. Japanese women in native garb bow repeatedly with the presentation of each new dish. To Captain Woods, familiar only with American travesties of Asian cuisine, the variety of flavors and textures comes as a welcome surprise. Other aspects of the native culture are less appealing, such as toilets set flush with the floor—"awkward at first but soon enough you manage." And the indifference of Japanese maids to male nakedness in the showers takes some getting used to.

Within a week, Woods is ready to hazard early observations about the defeated citizens of his new home:

December 22

The Japs are poverty-stricken. It is taking a large effort on our part to avert outright starvation. And I don't know how they survive the cold. It's been bitter.

These people are thoroughly whipped. Or else they quit because they were told to and would start in again tomorrow should the emperor say otherwise. For now, the Nips are all sweetness and light to a point that seems incredible. Since my job will call for close contact with them, it also calls for a tremendous amount of skepticism. Which fortunately I got.

The war will be this city's only story for years to come. But there is no sense of danger. There's no need to carry weapons—no one goes armed and somehow you feel perfectly secure.

But arms have been issued. My father signs for a blue steel snub-nosed Colt revolver, a .38 caliber Detective Special to be carried in a belt or shoulder holster when he wears civilian clothes. (I have the shallow cardboard box it was packaged in, marked "sterile." Untraceable.) When in uniform, he will strap on the standard army sidearm, a .45 automatic. But in Tokyo, these weapons were usually locked in a drawer.

Later, Korea would be a different matter.

Captain Woods is scheduled to attend a three-week school in a secret location, where the tradecraft he learned at Fort Holabird will be burnished and set in the context of the societies he will serve. Until classes commence, he is free to wander the ruined city. He continues his close study of the people and begins to pick up a bit of colloquial Japanese. (In time, he became fluent. He was a good linguist.) He also looks at art—scrolls, sculpture, painting, calligraphy—in a few small galleries that have somehow survived the bombs. He has no expertise, but he has seen similar work during many hours spent with his wife at the Philadelphia Museum, and he finds much of it attractive. He eats at street stalls, challenging himself with dubious offerings—rice, rat, soy sauce, shreds of unfamiliar greens. He rides the subway and records an urban adventure that would become quite familiar to his younger son nearly twenty years later:

December 3

Yesterday I rode the elevated for a few stops. Fortunately there's a car reserved for allied military—otherwise I would have had to claw my way aboard. That's not hyperbole. Times Square at rush hour is a pink tea by comparison. When the train stops, there's a huge collision as people pour on and off at the same time. A few are left hanging out the windows, some crowd the open spaces between the cars, the hardiest souls claw their way to the roof. And they murder each other for a few square inches.

On Christmas Eve, Captain Woods and his cohort were moved from the college to the Kempeitai building, where the rest of the counterintelligence detachment is quartered. "It's the former home of the Japanese secret police," he notes, "so it's fitting we should be there." "The Kempeitai were, and to some extent still are, the 'counter' in CIC in the Pacific. It would be hard for you to realize how scared the Japs have been for years of their own police and they are twice as scared of our MPs and ten times as scared of the CIC. In some ways that makes the work harder and in some easier."

One morning standing by the elevator in Army GHQ, Captain Woods is joined by a gaunt elderly man in a well-cut tweed suit. Civilian garb does nothing to conceal the identity of General of the Army Douglas MacArthur. The two men exchange courtesies and even have time for a minute's conversation as they wait for the car to rattle to a stop on their floor. My father was not easily awed, and I don't know that he had high regard for the general. But in his next letter home, he doesn't scruple to record the frisson he felt at this encounter with the architect of Pacific victory.

Practical matters do not escape notice. He comments on the exchange rate (15–1), and the design of the banknotes. "The money looks like wallpaper. I've enclosed one yen for young Arthur—about 6⅔ cents worth." He also sends his elder son a packet of stamps honoring the emperor; my brother is an avid collector. And he asks Louise to send him cigarettes—"but disguise the package, they're scarce and valuable."

Arthur Woods is beginning to sketch in the outlines of his new life. And there is much of interest to be discovered in the conquered city. But he's restless in the absence of any larger occupation and eager to take up the final phase of his training, to get on with the work he feels he was made for.

Early in January 1946, Louise writes to tell him that several prominent American journalists and politicians have charged that the Japanese are being treated too leniently by the Allied military government. His rejection of the charge is swift and categorical:

Don't let anyone fool you about a "soft" peace. They aren't getting one here in my estimation. The daily ration has recently been announced, and the Japs will get barely enough to keep alive on. There is some "fraternization" evident, but not much. In another sense of fraternization, well, that may be my job.

From all I can see, the CIC is friendly to the natives, and it has to be if we hope to suck them dry. And in yet another sense, that may be a good thing. Our choice was to wipe these people out or make some attempt to make decent world citizens out of them. Since apparently we have more or less embarked upon the latter course, the best weapon we have is example. It makes an impression, I'm sure, that an organization like ours, which in its Japanese equivalent would have brandished arbitrary powers of life and death, can proceed to work in an efficient fashion without robbery, murder, and torture and that we can go about getting what we want in a civil way. People who have lived here many years tell me that basically the Jap, though hard for Westerners to fathom, responds as any human organism would in a given situation. In other words, if you prick him, he bleeds; if you feed him, he may well be grateful. Anyway, the Army here is going on that assumption.

At last the three-week course begins. The only mention in his letters is a single line—"I'm still going to poop and snoop school, but in a couple of weeks I'll be out roaming the countryside"—but graduation is announced in a letter to my brother Arthur:

> Your old man finally and officially became a cop today. They issued us our credentials and badges. The credentials are in a folder like a wallet, which contains my photograph together with a statement identifying me as an officer in the Counter Intelligence Corps possessed of all attendant powers (whatever they may be). But the badge—ah, there is something. It's a gold shield with an eagle on top and the words WAR DEPARTMENT and MILITARY INTELLIGENCE circled underneath. It pins in a small leather folder and slips in your pocket. All I have to say is Dick Tracy had better look to his laurels when Sherlock Woods gets on a hot trail.

The implication is that he will be involved in routine police work. The reality is somewhat larger. As he tells Louise at about the same time:

> Our little outfit is doing an important job here. We are General MacArthur's eyes all over Japan. Our people are scattered hither and yon in twos and threes in remote places where they're the only Army there is. That's the EM. They're mostly sergeants but some corporals as well. When they're in uniform, they don't wear any insignia of rank, just an officer's "US" badge on the collar. They're addressed as "Agent Smith" or Jones, etc. The idea is that the less people they're talking to know about them, the better. Like officers, these guys sometimes wear civilian clothes to work.
>
> The officers are stationed in larger cities. It's our job to jump in a jeep now and then and see what's going on in the outlying areas. That can include anything from murder, counterfeiting, or the black market to ferreting out Jap war criminals in hiding to finding Russian agents up to no good—which is about as much as I'll ever be able to tell you about my work. But it promises to be remarkably interesting work.

It also promised to present an extraordinary array of challenges, especially once my father received orders for Korea. Operational security would have made it impossible for him to provide specifics at the time, and he seems to have had no interest in filling out the written record in later years (*there's* a ghost journal I'd give a great deal to possess), but Duval Edwards, a CIC agent who served in Asia in the 1940s, published a history of the Corps which offers an extensive account of the duties of its members.[13] From Edwards's story, we learn that Counter Intelligence Corps officers in Japan were expected to establish working relationships with local officials in every prefecture, and then move on to many different tasks: ensuring compliance with the terms of surrender, dismantling the Kempeitai, hunting still-hidden Nazi agents and suspected Axis war criminals, locating weapons caches, uncovering secret deposits of money and precious metals, freeing political prisoners, tracing Americans suspected of treason, uncovering black market activities, and thwarting the ambitions of Soviet spies. In their free time, they were also to investigate the origins of political violence, food riots, and labor strikes. Certain murder cases might come CIC's way as well. As to routine policing, that could be left to the MPs.

This was the world my father entered. He did so with enthusiasm, and evident success. To read between the lines of his necessarily circumspect letters is to conclude that his day-to-day work brought him into contact with many of the problems described above. Of course, each day was different. One might mean no more than eight dull hours at a desk. The next could bring a shootout at a shabby house where an architect of the Bataan death march lay in hiding.

That was Tokyo. In Korea, these duties would be joined to others yet more daunting. There were repairs to be made to a collapsing administration left a shambles by the departure of the Japanese. There was the abiding imperative to monitor the antics of the Russians. And, crucially, there was an increasing need to run agents into North Korea to assess the intentions of Kim Il-Sung. As Edwards puts it, "CIC agents in Korea lived an exciting and adventurous existence, probably more so than in any other occupied zone."

To my father, such an existence must have seemed a second chance.

---

13. Duval Edwards, *Spycatchers of the US Army in the War with Japan* (Gig Harbor, WA: Red Apple, 1994).

WOODS LOOKS to the details of his daily life soon after his arrival in Korea, expressing satisfaction with his quarters, a small bungalow built in Japanese style and staffed with a cook and a houseboy. He's also pleased with his prospects, since the officer in charge of the detachment, a Captain Guthrie, is to be reassigned, leaving my father in temporary command of the officers and interpreters at headquarters as well as of agents in the field.

Early in February 1946, a CIC sergeant reports an incident in Taejon that prompts Captain Woods to travel by train to the small city ninety miles south of Seoul to "assess the situation." He cannot describe the incident, but he does offer a vivid image of the terrain in a letter capped by a comic anecdote:

February '46

The car had long observation windows so I got a good look at the countryside. The roadbed ran down the valleys and through the passes in the hills. The hills have little vegetation. They look ancient and have all sorts of queer convolutions and parallel ridges. Almost all the low ground consists of rice paddies made up of small patches of sodden land separated from each other by ridges of red mud. Farmhouses —whole villages—are made mostly of packed earth huts, built close to the ground, thatched and grouped together. The ox is the work animal here and you see plenty of them carrying tremendous burdens.

About an hour before we got in, I was joined in the car by a dozen Korean railroad workers, some of whom had been looking at the hot sake overlong. Soon enough my friends started to belt out Korean songs, whose shrill tones claw at a Western ear, and they asked me if I would contribute a song or two. I obliged with a couple of popular numbers—Rogers and Hart, Irving Berlin—that they properly appreciated and then I tried them with a few strains of Mozart and they were enraptured. I had to sing an encore. Picture it—an American intelligence officer riding through the Asiatic countryside sampling The Magic Flute for a bunch of Korean drunks.

The issue resolved, Woods returns to the capitol a day or two later but is almost immediately summoned to Tokyo for a brief assignment there. Off duty, he manages a visit to the Great Buddha at Kamakura, a monumental thirteenth-century bronze, one of the treasures of the nation. He is duly impressed; his interest in the art of Asia deepens. There is something like reverence in the tone of his description of the scene. He strikes a lighter note when recounting his welcome from an elevator attendant at the General Headquarters building in Tokyo. With a deep bow, the woman murmurs, "Oh, my aching back." Someone had taught her the phrase was an American greeting. Amused, my father is reminded of a doorman at the Dai Ichi building who welcomes officers in the rank of major and above with "Come in, fathead." *His* instructor had clearly been some disgruntled soldier in the rank of captain or below.

It is still February when Woods returns to Korea, a ragged journey he depicts with offhand nonchalance. This letter is notable as well for the first appearance of a nom de guerre and the suggestion that security measures need to be observed on both sides of the ocean:

It was a long trip over, but down through Japan everything was worked out—no trouble with luggage, comfortable compartment on the train, good car porter, and station porter service. The boat trip over to Pusan was fairly rough so I took a nap and along about evening arrived. From there on in it was like old times. They did have a truck to meet the boat but we had to sweat out our own luggage, even the officers, and when we got loaded on the truck it wouldn't start— someone had drained the gas out of the tank. I heard one of the old hands mutter "Well, now I know I'm back in Korea" and he's about right. All the rest of the way it was do it yourself under handicaps. They'd stopped running the night train so I had a ten-hour daylight ride looking at the same scenery. Of course, I stopped off for some time to see Kim and the rest of them and they seemed quite delighted to see me. Arrangements have been made for me to renew my contacts with most of them a little later here in Seoul.

P.S. If you have already sent me any mail with a different address, it's all right, but you can now address your envelope as follows: S/Sgt Stanley L. Babberl RA37678944 HQ XXIV Corps G-2, APO 235 C/O Postmaster San Francisco. Best use something other than your own name for a return address—maybe your mother's.

Throughout that winter and into the spring, his letters continue to provide notes of local color, often in telegraphic style: "street scene: chimney sweep beating a gong, taffy salesman clashing his scissors together." "Costume notes: flock of local gentry dressed in white, braided rope circlet around the head, another one around the middle." "Tall man in white robe and stovepipe hat, woman in pale blue smock spotted with mud." "Children with butterfly nets chasing swallows." "Man with a collection of 600 tiny jars used for pouring water to soften blocks of ink." His other subjects include his hopes for a transfer to the regular army ("but it's unlikely—there are simply too many reserve officers seeking too few places"), his concerns about the growing cholera epidemic ("but I'm not personally worried about it"), his routine travels ("I expect to drive up to Chinju tomorrow to check out our sub-office there"), and his anticipation of the first anniversary of VJ Day, which seems likely to trigger demonstrations throughout the country.

August 8, 1946

Everything remains quiet locally, but we anticipate a little amusement on the fifteenth of August—Liberation Day. The right-wing boys and the southpaws are at present calling each other national traitors and pro-Japanese and "threatening to do terrific things severely" as the local phrase goes. I doubt seriously if any Korean on that day will be able to scratch his ass without some of our lads being present to help him.

At which point the letter shifts abruptly to a new subject. Captain Woods reminds his wife of a Hertford neighbor who dabbles in amateur shortwave radio. "If you can recall for me his name, we might get in touch. Anyway, it would be interesting to try." This casual notion seems a strange lapse in security but coming across these lines made me remember that I once heard my mother reminisce about such a project, so it may have borne fruit. But for what reason? It presses the limits of plausibility to suppose Captain Woods hoped to transmit intelligence outside official channels to an unvetted civilian, but in truth Louise is not entirely detached from the world of her husband's work. A spy's wife is like an army wife: they also serve who only stand and wait. I think, though, the shortwave gambit was more likely the occupation of an idle hour—not that A. R. Woods had many of those. If he wasn't in the field, he was usually preparing the next mission, and if he wasn't doing that, he was evaluating the outcome of the last. "Right now

I'm spending most of my time doing background studies," he writes in April 1946, "reading up on players in the region who seem likely to become of operational interest fairly soon."

> Meanwhile I wait for things to develop, and when they do I snap
> like a frog at a fly, hoping it's not a hook concealed by red flannel.
> So far, no hooks. And I have nailed a few flies. Even so, I'm still in a
> curiously nebulous position here. Only a few people know that I <u>am</u>
> here, and the minute I try to do something which is relatively easy
> for someone not a disembodied spirit to do, all sorts of embarrass-
> ing problems come up. It's almost impossible to make contact with
> anyone who is not in uniform, or known to the director of civilian
> personnel, or a missionary, and since none of these is true of me, well,
> maybe I'm not here at all.

The concluding phrase evokes the mystery in which he must abide, but even a spy knows ordinary hours—until he doesn't. Now and then Captain Woods's domestic life possesses drama of its own. On two occasions his house is robbed; another time an explosion tears the floor from under him. The first instances are never solved, so he starts sleeping with a revolver under his pillow. The second is explained when my father and a visitor "grabbed our pistols and took off to find the culprits, only to discover the houseboy had been monkeying with the water heater until it decided to explode." Remarkably, there are no injuries, but these instances of incompetence and home invasion, combined with an ongoing pattern of corruption in local government and petty larceny among the staff, produce a disillusion with Korean life that, despite his professional successes, has Captain Woods plotting a permanent return to Japan.

> I get more and more disgusted with this country daily. As you know
> I've made a few particularly good friends here but most of these
> people, I think, are hopeless. They don't know from one day to the
> next what the hell they want, except to cut the throat of anyone who
> has a better job. The idea of doing any work is repugnant apparently.
> The corruption is extensive and runs very deep. I am on the verge of
> pulling every wire I know how to pull to get back to Japan, where for

some inscrutable reason it seems at least cleaner. Over there we run the show, and that makes life a lot easier. Here in this godforsaken country you can't trust the gooks as far as you can throw them.

Though temporary duty takes him frequently to Tokyo, his hope of a permanent reprieve from service in Korea is never fulfilled, but in the course of his tour he will become reconciled to life in Seoul and adept at maneuvering through its corrupt labyrinth. "These people have organized their world this way for a thousand years," he notes, "and I've concluded that it's wiser to follow than to fight them." He especially makes peace with his household staff, who rob him almost daily.

Squeeze is an ancient prerogative in the Orient; when I buy twenty-five candles I get to burn twenty, and likewise with such articles of my diet as appeal to them. On the other hand, I can't get along without them—and I don't have to pay them myself.

They do very well by and large, especially considering my highly irregular habits and hours, and the strange people who keep coming in and out of the house at any time of day or night.

ON JANUARY 12, 1946, Captain Woods received his orders for Korea. He was to be based initially in Seoul, but expected to be sent to trouble spots here and there around the countryside. He had yet to learn the precise nature of his duties. "More on that when I find out," he writes, "to the extent that I can tell you."

The flight from Tokyo took two and a half hours. Crossing the Korean coast, Woods glanced down to see small farms terracing the mountainsides, "veined and netted like a butterfly's wing." The plane landed safely and the passengers bounced through a twenty-minute ride in an open truck to the city, where they were quartered in a comfortable hotel. The rooms even had private baths, a luxury the new arrival comments on. "I've finally arrived on the mainland of Asia," he concludes. "I surely never expected to be here—but here I am."

MERCHANTS AND MISSIONARIES ASIDE, few Americans expected to set foot in Korea until the end of the Second World War also ended thirty-five years of Japanese colonial rule on the Korean peninsula, swiftly followed by the partition of the country into northern and southern occupied zones, the first to be administered by the Soviet Union, the second by the United States. The dividing line was set at the thirty-eighth parallel. This trusteeship suited both world powers, Russia because it wanted an ally in the region, America because it needed a buffer between revolutionary China and a pacified Japan.

But many Koreans who sought an independent nation formed factions that immediately challenged the new status quo. In northern Korea, the Soviets supported a communist revolution. In the south, by 1948, left-wing groups had opened a guerrilla war against the American-sponsored government of Syngman Rhee. The Truman administration, whose focus was almost entirely on Soviet threats to Eastern Europe, proposed a UN commission that would supervise a national election to unify Korea, thus ending the occupation. But without the support of Kim Il-Sung, who refused the entry of UN supervisors into North Korea, the election of May 1948 took place only in the south, establishing the republic, the presidency of Syngman Rhee, and the swiftly staged withdrawal of American combat forces. By September, most Soviet troops had been withdrawn as well, and the Democratic People's Republic of Korea proclaimed.

Though South Korea was now confirmed as an independent country, the political situation there remained chaotic. Within a month of the end of the war, the United States had imposed a military government that would last only until 1948. That government failed to reconcile the warring factions and failed as well to halt a growing underground communist movement. The division of the peninsula also caused economic chaos in the south, whose industrial base was crippled by the departure of the Japanese and whose citizens were under siege from inflation, overpopulation, food scarcities, riots, and labor strikes.

Syngman Rhee, whatever might have been hoped, proved a repressive dictator more than ready to massacre his enemies. Such were the conditions under which the American military commander, Lt. Gen. John Hodge, was obliged to labor, with limited resources, during the years of occupation. And as the two Koreas moved closer to war, the fuse may have been lit when Secretary of State Dean Acheson publicly announced that South Korea was excluded from the American defense perimeter in Asia, thus emboldening the north to think seriously about invasion plans.

The above sketches the picture in the broadest possible strokes. The details have been filled in by many historians, notably Allan R. Millett, from whose comprehensive work I have largely distilled my capsule history. His summary of the situation as it stood in the late 1940s can hardly be improved on:

> The ROK government had developed all sorts of rivalries that made it weak and ineffective. There were personality clashes, presidential-legislative battles, Korean-American disagreements, civil-military tensions over conduct of the counterinsurgency campaign, police-Army feuds, schisms between southerners and northern refugees, city-rural tensions, and an unsettled waxing and waning of coalitions of political parties and youth associations. The economy was plagued by inflation, rice shortages in the cities, a lack of consumer goods, and no capital accumulation and investment. In contrast, the news from North Korea suggested a firm bond between the Soviet Union and the Democratic People's Republic. After the Red Army's withdrawal, an invasion had to be considered a real possibility after all the American forces departed later in the year.[14]

This is the world Woods lived and worked in during his four and a half years of service in Asia, a petri dish for spies and counterspies. Even a superficial account of its history is sufficient to explain why army intelligence officers were tasked with such a chaos of chores early in the occupation. To trace conditions back to the end of the war reveals why CIC agents must occasionally have felt overwhelmed by what they faced.

On August 15, 1945, preparations for the invasion of Japan had been transformed into plans for the occupation. CIC detachments, serving alongside combat units throughout the war, now entered the home islands with an ill-defined mission complicated by overlap with other agencies. Relative chaos prevailed for the first few months, but by the time of my father's arrival in December that year, the duties of the CIC had been more precisely defined, so that what one history of the unit calls "an uncountable number of investigations not of a counterintelligence nature" were eliminated.

Even so, the work that remained would require CIC agents to enjoy the

---

14. Allan R. Millett, *The War for Korea, 1945–1950* (Lawrence, KS: University Press of Kansas, 2005).

greatest possible latitude for their actions, a freedom not always easy to achieve within the army hierarchy. But Douglas MacArthur, who had come to appreciate the value of counterintelligence throughout the Pacific War, eventually saw that they had it. In a directive issued in June 1947, he ordered that CIC personnel operate with "minimum restrictions of movement" and without the burden of "standard military customs or prohibitions" being imposed on them. Encountering CIC operations, American military police were specifically ordered to stand down. "Counter Intelligence Corps badges and credentials," the order concluded, "will be honored at all times."

Woods and his fellow officers and agents took full advantage of this freedom, whose effect was to empower them to conduct solid operations before the Korean War, and indeed throughout it.

DROPPING OFF HIS B-4 BAG at the hotel, Captain Woods makes his way to the headquarters of the 441st CIC Detachment. The outer office is lively. He sees a sergeant leading a handcuffed prisoner to a holding cell, one officer questioning a suspect in a black market deal, another on the phone taking down an account of a politically motivated murder. Woods leaves his personnel file with the duty clerk before reporting to the Officer in Charge, a gaunt Negro in civilian clothes chained to a shabby desk by a brimming coffee cup and the stub of a reeking cigar. The officer offers a bleak smile but a genuine welcome.

"We've been looking forward to your arrival, Captain. Been pretty short-handed here."

"Yes, sir."

"Take a chair. Heard good things about you from Tokyo. Quarters okay?"

"Very comfortable."

"Good, good." The OIC manufactures a frown. "Now what will we do with you? Town's pretty quiet right now so most of our people are trying to catch up on old casework. But there's going to be a big demonstration in a week or two—all the usual factions snapping at each other—and there's no doubt Ivan will be in on the action. I'll want you keeping an eye on that."

"Yes, sir."

"No need for sir, I wear the same bars you do. Sorry, do you want some coffee?"

"No, thanks."

"In the meantime, there are a few loose ends you can help us tie up. We're still scraping the Japs out of the city administration and there are odds and ends of Kempeitai. But mostly I want you to spend time getting a feel for the detachment: who we are, how we do things." The OIC studies his cigar with evident dismay and plunges the ashy tip into his coffee. "In a few weeks we'll turn you loose in the countryside." He grins. "Work in the boonies is full of surprises. You'll like it, I think. Most of us do."

Captain Woods is given the rest of the day to himself and told to report back in the morning. "So I left before they could put me to work," he writes blithely. "It was getting on toward my bedtime anyway."

That night was the last good sleep he was to have for some time. The next morning he plunged into his new duties, sending home a report on January 26 that has more the tone of a seasoned agent than a new arrival:

Koreans love large events—parades, demonstrations, meetings. They had a giant pro-trusteeship show here yesterday, thousands of paraders who shuffled along in clumps. One clump had a cheerleader with a megaphone who honked out something or other at intervals. Another clump sported triangular paper hats decked out with elaborate colored flowers. Then came a clump of young girls in middy blouses. There was a band clashing cymbals and gongs with woodwinds wailing oriental snake charmer music. Mounted MPs rode herd on the line—still, at the end, there was a small donnybrook—broken bones but no fatalities. Even so, some of our boys are investigating. We like to know when these spats arise organically and when they're prompted by powers unknown

A steady wind lifted innumerable flags and banners—mostly US, many Russian, some British and Chinese.

The Russians are thick around here, conspiring—to what end, nobody knows. Most Koreans are scared to death that we'll pull out and let the Russians in. The Sovs let go a blast in Tass yesterday condemning the US occupation—tied with upcoming conference and everyone here knows it. I talked for a while with the <u>NY Times</u> correspondent here and that's the way he wrote his story.

During his years in East Asia, my father would spend a good deal of time tracking the activities of Russian agents. But we will also see him involved in the capture of a Japanese war criminal, the dispatch of spies to North

Korea, and the unraveling of complex political and economic problems in the south—all the while shuttling between administrative tasks in Pusan and Seoul and tactical operations in the field. We can never know the details of this work, but Captain Woods has a gift for evoking the tone even as he obeys the imperative to conceal the specifics:

> My job, about which I can perforce write little, is coming along with various ups and downs. Sometimes when I think things are going well my small schemes blow up in my face, and then all of a sudden an apple drops in my lap. I've almost come to the conclusion that working and planning is a waste of time, and that I get equally good if not better results by just waiting for what comes. I figure out a brilliant move and then the character I'm after gets pinched for graft or theft and so is lost to me. Or I make a long trip to get something only to find out that if I'd stayed at home one gent was only too happily bringing it to the office. This sort of serendipity is at least as common as a well-executed op. So there you are.

Of course, he can give a much fuller picture of his domestic arrangements, which feature on the one hand a degree of deprivation ("a cigarette shortage is staring us in the face again, and fresh foods have been cut off by the floods") and on the other a measure of luxury.

> Then there's Mr. Kim. I wish I could bring him back with me. He is the nearest thing to a body retainer I have ever run into. Never wants a day off, very handy with tools, likes to work, lets me practice my Japanese on him, always good tempered, and very happy to brew a cup of coffee at odd hours of the day or night, and that's not really such a simple task. He's forever mopping or scrubbing something with no word from me. In fact I don't remember ever telling him to do anything—he usually has it done before I think of it. You may form an image of Victorian India, the British subaltern being followed about by a turbaned servant with a fly swatter or a cup of tea. Strange for a modern American but I have to say you get used to it.

Mr. Kim is only one member of a larger staff. At one point my father apparently shared quarters with at least one other officer, and they thrived on the attentions of not only a cook and a valet but a squadron of houseboys.

The Americans have been drugging themselves against malaria, a far less fearsome foe than the cholera that would soon afflict the region.

I've been taking atabrine faithfully now for a month on Sixth Division orders, and was starting to turn a little yellow when word came down from XXIV Corps to stop. Which suits me fine—haven't seen a mosquito yet. We're way up on a hill overlooking the harbor with a good breeze all the time which apparently discourages insect life. We have a rather nice enclosed garden with pine trees, rocks, and dozens of azaleas now in their second bloom. The house is becoming more livable as well. We snitched some confiscated silk from Materials Control and the houseboys made curtains. I've got a good bunch here, willing to go to a lot of trouble to fix the place up.

It's good to be back. My stay in Taejon was beset with inconveniences. At one time there was not much down there but me, my interpreter, and a few broken jeeps. Here I have fifteen men and several interpreters, twelve jeeps in good condition, and sub-offices in Chinju and Kyonju staffed by capable agents. We're getting quite a bit of good work done. I'd still rather be in Japan, but for Korea this ain't bad.

As the months wear on, much of the work would call for a long, slow patience.

At the moment I'm in a more or less standby capacity, once again waiting for things to show up and shape up. I've re-met some of my old Korean friends on a social basis and I've been writing up some projects I'd like to undertake, one concerning a new arrival from another nation that also takes a certain interest in Korea. But overall the country is relatively quiet—with no immediate prospects for anything more than a hot-headed political clash. In Korea, of course, these can always turn violent.

Yet even much later Woods remained sanguine about the possibility of maintaining peace between north and south for at least the next few years, writing on March 16, 1948:

You can discount most of the junk the newspapers put out concerning events in Korea. Most of it is not fully accurate and much of what

might be probably doesn't even get printed. I saw a choice example of this yesterday. Someone had sent back a copy of the *Baltimore Sun* which had a front page banner headline AMERICAN TROOPS DIG IN IN KOREA followed by a long story about heightened tensions along the 38th parallel. The correction, printed a day or so later, was buried on an inside page. Even then the follow-up didn't explain that the original reporter got his info from a courier who saw someone digging a latrine that somebody else said was a trench and so it goes.

The distance between the alarmist reporting he sees and the facts on the ground as he knows them is wide enough for him to reach a confident conclusion: "All is still quiet here. There are those who say it's the lull before the storm, but I don't think so. I believe the coming elections will straighten things out with little or no trouble at least for a couple of years. And then who knows. When and if trouble comes, it will probably hit somewhere no one has ever heard of—and I don't mean Korea."

CAPTAIN WOODS spent much of the spring of 1946 testing the dimensions of his job. He'd been cautioned by his instructors and by old Asia hands that the drama of counterespionage could be deceptive, that for every fraught meeting with a spy in an alley or breathless hour passed waiting by a border for an agent to cross, there would be a long parade of numbing days spent fitting together scraps of information, making phone calls and protocol-dictated visits, filing paperwork, fishing through stagnant ponds of data and detail. This proved true. But even such routine days were not always unre-warding. My father's legal training supported an analytical mind that could take pleasure in the meticulous assembly of orphan points until a pattern began to emerge, until a watch long silent suddenly began to tick. Still, the hours at his desk took their toll. He became restless for action, and one day in July 1946 he found it.

For several weeks, American intelligence analysts had seen the danger mounting. Heavy rains and flash floods had torn up telephone and telegraph lines, closed roads, and washed out railroad bridges. Rice paddies had been submerged, wheat and barley crops destroyed. Cholera had ravaged whole communities, drawing a strict quarantine. Supplies of rice reaching Pusan had dwindled and black market prices sharply increased. "There are people in this city at risk of starvation, and those who aren't are at best continually hungry. So there was a food riot here yesterday."

Three thousand desperate Koreans were thronging the streets around city hall when a small force of American MPs and a company of provincial police arrived to confront them, too late to prevent the savage beating of the official in charge of rice distribution. Captain Woods and a small con-tingent of CIC troops appeared on the scene minutes later. Woods watched the struggle evolve out of a strangely static moment: the mob swaying and sullenly muttering but held in place by the raised rifles of the MPs and the local constabulary, the Americans with their fingers on their triggers but dreading the order to fire—no one wanted to shoot starving people driven by desperation to an action that can only end badly for them.

Captain Woods considered his options. Ordinarily, counterintelligence soldiers had no role in riot suppression unless there was evidence of an attempt by Soviet or North Korean agents to discredit the American military government. But the MPs were greatly outnumbered and my father had no intention of standing by idly if the situation deteriorated. He and the Military Police commander, a Major Atkinson, swiftly agreed that the mob had to be sent packing, without shots fired if that could be achieved.

Rocks and bricks started flying. A small paving stone smooth as a cannonball caught my father on the side of the head. He swayed on his feet but stayed conscious and a moment later plunged into the crowd, emerging with his attacker, whom he turned over to an army cop to handcuff and drag to jail. The encounter seemed to elate him. He moved swiftly back into the scattering mob, spotted a man wielding a ten-inch cold chisel, and subdued and arrested him as well.

Similar small actions were playing out all along the street, but, remarkably, the troops maintained fire discipline. Batons break skulls, broken bottles slash the soldiers, there are cries and curses—but no shooting. And the struggle is already starting to fade when a convoy of jeeps and armored cars pulls up before city hall and disgorges enough American infantry to quell the riot altogether. Over the barrels of their machine guns, the mounted soldiers watch the mob drain away down the side streets. And my father becomes conscious of the throbbing in his head.

"It hurt like hell," he notes cheerfully, "but no blood, no scars, and no Purple Heart." "This sort of thing I don't like very much—chasing hungry people—but all they were doing was raising hell to no advantage, and no profit, and creating a potentially dangerous situation, possibly encouraged by some outside Agency. So they had to go and I know that every effort is being made to alleviate the crisis."

In the morning, he questions the men he had arrested. Satisfied their actions were spontaneous, he turns them loose.

The Pusan riot was hardly the only violence Woods would encounter in his years in Korea. As tensions between north and south tightened toward war, his work took him to points along the thirty-eighth parallel where border skirmishes ignited with increasing frequency. Food riots like the one in Pusan became common; arrests of war criminals and black marketeers were not always free of the threat of violence; and anti-government guerilla campaigns in the south drew counterinsurgency responses that required counterintelligence support. But the most savage bloodshed recounted in any of the letters took place in November 1948 at Taegu. My father's notes on what amounts to a full-scale battle are worth quoting at some length:

These are troublesome times in South Korea. For the last three weeks we have been working 18-hour days trying to keep up with current events. Before that I was out in the province for a couple of weeks talking with agents in the field covering some of the most desolate and god-forsaken country you could possibly imagine. I'll tell you what I think of the local situation, but I can't be sure I'm right.

The tensions mostly grow out of the rice collection program. The people here are dead set against it and are resolved to oppose it. But the facts as established by a joint board of US and Korean agricultural experts show that this country is faced with starvation, particularly in the cities, by March if the program is not carried out. The details are complex but the fundamental facts seem clear. Even so, the average Korean doesn't buy the argument and feels he's been shopped.

On top of that our left wing boys (and I have a great deal of documentary evidence) are doing all they can to stir up riots and demonstrations regardless of the inevitable cost, their purpose being to discredit military government and embarrass the occupation. In addition, the Korean police have been thoroughly hated by the majority of Koreans for a long time and there has been no recent change.

All of which resulted in a serious outbreak in Taegu recently— about fifty police were killed, some of them brutally, and the troops had to be called in to take over. Other attacks took place in the western part of this province, in Chinju and Masan, where in the remote villages there has been some mob violence resulting in numerous casualties. Nothing further has happened in Pusan to date, but we have US soldiers with machine guns in the police stations in support of the police, and tanks and armored cars patrolling the streets. Two days ago, I picked up a rather detailed map showing arrangements for a raid on the north Pusan police station but to date nothing has come of it. Last night I worked out in the country around Pusan and found that the cops in Tongnae had picked up twenty customers holding a considerable supply of dynamite and grenades.

If it seems curious that the mob has in no instance attempted violence against US troops, I can tell you that instructions have gone out from the headquarters of the provincial communist party that their people are to avoid clashes with Americans, and whenever they come in contact with our people they're to take for the hills. And this they have done so far in every instance.

All in all the present situation is a mess and seems likely to continue that way for a while. I don't know who's right or who's wrong but I have seen some of the police who were killed, and it ain't pretty. We'll just keep plugging I guess until this is settled.

Tales like these made me wonder how often my father's Korea was more like a combat zone than an occupied country. Like many soldiers in their letters home from dangerous places, he had tempered his accounts of violence to ease his family's fears. But now I'd read some background to the letters and could read between the lines—the riot in which he'd been wounded was probably more fraught than he acknowledged, the rows of dead constabulary put him closer to the action than he'd admitted, and the armed midnight meetings with mysterious figures who might be friend or foe spoke of tense experiences that stayed with him for years after his Asian tour.

I remember one night at dinner when I was perhaps ten years old, I was prattling on about the thrilling action my friends and I had witnessed in some war movie we'd seen that afternoon—it was probably *Battle Cry*—until my father had heard enough. He knew the films of the day were utterly bloodless, the wounds of war invisible, that the dead toppled tranquilly to the ground with faint patriotic smiles on their faces and passed into Valhalla to the strains of the Marine Corps hymn. He put down his fork and said in a cold mild voice: "If you'd ever seen a man holding his guts in his hands try to push them back into the hole in his belly, such scenes might seem less glorious." My mother cast a warning glance into the ensuing silence, but I'd been left speechless though I was more puzzled by his anger than abashed at my own bloodthirsty glee; and if the reaction was out of proportion to the offense, it offered the shock my illusions needed, and the moment has stayed with me for more than sixty years.

BY JANUARY 1950, Woods feels compelled to offer a bleak assessment of the prospects for Korea:

Life goes on about the same here. I see many of the same faces, hear most of the same lies, deal with mostly the same gremlins that I dealt with in the past. However the fiasco[15] in China hasn't made our job any simpler. Many of these people figure, and perhaps rightly, that we might pull out any day and throw them to the wolves. I don't know, of course, but the Chinese business plus Royall's crack about getting out of Japan—those things, believe me, do not go unnoticed. Currently the Korean Investigating Committee is busy chasing pro-Japs, and there are quite a few people who feel that perhaps two or three years hence a similar committee may be chasing pro-Americans.

Well, those problems are for the high-level policy boys and not for me. I'll just keep on sweating out the best job I can, and, if the worst comes to the worst a few years hence, we may have something left here we can build on.

Despite the political unrest, he still considers conditions—certainly in Japan—stable enough to want to bring his family to Tokyo to join him. On January 28, 1950, he writes, "We've all been apart much too long and I've put the machinery in motion to bring you and the boys out here sometime in the spring, for a year or so. Believe me, the only risk you'll face in Japan is being spoiled by the luxury." He has arranged for Louise to travel as the wife of a Department of the Army civilian executive holding rank equivalent to a lieutenant colonel, guaranteeing a certain level of comfort both aboard the ship and at the guest quarters where they—we—will await housing. She won't need to pack much—the PX, he assures her, is the size of Wanamaker's. Her husband advises her to bring all the cash she can carry in a money belt and not declare it when she lands. He plans to take two weeks' leave when his family arrives but cautions her that this may not be possible.

"Believe me," he persists, as though expecting resistance, "in Japan you will never have had it so good. You'll have two servants and if we want to pay an extra ten bucks a month, a Class A cook as well."

At the same time, he doesn't downplay the developing peril on the Korean peninsula:

---

15. The "fiasco" he writes of is the revolution that established the People's Republic of China. Royall is Gen. Kenneth Royall, the last American secretary of war and first secretary of the army.

The situation is quite precarious. There's no immediate danger of war but the risk is very real and I am in the process of putting the finishing touches on some rather important and delicate projects. There is literally no one else qualified to take over here for some months to come and my years in the Far East will not have been as productive as I could wish if I don't see this job through to the end and I really feel I should.

Again, there's no immediate danger, but the situation is very fluid and for the next six months I'll need to split my presence between Korea and Japan, most of the time in Korea at first, gradually phasing out of Seoul to direct operations from a Japanese base.

But before six months have passed, my father will be out of the army, out of the Agency, and out of Korea and Japan. He will be back in America, looking to build a new life for himself and his family. In time I'll speculate on a possible reason for this swift sea change, but—as with the silence that takes him from civilian to soldier and from soldier to spy—I have to work in a gap the letters leave; in this case, the largest one of all.

Were he to look back two years, this outcome would have appalled him:

December 11, 1948
Went with Vanderpool to the Corps Club last night to bend an elbow. When we left at 10:30 I had consumed no more than three small Scotches and one beer and—disgustingly sober—decided to just go to bed. Vanderpool had been a bit more vigorous than I in his imbibing—he made his drinks doubles all evening. Anyway we took off. The streets were dark and one of the gremlins apparently had decided he could peddle the sewer grating just outside. I promptly fell in the gaping hole, painfully barking both shins. Vanderpool, somehow missing the hole, had gone on ahead of me to fetch the car. He turned around and, in the darkness, could see that only half of me was visible, the other half having somehow disappeared. He raced madly back to the rescue and, of course, also violently toppled in. No injuries whatever. Next time I'll make mine doubles. Anyway, we got home.

References to drinking are not infrequent in my father's letters. One of his burglars had escaped with a bottle of whiskey ("He kindly left the Coke"), and the drunken railroad workers who joined him in song were soon abetted by one Mr. Ri Bo Young, who made free with his host's liquor locker, solemnly announcing the next day, "Electric poles go back and forth, streets go up and down." At a Chinese New Year's celebration, "It became," Woods reported, "my sad duty to get a few of my Korean friends plastered by swapping cups of sake with them." They collapsed, he didn't. And at a graduation party for a Korean police school where Woods had been an instructor, the class president "'shinda'd'—passed out—early."

Earlier that year he had seen a more charming example of what may have been a Korean cop tradition:

> As to what so many westerners are pleased to think of as Oriental impassivity, I was out with the local police department at a party the other night and the chief of detectives burst into tears after three short sakes because someone had spoken harshly about him. Three more and he wanted to fight. His friends fed him six more and he put his head on the table and went to sleep. Seems to me I've seen drunks like that in San Francisco and New York.

This hard-drinking highlife surprises me a little. My father's bedside bottle did not follow him from Seoul to Bethesda, and at home I rarely saw him take a second drink before dinner except on festive occasions; he almost never drank wine with his meals. The overseas alcohol would seem to have been situational. The sustained tension endemic to his work could certainly find relief in a few slugs of Suntory at the end of the day, and in the 1940s, army officers were still expected to be able to hold their liquor, such fortitude being almost a second badge of rank. But what's most crucial is that Korea was (and is) a hard-drinking culture, where the social and professional connections an American agent had to maintain in order to further his projects were necessarily lubricated by nights of scotch and sake in quantities unfamiliar to milder climes.

Col. Jay Vanderpool shows up from time to time in my father's letters. They had become friends after jointly mounting a successful operation whose details remain obscure. Vanderpool was a considerable figure. Chief liaison between the army and the guerrillas in the Philippines during the Second World War, he would go on to mastermind a number of covert operations during the Korean War, and still later—though not an aviator—would become a key player in the development of the air assault doctrine that shaped American tactics in Vietnam.

My own memory of the friendship between our families produces an evening in 1954—I would have been ten years old—when Jay Vanderpool came to dinner, carrying in a wire cage a caiman, a small crocodilian a foot or two long, fierce in demeanor and possessed of a mouthful of thin, menacing teeth. After a few drinks, my parents decided to give the creature the run of the house—the cats promptly disappeared—and it scampered around the living room for a while before slithering under the sofa. None of us knew where it was until it bit my mother on the heel. She yelped but took the attack with aplomb, forgiving the creature—and the colonel. After all, she had spent much of her adult life in the company of faintly raffish military types.

One afternoon toward the end of April 1949, my father sits alone in his garden, comfortably dressed in a subdued *yukata*, a pack of cigarettes and a cup of whiskey close at hand. He has been tasked with planning the abduction of a North Korean spy from a conference in Seoul, which the man will attend in the guise of a diplomat. There is to be no violence and no harm is to come to the target, so the approach will call for a good deal of finesse. Woods has a few ideas but finds it hard to keep his mind on the problem. Lately, he has been thinking that his years in Asia may be drawing to a close.

He is fairly sure he wants to remain with the Agency. The work has been interesting and clearly important and in the years of struggle that lie ahead can only become more so. As he had written Louise the week before:

Since I last wrote I managed a four-day trip to Japan. Felt like it was time to talk to George—you'll know who I mean. For obvious reasons I don't see very much of him and when I do it's usually at night in a dark alley.

He asked about you and about our plans. I had to tell him that as far as Korea is concerned things looked very dim. We agreed that if after my return to the states they once again wanted to reassign me to foreign duty he would heartily second any request of mine to work with him. One of the larger wheels from home—a man I know—was in Tokyo on his way to China. He'll be passing through Korea in a few weeks. I had a chance only for a surreptitious handshake but we'll have time to talk on his return trip. I'm quite sure he'll view with favor any request from me to get back to the US before Christmas. I'm physically healthy but my nerves have been on edge recently—one of the reasons for the Tokyo trip.

But there is no guarantee "George" will prevail. Then there is the question of the coming war, which Woods believes to be no more than a year away. He feels some desire to play a role in it. He could ask to be recalled to active duty, and as a major would rate a battalion, but he's five years gone from field command and there's almost no chance he would be offered such a position. Once the shooting starts, he has no interest in passing the war in an office in Tokyo. And there are other considerations—he'll soon be forty, he's not in the shape he was when he left OCS, he has a wife waiting, and two sons—one in his mid-teens, one not yet of school age, both of them at stages where the presence of a father would seem desirable. If he returns to active duty, he'll have to go where the army sends him. If he stays in the CIA, he'll remain a civilian, with a bit more say in where and how he spends his days.

But—again—there are no guarantees. Whether he's working for the army or the Agency, A. R. Woods is only one of uncounted players trying to reach consensus on the risk of war. CIC or CIA, intelligence analysts are divided, some convinced Stalin will never turn Kim Il-Sung loose, others that North Korea is an independent actor bent on invasion. Woods is inclined to believe the optimists are wrong. He also believes they will carry the day for one simple reason: intelligence analysts too often bring dire news to clients whose political futures depend on their rejecting it.

He lights another cigarette, barely realizing that he's using the burning stub of the last to do it. He has always been a heavy smoker but not a chain smoker. He inhales the smoke gratefully but with a mild sense of dismay. The daytime shots of Suntory are a new development as well.

Woods's letters are discursive, passing through six subjects in three pages—his work; his state of mind; his domestic life and social relations; his concern for his family at home; the political background to the evolving tensions in Korea; and, rather touchingly, requests for treats like candy and cigarettes, as though he were a lonely kid adrift in boot camp instead of a freewheeling secret agent, king of much that he surveys.

One of these themes usually dominates, but whatever the primary subject many of the letters are salted with references to a growing collection of Asian art, some of which he alerts his wife to look for in the morning mail, some of which he squirrels away in his quarters, either to protect it from the risks of transit or to brighten his own rooms. He has no history as a collector or a connoisseur, but his confident tone when he describes his holdings suggests he is developing a discerning eye:

I've been thinking about that junk that I hope someone has mailed you from Seoul. I had to leave it there when I came down here. I had too much to carry. The bear, the pottery, and the Buddhist beads are all right, but the kimonos are nothing much. I'm mailing you a much better one today. But I've either lost my pornographic scroll or stuck it in the Seoul box. Better watch who's around when you open it.

I've also picked up a rather beautiful plate with dragons and things on it, three exceptionally good sake bottles, and a fine female Buddha, probably an image of Kwan Yin. It's a china figurine about a foot tall, and very fragile. I'm reluctant to trust it to the mail, the more so as I was recently beset by a minor tragedy—bought a superb vase for 150 yen which was broken by the housemaid, one Yusan, who is about as clumsy as anyone I've ever seen. She's in love with a local dashing police sergeant and I think spends most of her time dreaming of him. She's very good-natured and tries hard, and one harsh word would send her packing, so I don't bother her over much. Anyway, she washed the vase, found some flowers to put in it, and in the process managed to drop and smash it. She was properly contrite, and I muttered the inevitable phrase *shi kata ga nai*, which means "It can't be helped." You hear it all the time. I was mad as the devil but concealed it. *Shi kata ga nai.*

The loss of the vase prefigures the vanishing of another object whose worth was to be measured in far more than money:

I mailed you another package from Seoul the other day, and I'm on the verge of making a Shanghai connection for some really first-rate stuff. My major trophy I won't trust to the mail. It's a short sword forged by one Sadamune some six hundred years ago, and I find by checking a reference book that prior to the war it would have commanded "a fabulous price and would be probably unobtainable, being in the category of a national treasure."

As far as I know, the Sadamune blade never made it to America. It's too hideous to imagine this priceless object lost in transit, so I prefer to think the customs charges proved prohibitive, or that the Japanese government blocked its exit, or even that my father, grace overcoming greed, came to think better of so large an act of cultural theft. But many of the pieces described in the letters did remain in the family and provided a design aesthetic for my childhood homes. These spoils of war melded smoothly with prints of the subdued Post-Impressionists my mother favored, and the result was a degree of elegance rare in suburbia. As a kid, I took no notice of this; my own room boasted reproductions of Jackson Pollack and posters of Monroe, Brando, and James Dean. But the expanding impact of my father's loot became clear to me only as I was working on his section of this book, when it seemed to me at first that my workspace was missing his totemic imprint.

Because while writing a rough draft of the first two sections, I found myself creating small shrines to their subjects, setting aside a part of my workroom as a space for objects that spoke of their lives. For Louis Crawford, the red leather journal he had carried in the Philippines, his spurs, his sword, a photograph of him on horseback in Arizona, a model of the Jenny. For his son William, his West Point ring, his jump wings, his 11th Airborne patch, a dance card from a regimental ball, his Silver Star.

But the trunk that held my father's relics yielded little I could use. I had the cardboard box that packaged his .38, but not the weapon itself. I had some photographs, but they were mostly of Korean landscapes. They might as well have been postcards; some were. I could find little else, and decided to settle for the symbolism of what the empty space told me—that my father's work necessarily left few traces, and that there was a mystery in his life I could not hope to plumb. I was some weeks into my third task before I realized I was in truth surrounded by the major's artifacts—the *kakemono* (mist, mountains, streams) that hangs on my dining room wall, the Korean drum that serves me as an end table, the tall carved figure of the wandering Asian scholar that stands on the mantle, the graceful ceramic form of the female Buddha in the music room, the ancient lacquered Chinese box that crowns a bedroom shelf. I didn't need to fashion a temple to my father's life. I was living inside one.

The letters sometimes reveal the tension Captain Woods felt at trying to maintain his position as head of a household when the household is seven thousand miles away. He sometimes writes at length about finance—speculating on raises and promotions, advising his wife about insurance policies and banking practices, weekly budgets and tax preparation. It makes for dull reading now and must have done so even at the time.

Now and then he seems aware of this, once even referring to himself as "Money Mad Woods." But his tone is more often hopeful than hectoring, and he doesn't exempt himself from his own strictures, writing on one occasion: "I just bought two summer suits—one seersucker, one tan. Together they cost about fifty dollars. I must admit my mania for clothes does play hell with my banking arrangements. But, as you know, we're often in civvies." Other purchases included occasional small gifts for his family, most often to his older son.

During A. R. Woods's years in Asia, my brother was in his early teens, and our father maintained a fragile connection with him by sending him paper currency, carved wooden figures, and even an army field jacket. He often sent young Arthur stamps. I remember the worn fat pale blue volumes in which my brother kept his extensive collection. The exotic Asian postage was a special treasure. First to arrive were *showa* stamps, all issued during the reign of the present emperor. "'*Showa*,'" Captain Woods noted, "means 'radiant peace,' and is the curious name Junior across the street picked out for himself."

> A note to go alongside with the stamps I sent by registered mail today: I got them from a Mr. Ashida, the man who writes the Japanese stamp catalogue. He works in the telegraph office in the Imperial Hotel. I've tried to have some of them identified and I hope you can figure out the notes on the packets. I don't know what this last batch is worth, possibly 150 yen, but Mr. Ashida was glad to swap them for some Hershey bars, peanuts, and soap.

My brother was also first to receive the glad news of our father's official appointment as a Counterintelligence Corps officer, but the tone toughens when Captain Woods learns that his son's interest in sports is beginning to play havoc with his scholarship. "I will not tolerate anything less than first-class work," he writes Louise. "He's old enough to realize the importance of a decent academic record, or he should be. If he's unable to manage both school and sports, he'd better face up to it like a man and drop the football."

When my father attends to the other shore of his transatlantic life, a note of strain appears in the letters. Cautioning my brother about his high school grades and calming my mother's frets over household finances, he sinks to conventional wisdom: put your homework first, make a weekly budget. The light humor with which he assesses much of his daily life in Korea, together with the darker notes of his clandestine employment, evades him, giving rise to the thought that his American life may feel a little unreal. Mom, Dad, Buddy and Sis, Mittens and Rover, the house in the suburbs with its white picket fence—this may not have been a world he was eager to return to. On rare occasion, he does betray a wisp of longing for domestic life, but for the most part the world of espionage and the lure of Asia seem to have claimed his loyalty.

PUSAN. MAY 1946. A. R. Woods approaches the jeep parked by the curb, its motor idling, its windshield folded against the hood combat style. Jay Vanderpool is at the wheel. He wears a pale blue Hong Kong suit and a sidearm in a shoulder holster. In the back of the jeep sit two CIC noncoms, a sergeant and a corporal, both in uniform, one gripping a carbine, the other a Thompson submachine gun. The corporal with the Thompson gun is a black kid from Pittsburg with orange hair and an offhand manner that announces his indifference to his work, in which he is in fact expert. My father has sometimes thought about why this man, one Solomon Jefferson, finds it important to represent himself as less than he is, but he hasn't been able to reach a helpful conclusion. The two noncoms have the raffish air of the enlisted men of the Corps—hair a little long, khaki shirts rumpled and conspicuously bare of decoration. Woods nods at them as they sketch casual salutes.

"Bit of overkill, don't you think?"

"SOP, buddy," Vanderpool tells him. "And this guy is known to be a little volatile. But I think it was his nickname that convinced me we needed to bring some firepower. Hop in."

My father settles into the jeep's front seat. "Refresh my memory."

"The Butcher of Shanghai." Colonel Vanderpool puts the jeep in gear and fits it skillfully into the surging traffic. "Got your gun, Annie?"

The musical *Annie Get Your Gun* had just opened on Broadway. Captain Woods, also in civilian garb, touches the left side of his jacket. Thirty minutes later, Vanderpool jerks the jeep into a parking spot across from the building where their spider waits in his web. A shabby elevator shuffles them up to the fourth floor. The officers enter the room with their weapons holstered, but the sergeant, standing just behind and to one side of them, levels his carbine at the man behind the desk. The corporal with the submachine gun remains in the doorway, his eyes on the hall.

The man is a gaunt Korean wearing a threadbare white shirt, frayed at cuffs and collar but starched to a stony edge. His hands are folded before him on the blotter. He does not move or speak. He raises expressionless eyes to my father, who promptly matches the empty gaze. There is nothing on the desk but the blotter and a gooseneck lamp whose light falls on the desk's top drawer. The drawer is open by perhaps four inches.

"*Tachiagatte kudasai.*" Stand up, please.

The man remains motionless. The CIC sergeant lifts the muzzle of his weapon twice, causing the Korean to stand slowly, as if raised by an invisible lever. "Step slowly away from the desk." Still in Japanese. "Face the wall. Lean forward and put your palms against the wall. Keep your legs well apart."

Colonel Vanderpool signals the sergeant to come forward. The sergeant rests his carbine gently on the desk and approaches the prisoner. He puts a foot between the man's legs. Then he handcuffs the prisoner, who has yet to speak, and leads him into the hall.

"Make him snug," Vanderpool says, "but I don't want to see any bruises. We'll be down in five."

"Yes, sir."

The two officers conduct a cursory search of the room—there's a file cabinet as well as the desk, a bookshelf, a low table with scattered papers on it—but find little of interest. It doesn't much matter. The evidence that condemns their captive is copious and overwhelming. Captain Woods, sliding open the desk's top drawer, sees light falling on the grooved grip of a Nambu pistol, which had lain concealed a few inches from the hand of a doomed man who had very little to lose by reaching for it. Vanderpool glances with some interest at the find.

"Huh. These guys usually carried Lugers. The Parabellum P 08," he murmurs, almost dreamily.

My father glances at him. Sometimes Colonel Vanderpool seems a little too fond of the hardware. "The Nambu is a reliable weapon."

"Yeah, early in the war it was," Jay Vanderpool persists. "The Japs made good automatics in the thirties but the workmanship got pretty shoddy toward the end once we'd bombed their factories." In the colonel's voice is an irrelevant intensity that signals the relief of a mission completed, a danger passed. "What would you carry if you could have any piece you wanted, Hank?"

"The Colt is fine."

"Think I'd go for something exotic. The Czechs make some nice handguns."

In the jeep they find the gaunt Korean secured in the rear, so slender that he is barely cramped between the two Americans. "So who is this guy, anyway?" Some confiding mood has been released in the corporal. Neither officer sees fit to answer, but the brusque youth presses on. "What'd he *do*?"

"Earned you a three-day pass."

When Woods writes home the next morning, he makes no mention of the pistol:

CIC may have justified its existence here in Pusan. The other day we managed to pick up an alleged war criminal whom the Chinese want pretty badly. There have been many wireless messages popping back and forth. We located him here, identified him, and arrested him, and sent him back to Seoul for transportation to China.

He seems to have been a Japanese intelligence agent in Shanghai (he's a Korean) during the war where he made life rough for a number of allied prisoners and managed to squeeze many many yen selling immunity to the local Jewish colony.

I don't know what a war criminal looks like. This gent was very quiet, and well-spoken under interrogation, and didn't seem as if he could hurt a fly, but where there was so much smoke there must have been plenty of fire, so I was very pleased we could nail him.

I KNOW my father enjoyed at least one home leave during his years abroad because I remember it—remember not so much him as Hong, a very tall and gentle Korean who gave me a set of Bill Ding blocks for Christmas (I still have one of them). It was probably Christmas 1948. Hong must have been an interpreter, or one of my father's agents. I don't know how it came about that he accompanied Captain Woods to America on that occasion, whether there was work that would take them to Washington or simply a few weeks of freedom from the tension and turmoil of their duties. That year, I would have been three. I'm sure I found nothing surprising in Hong's presence—kids take what comes—but now I wonder what the white citizens of rural North Carolina would have made of him. I doubt he would have been subject to their racist scorn.

As with Bill Crawford's easy accommodation of foreign *gens de couleur* at West Point, the Hertford folks would have seen Hong as a benign exotic. In any case my father would have tolerated no disrespect. He was well liked in my mother's circle, though regarded at first with certain skepticism—like Louis Crawford, another Yankee blade come to town to snatch up one of their Southern belles. Hong is mentioned now and then in my father's letters, but his name never came up in conversation in later years. I don't know what became of him once the war began. After that Christmas, I never saw him again.

THE LETTERS my father wrote during his first two years in Korea are optimistic as regards the country's prospects. He is never unaware that the peninsula exists in a continuing state of barely controlled chaos, but until the tensions of the Cold War tighten toward the seeming inevitability of armed conflict, he apparently feels confident that both the United States and the Soviet Union can control their client nations. By the spring of 1948, that confidence has been shaken.

You may have seen in the papers that General Hodge has set the election date for South Korea as May 9th. It is far from clear how that will affect my outfit but maybe matters will clarify themselves. The UN committee was stopped short at the border by our friends to the north so the formation of at least a tentative South Korean government is almost certain. Just how much autonomy it will have or exactly what effect it will have on the military occupation is quite uncertain. Rhee and his chums—he's pretty much a shoe-in—may settle for a substantial military mission, but anything could happen—I just can't give an intelligent guess. At any rate I think the situation will probably jell in the next three or four months.

The situation does jell. Korea shapes itself into two hostile nations, and an apprehensive American public submits to a toxic drone of news. Louise

Woods must have written her husband her fears for his safety, because he begins a letter that captures his sense of the Korean status quo with a hasty note of personal reassurance:

> Despite all the tales of riot run rampant in Korea—and they are to a large extent true—I personally have no more contact with the violence than you in Hertford have with a gang war in Chicago. I feel sorry for the farmers, though—the cops beat 'em up if they don't vote and the commies burn 'em out if they do—and they mostly don't give a damn one way or the other. Like peasants everywhere, they're caught in the high tides of history—crushed between contending forces that promise much, deliver little, and ultimately are no more than the agents of mass murder that form the politics of the present day.
>
> Enough preaching. I expect to go to Japan for a few days next week—have to transport a body (a live one) and handle one or two other matters concerning which I must as usual maintain radio silence.

Six months later, he will contest the accuracy of the stateside accounts of insurrection, while again admitting the accelerating collapse of civic order throughout the countryside.

November 22, 1948

I can understand your concern about the recent political difficulties here not to mention riots and such. However, a reading of the accounts as they appeared in the US press and in *Time* and *Newsweek* made me wonder if those estimable publications are equally accurate in their reporting of other news. I can assure you that—except in the minor respect I wrote you about in my last note—US personnel, far from being wounded or killed or run out of town, were in fact not involved at all. It was an unpleasant mess to be sure but strictly, as in every other instance, a Korean mess, and we have every reason to believe that in the unlikely event of widespread difficulty, that difficulty will continue to be a domestic deal, and only indirectly of concern to us.

I can't blame the reporters too much since they probably were unaware how notoriously unreliable Korean sources are, and those were the only sources they had until the mess was mopped up (by Korean police and Korean constabulary). The moral is—don't trust alarmist reporting out of this country.

But the anodyne reduction of a chain of destructive events to mere "political difficulties" is readily disputed by the local history, which by the fall of 1948 had seen full-scale guerilla warfare on the island of Cheju-do, where a popular uprising against Syngman Rhee's oppressive republic would claim as many as sixty thousand lives before spreading to the mainland. Cheju-do may have witnessed the worst of the violence, but small battles between peasants and police are common throughout the country during this period. And my father is not entirely candid in calling the struggle "strictly . . . a Korean mess" since American advisors were often attached to Rhee's rabid army.

Other events added their poisons to the broth: the Soviet Union became more aggressive in Europe after successfully testing an atomic bomb in September 1949, and Mao Tse-tung proclaimed the establishment of the People's Republic of China a month later. (Ho Chi Minh had achieved a similar goal in Vietnam four years before.) And to all this may be added the frequent border skirmishes between northern and southern Korean forces that flared up for more than a year before the actual beginning of the Korean War.

My father's account, then, feels to a degree disingenuous. But, again, I suspect his chief concern is to offer reassurance to his family, and it's possible as well that his own work didn't often bring him into direct contact with the turmoil he accordingly declines to describe. Indeed, a letter of August 1948 depicts Seoul as a relatively peaceful city whose civic life is an appropriate subject for satire:

Things remain comparatively quiet here. The main part of my job right now is to check up on local political activities. I could run for office myself since I know exactly what to put in the platform no matter what party you belong to. You first applaud Korean independence and then for five minutes waffle on about the pro-Japs and the traitors, after which you're elected to the office of honey-wagon driver. As the weather grows warmer, that promises to be one of the really first-rate jobs.

Still, the more I have to do with these people, the more I find they

are even as you and I in most regards, and that our lack of understanding is due mostly to a lack of knowledge. I don't know how long
it would take us to get that knowledge, maybe longer than any of us is
willing or able to spend.

He is being modest about his own intuitive empathy with the Asian mind,
for this is the month during which he will be sent to confer with Syngman
Rhee, a meeting he mentions to Louise only in passing, as though his access
to the high councils of the new nation is worthy of no particular note: "Paid
a call on President Rhee the day after the inauguration and had an hour's
private conversation anent current work. Can't tell you too much, but it
looks as if the visit may have been well worthwhile in many respects."

Indeed, August 1948 is clearly a month in which Woods's work is thriving:

It has been filthy hot, dusty, and dirty here and I've been handling
quite a few arcane chores at odd hours.

One small reward—we got a cable from our headquarters a couple
of days ago praising me for the "planning, progress, and development" of a project that's been of primary interest to me now. If this
were a more usual sort of army work I suppose I'd be up for a medal
of some sort, but of course that kind of thing doesn't happen in CIC.
What does happen is paperwork and tedium and empty hours punctuated by the occasional moment of minor drama. It seems a little
theatrical at times, as when I find myself lurking in an alley wearing
a seersucker suit and a sidearm in a shoulder holster on the alert for
some Korean gentleman with whom I'll exchange sign and coun-
tersign and then wait to see to what extent he plans to reward my
patience or complicate my life.

Captain Woods was promoted to major in July 1947, but the promotion
was not made secure through appointment to the regular army. Absent such
a commission, he saw no great future in uniform. But he had been enjoying
his work, and there chanced to be another government Agency, very new,
where he could turn his experience to account.

If my father had any doubts about going into the CIA, they could have had
very few about him: an Ivy League infantry officer of impeccable background
with language skills and a law degree plus five years in counterintelligence?

He was born for it, exactly the applicant the Agency was looking for, and indeed the transition from soldier to spy was so effortless that the only reference to his new master in his letters notes simply, "Well, I'm no longer in the Army but the work is much the same." At no time thereafter will he again identify his supremely secretive alliance: we may not know who he is. In the army, after all, he had sometimes openly been Lieutenant or Captain Arthur Woods of the ____th CIC Detachment. Now he would be an anonymous civilian in a shabby suit, carrying out shadowy missions for an obscure force steadily gathering to itself the increasing powers it would deploy throughout the Cold War, and after.

My father's promotion may have been only days ahead of his release to the reserves and appointment to the Central Intelligence Agency,[16] if indeed the events were not simultaneous. And there is good reason to suppose that Jay Vanderpool, an Agency asset already, was instrumental in effecting the transition. He and my father had worked well together on difficult and sometimes dangerous projects, and the storied colonel, who agreed with his junior that war was inevitably coming, may have wanted a tested companion beside him when it came. Perhaps he put the option to Major Woods directly, or he may have invited his CIA superiors to test the waters. I envision a slightly serpentine approach, like that of the Penn professor that brought my father into the CIA. Did the army absolutely require Major Woods's talents any longer? If not, should the new major find further advance through the ranks unlikely, perhaps he might entertain the idea of another form of government service—something that could draw strongly on his particular set of skills? It is not hard to envision an enthusiastic answer. He was still a relatively young man of adventurous spirit and a desire to serve where needed, and he had no doubt the secret war still needed him.

But he was still in the army when a staggering coup dropped in his lap one afternoon during an idle hour, just as he had earlier predicted to my mother that it might, the product not of search but of serendipity. My father was sitting at his desk, chain-smoking and reading a Naigo Marsh mystery when Hong approached, dropped a thin manila envelope on the blotter, and left without the usual exchange of pleasantries. Woods opened it. Inside were two long sheets of rice paper, clotted with kanji and English and bordered by crudely drawn maps of the eastern Chinese and western Korean coasts.

---

16. He would not be discharged until 1953.

The document was a detailed plan for the deployment of the Chinese army in the initial stages of the coming war.

At CIC HQ, analysts vetted the two pages in different ways, finding the source of the paper, the origin of the ink, the hand behind both the English scrawl and the Chinese strokes, the courier's history, and the path the text had probably traveled before ending up in Captain Woods's office, before turning to the contents. They concluded the document was legitimate. Under maximum security, it was passed on to 8th Army GHQ, where it vanished without a trace. A month later it was returned to Captain Woods for his files. He would never know what effect, if any, these extraordinary pages had produced. But when I found them among his papers, I was stunned to realize how narrow was the distance between my father's undertakings and the cataclysm about to unfold, and once more I marveled at my memory of him as a corpulent old man trudging about his garden while *he*, perhaps, entertained memories of a time when he was one of a handful of people standing in the path of history, trying to block an all-out war.

ON MARCH 22, 1950, the army authorized Louise Woods to proceed to Fort Lawton, Washington, with household goods, hold baggage, and dependents, prepared for an April 17 embarkation from the Port of Seattle for Yokohama, Japan. On March 30, I turned six. My mother, my brother, and I shared a comfortable suite of senior officers' quarters on an army troop ship, the *David C. Shanks*.

The only memory I retain of the voyage is provided by a yellowing snapshot of a little boy on a sun-scarred deck waving a handsome wooden sword, saber-shaped and painted silver, that some family friend had given him in bon voyage. You may be sure it resembled the dress sword I had long coveted that hung on the wall in the entrance hall of the Hertford house.

In Japan, my father had secured us accommodations in the Mampei Hotel while we awaited permanent housing. An old alpine resort in Karaizawa, the Mampei was surrounded by forest and graced with hot springs. Our rooms, in the half-timbered main lodge, made some concessions to Western ease—we had beds, not futons—but they were largely traditional, with *tokonoma* alcoves and sliding *shoji* screens whose frail paper walls I found fascinating. I have a guilty recollection of putting my tiny fist through one just because I could.

My memories are fragmentary, but some are vivid. There was the day our family took a long train ride in mountains woven together by mist. I remember Buddhist shrines scattered through groves of cedars dripping with rain, and the scent of the fat waxed-paper umbrellas carried by the small black-clad men and women who filled the carriages. I think I remember the whirling, pulsing landscape of lights scrawled across the office towers of the Ginza in downtown Tokyo, though now I wonder whether the district could have become a palace of neon so soon after the war.

My father taught me a few phrases of Japanese, and it seemed to delight the maids and bellhops at the hotel to hear a small American boy attempting to employ them: *Konnichiwa* for greeting in the morning, *konbanwa* at night. For some reason, I was taught to say in Japanese "The flower is not white," a phrase for which you might think there would be little use. But once, in the hotel lobby, faced with a display of pink chrysanthemums, I stumbled through it for an attentive concierge, and he was hugely entertained. My father seemed amused as well, as, in general, he seemed pleased with me.

For my part, caution reigned. I was with my father for the first time in years. He had been away when I was born, and he had lived overseas almost my entire life. I wasn't altogether sure what his presence boded for my future, but I somehow understood that he would be resuming his role as the dominant male of the household, a role that had heretofore been mine. I felt some apprehension as I pondered the complex negotiations that lay ahead. My mother, well aware of this, sought to ease my fears shortly before our arrival. "Billy, your father will be so proud of how you've grown," she said, and I'm told that my answer was "Has he grown, too?"

He had.

At six, I knew my father had been in the army, but I didn't know what he did. I understood that he was now a civilian, but I didn't know why he spent part of each week in Tokyo while my mother, brother, and I remained in the mountains. I had been told that after our year in Japan, the family would be returning to America to a new home and a new life I found hard to imagine. I knew my parents and other Americans living in the Mampei regarded the situation in Korea with foreboding, but I didn't really know why. And I certainly didn't understand why the twelve months we were to spend in East Asia abruptly dwindled to less than two, or why I found myself on a transpacific luxury liner just as I was getting happily accustomed to life in a luxury hotel.

The fact is that during those few weeks our family lived in Japan—weeks that saw my mother enchanted by *ikebana*, my brother flirting with the chambermaids, and me darting about the dark halls of the old hotel brandishing my wooden sword—my father reached the decision that would conclude his Asian duties and lead to his third and final form of government service. I can't now retrieve his thinking with anything like certainty. He may have wanted to rejoin his scattered family in the promise of postwar American life—he'd lived in exile long enough! Perhaps he hoped to return to the practice of law shorn of the trappings of violence. Or maybe he had become so well known to his opposite numbers that, like an actor grown larger than his role, he could no longer function effectively on the secret stage. But what seems certain is that he saw war coming, but couldn't see a way to serve in it, or to stop it.

His letters make clear that he had become disenchanted with the inertia of planners and policymakers in Tokyo and Washington. The official position of some part of the CIA had long been that, despite evidence of a military buildup, there was no possibility of invasion because North Korea's status as a Soviet client state rendered it unable to act independently. Though Kim Il-Sung was rabid to attack, the logic went, Stalin would not turn him loose and so risk war with the United States. And there was always the question of China.

In Washington, the argument looked sound. But Woods seems to have been one of a handful of experienced officers who, noting the exclusion of South Korea from the American defense perimeter, had become persuaded otherwise. "The Agency is telling the administration what it wants to hear," he noted in a letter to a friend, "but not all of us are on board."

At that point, according to my mother's memory many years later, he had been ready enough to return to active duty and serve in a war he had worked to forestall. She countered with the same objection Kate Crawford had urged on Louis in 1917—that her husband had given years of his life to his country, that he had faced his share of danger, that he had a family which now needed him more than the nation did. But her pleas were hardly required. As I've noted, as an infantry major Woods rated a battalion, but as an intelligence officer he had been five years divorced from troop command. No such appointment would have been forthcoming, and he had no interest in repeating the vain pursuit of combat that had evaded him throughout the Second World War.

So. Nothing doing with the army. And I suspect that *he* suspected his path had narrowed in the CIA. If he had argued the case for the risk of war forcefully with his superiors at a time when they were selling a different story, his future in the Agency might be no more promising than his fortunes in the army would have been. I like to think he resigned on principle but find it almost more satisfying to imagine a large unlikelihood: that his professed departure from the CIA was no less than a cover for his deeper immersion within it, that his subsequent government career marched in lockstep with his secret one, and that, like the Korean War itself, my father's war never ended at all.

Our voyage east put us in first-class cabins aboard the SS *President Cleveland*, an elegant liner that boasted many more amenities than had the *Shanks*—theaters and restaurants, cocktail lounges and a formal dining room. The theater showed two movies a day, one in the afternoon, one in early evening. Just as in America, the rattle of the projector was muted by a soundproof booth and the cushioned chairs stood in deep ranks, though smaller numbers. One feature stayed with me as fragmentary images: coffins lined beside open graves, a flapping sign reading VACCINATE NOW.

I have more vivid memories of the festivities that accompanied our crossing of the International Date Line, and I remember being pleased to have the undivided attention of my brother, who cheerfully accepted the role of babysitter so our parents could dine and dance each evening though I'm sure at seventeen he could have made better use of his days at sea. The only other memory I have is of eagerly trading my beautiful handmade wooden sword to another little boy for his cheap metal cap gun and being mildly reproved for doing so.

We disembarked in San Francisco on June 11, 1950. Exactly two weeks later, troops of the Democratic People's Republic of Korea crossed the thirty-eighth parallel.

The family spent that summer in Colonial Beach, Virginia, tucked into two rooms in an old hotel on the Potomac River where my father housed us to spare us the heat and damp of August in Washington. He lived during the week in the Wardman Park Hotel on Connecticut Avenue while he looked for work, joining us on the weekends. If he was uneasy about his prospects, he remained jovial, and the nervousness I'd felt faced with his large presence in Japan eased a great deal. Our time fishing together began that summer. We sought flounder, croakers, and perch from the long hotel dock that pierced the river; now and then we went out in rented boats. On weekend evenings, my father read Dickens in an Adirondack chair on the hotel veranda, smoked Camels, and drank scotch while fireflies crept around the screen. He had come to the end of his adventures.

The more I learned about my father's army and Agency years, the more I felt I was being guided toward a hitherto-obscure aspect of his personality. I had known him to be for the most part an affable man with an even temperament, though I had also seen his equanimity punctured by occasional flashes of fathomless anger. And I had known him as a social being, capable of both close friendships and casual connections. But he had a private side I rather admired, probably because I could sense its same steady growth in my own personality. He was happy spending hours alone, sitting on the porch in fine weather gazing pensively into his well-kept garden, or in his armchair with a drink and a book, largely oblivious to the comings and goings around him. Finally, a private man. Now as I pondered his story I was led to wonder whether his education in the clandestine arts had fashioned the guarded aspect of his character or whether he was born with a secret self that fitted him for his covert calling.

Now and then a colleague from A. R. Woods's days in Korea would turn up in Bethesda and address him as "Hank," evidently his nickname in country. But my family had never heard of it, no one else ever used it, and he never explained it. My father had employed various noms de guerre in his work, but I don't think Hank was one of those. I think it was part of his pleasure in constructing a life, another way of adding distance between himself and the world—or of creating a connection with it whose nature only he could know.

IF MY FATHER didn't often tell his stories, my mother sometimes did, and as a kid I was dubious about the details precisely because I was eager to believe them and they seemed too romantic to be altogether real, also perhaps because the Oedipal romance required that I slay the king, and the more compelling a character he became the more complicated that task would have to be. So I listened with a grain—with two grains—of salt to her claims that he had enlisted her help with a secret short-wave radio operation, that he'd captured a notorious war criminal, that he'd been wounded in a riot, even that he'd survived a shootout in a Pusan alley with a Soviet spy. (This last story amused him and he got the best possible mileage out of it by refus-ing to either confirm or deny.) But Louise Woods was the soul of probity. If she pressed a story toward fiction, it always grew from a seed of fact. Still, I did think her capable of enhancing my pleasure by sometimes magnifying her tales.

Then letters from the footlocker began to emerge that showed there was substance to most of the stories and I was obliged to amend my memories of a chair-bound emphysemic drowsing through *Star Trek* to include a dapper secret agent prowling a kimchi-reeking alley with a Colt revolver in one pocket and a volume of Basho in the other.

That footlocker, exiled for decades to the Hertford attic, had been yielding a peculiar bounty, trash and prizes in nearly equal measure. Under the first heading I might list empty envelopes, Korean banknotes, language-training booklets, weekend passes, blank Japanese notepaper, ads for whiskey, and invitations to a "free 'cooktail' hour." Promotion records, discharge papers, and travel orders offered little more, though they did help me keep the time-line of his story sorted out. But other items, often floating free of context, proved deeply rewarding. There is a mysterious letter from a Japanese offi-cial thanking my father profusely "for all you have done for me, despite all the troubles I have caused you." There is a paper target, punctuated by five shots, all in or near the bull's-eye—his Colt revolver. There is a certificate from the Engineer School at Fort Belvoir, Virginia, establishing "this officer's mastery of mines and demolitions, Japanese and American." And tossed in the midst of such indifferent litter is the rumpled rice paper document titled "Plan for Collecting the Informations [*sic*] of the Chinese Communist Army," dated only months before the outbreak of the Korean War.

And, atop it all, some bits of colored cloth.

My father earned a number of campaign and theater medals for his ser-vice and suggests in one letter that a particular covert operation might have put him in line for something higher—"but in CIC, things don't work that way." General Hodges stated as much in a commendation of July 1, 1946, sent to each member of the clandestine force: "The fact that much of the work of the CIC must remain obscure because of its confidential nature in no way lessens its importance. . . . The contribution of your organization to a proper understanding of the political situation, the suppression of espio-nage, subversive activities and illegal organizations have been major factors in the establishment of an orderly and peaceful administration for South

Korea." This is a perspective confirmed in Major Woods's separation orders, where his career is described only in the most general terms: "Collected, evaluated, and disseminated information pertaining to enemy activities, sabotage, and subversion. Confidential nature of assignment precludes detailed description." In this, the official record resembles his letters.

There was more. A yellow cardboard box of color Kodak slides I put aside to look at later if I can ever track down something as antique as a slide projector; and the box that held my father's Colt revolver, now home to a stack of small black-and-white photographs remarkable for the way they conceal their meaning: Asian and American figures, some in uniform, some not, standing by threes and fours against a backdrop of anonymous buildings; low mountain ranges; derelict Jeeps; a stone Buddha in a grove of sickly pines. If these snapshots have stories, they're not telling them to me.

IN WASHINGTON, by the early fall of 1950, my father had found work at the American Enterprise Association, a conservative think tank whose name sounded so vague to me when I was older that I sometimes wondered if it was a CIA cover, though I now recognize that as my attempt to restore to the major the black magic of his former life. But within a year or so he joined the Federal Trade Commission as a staff attorney, where he remained for the rest of his career. In 1952, our family moved to Bethesda, Maryland, in the Washington suburbs, where I lived until my adult life began.

As far as my relationship with my father is concerned, those years from six to twenty can be passed in a paragraph, and most of that may be summarized in an invaluable chestnut often attributed to Mark Twain about how dull he thought his dad was when he was ten and how startled he was to find how much the old man had learned over the next decade. I remained largely ignorant of my father's infantry, military intelligence, and legal careers and took little note of the successive avocations that claimed him—high-stakes poker, powerboating, gardening, music, model trains. We did keep in common a love of books and fishing, and those passions bridged some rough spots over the years.

As I entered my haughty adolescence, my father had the wisdom to adopt a reserve that protected both of us from his occasional anger and my contrived disdain. Our mutual caution cost us, among other things, those intimate conversations through which an approximation of wisdom is passed down the generations. So I didn't often ask him for his stories, including his war stories, though I must have known he had some good ones to tell.

Even so, our truce could be bridged by moments of conviviality, which were often founded, as they had been in my childhood, on our shared love of books. Then the preferred genre had been science fiction; now it was novels of suspense. John Le Carré was a mutual favorite and his great *Tinker Tailor Soldier Spy* a special treat. I had the central tension of that novel in mind when one evening, deep into my father's final illness, I decided to see whether I could prompt an anecdote or two from his sojourn in the secret world. I somehow came up with the name of Edward Landsdale, I'm not sure why. My father said, "Well, you *have* done your homework."

"Did you know him?"

"We met once, socially. But we all knew his legend. Though I shouldn't call 'legend' what in all simple truth was . . . truth."

"Some of his story is hard to believe."

"Then don't believe it." My father was showing the weariness of the hour. It was inscribed on his haggard face and evident in his shortness, his terseness. So we left it. I knew there would come some other times when the silence between us would shatter and I could elicit the stories I'd been too self-engrossed to value on other occasions.

Once I was out on my own, our relationship grew easier, but too much still remained unsaid when, in the spring of 1976—I would have been thirty-two—he reluctantly decided to take himself to a physician to have a chronic cough checked out. "I hope it's not bronchitis," my mother said. But the major already had his suspicions. "You know," he said, "I kind of hope it is."

A lifelong heavy smoker, my father gave up cigarettes for cigars after a gallbladder operation. He inhaled them. The lung cancer that followed was complicated by heart disease and emphysema, which finally kept him tethered many hours a day to an oxygen tank that eased his struggle to breathe. But in the early stages of his illness while his strength permitted, he changed nothing in his routine—fishing and gardening, reading and music, entertaining visitors from his easy chair with drink in hand, a jaunty beret draped over his chemotherapeutic baldness. He was largely cheerful. Such fears as he felt, he never spoke of.

My parents grew closer in my father's final days, which I believe is not uncommon. He and I were at peace as well. Still, there were subjects left untouched. I had by then achieved some professional recognition, but if I had ever impressed him, I was not to know it.

That fall, I was teaching at a college three hours south of the city, but I came home as often as I could, twice for false alarms before the final time for his funeral. We had some good conversations during those visits. Topics varied. He didn't speak often of his illness, and nostalgia never claimed him, but he was sometimes willing to provide anecdotes from his earlier life, and I had become more eager to request them. His years in Japan and Korea came up on occasion. He was circumspect in discussing them, as though even at this late date the rules of operational security still prevailed. But he would talk in general terms, and I stirred his amusement one weekend when his health seemed strong and his mood especially good by idly remarking that I supposed there was less weaponry on display in Agency precincts than there would have been in CIC.

"Christ," the major said, after he had tied off his choked chuckle, "CIA must have showed six guns for every one in counterintelligence, in terms of pistols alone. In Korea, we carried Colt police revolvers or Army .45s, never both." He stopped for a savage cough. "Sure, we could get such weapons as we wanted, but the occasions were rare. In Central Intelligence, I was offered stuff from the US, Britain, Russia, China, and the UAR and encouraged to qualify on all of it. That's handguns alone, remember. The sky was the limit on other armament."

I showed my surprise. "Why so? You weren't paramilitaries, exactly."

"Depends on who you asked. Some fireballs thought we *were* paramilitaries, exactly." Under his surge of energy, I could see his growing weariness, so I led the conversation into more anodyne paths until the evening ended, raising the possibility of a Soviet secret sharer, a counterintelligence counterpart on the other side. He shrugged the question off at first, then retrieved a casual anecdote that still can give me a satisfactory chill.

"Did you have that kind of opposite number?" I persisted. "A Karla to your Smiley?"

He smiled slightly. "You're giving me too much size, William. I was just a foot soldier in the Great Game. Still . . . " He halted. "There were Russians all over the place and some of them made an impression. I did take note of one gentleman who showed up just as things were getting interesting right before independence."

There was a pause while he seemed to be deciding whether to say more. I let it linger until he spoke.

"This fellow was supposed to be part of a trade delegation or cultural exchange program or some such." My father smiled. "Which was a bit like wearing a blazer with a Ministry of State Security badge on it. Anyway, it became clear he was trying to do for his side what I was trying to do for mine—a double, if you will. We left him alone at first but after a time he became too troublesome and I decided I would very much like to have a talk with him." The old spy paused again. "We put feelers out but he wasn't interested in opening a dialogue."

"So you never dealt with him?"

There was a silence. I was about to break it when my father said, "Oh, we dealt with him. I just never got a chance to *talk* with him."

For the longest time I had wanted to ask my father if he had ever killed anyone, eager to ask and dreading to ask, eager because I hoped he had and hoped he hadn't, dreading because I feared he hadn't, and would that reduce him in my eyes? There was also the fact that it was not a question you could ask, though I now feel sure he would have answered with honesty and candor. He must have been ready to kill when he was an infantry officer, or in CIC. In the Agency such a moral choice would have been taken for granted as long since made, and in the field the opportunities were many. Yet I persisted—I *persist*—in thinking that he had not, did not. This can only be for queasy reasons of my own, and *that* must have to do with what my own answer would have been.

MY FATHER DIED in the fall of 1976, within weeks of our last long conversation. His funeral was held at St. John's Church in Bethesda, where the choir sang some of the hymns he loved, but they didn't include Blake's "Jerusalem," his favorite. That day I wished I could have heard his powerful bass hovering above the other voices.

> Bring me my bow of burning gold!
> Bring me my arrows of desire!
> Bring me my spear! O clouds, unfold!
> Bring me my chariot of fire!

Several of my friends were pallbearers, including John Holland and Toby Thompson, for whose father I would one day perform the same melancholy chore.

We buried Major Woods in the churchyard behind Holy Trinity in Hertford. It was a modest military service—a flag on the casket, properly folded and presented to his widow by a brother officer who had come down from Norfolk to perform the ritual. No more than that, no Taps, no honor guard. It was a smaller ceremony than had been laid on for his father, Captain A. R. Woods, MD, buried at Arlington with full parade—the riderless horse, the rifle salute, the army honor guard in dress blues—a noble pageant I remember well. There would have been no way to fit all that in behind Holy Trinity. I think it would have embarrassed him anyway.

My father had played several roles in his life. Son, husband, parent. College instructor and government lawyer. Medical student, railroad laborer, sport fisherman, gardener, friend. Musician and spy. Scholar of medieval languages and connoisseur of Asian art. The list could be lengthened. But there was only one title he chose to carry into eternity. His headstone reads:

ARTHUR ROY WOODS JR
MAJOR US ARMY
JUNE 9, 1908 OCT 28, 1976
A soldier.

AFTER ACTION REPORT
Rumors and Random Intelligence

Years hence of these scenes, of these furious passions . . .
Now be witness again, paint the mightiest armies of earth,
Of those armies so rapid so wondrous what saw you to tell us?
—Walt Whitman, "The Wound-Dresser"

DURING THESE REVERIES of his final days, my father had mentioned his grandfather's Civil War service, but he had not dwelled on it, and indeed the story of Benjamin Woods looked to be lost in the long recital of the names of the men of my family who had taken up arms for their country before they even had one. All I could remember about this great-grandfather was that he had served as a sergeant, something of a relief to me in that I had long believed myself to be the only male of my line never to have known the glory of commissioned rank. I had not supposed Benjamin's story was retrievable until, years after my father's death, I came across a book that stood neglected on his crowded shelves and found in its pages not only a detailed record of my great-grandfather's war but a celebration of his extraordinary talent for survival.

A thick volume bound in worn blue cloth, title stamped on the spine in gold, the *History of the Eighth Regiment, NH Vols.*, was published by subscription in 1892 as a memento for veterans. The text ran to nearly six hundred pages of small print—my curiosity would hardly carry me through all of it—but I was determined to ferret out the bones of the unit's story and to take a closer look at my great-grandfather's role. Unsurprisingly, the *History* fell open at my great-grandfather's page, which was prefaced by two photographs:

Enlisted as a recruit in Company D, August 20, 1862, at the age of seventeen years. Joined the regiment at Camp Parapet, La., September 30,

1862, just in time to go in the Bayou La Fourche expedition and take part in the battle of Georgia Landing. Thenceforward he was in all battles and skirmishes in which the company or regiment was engaged, up to his muster out at Natchez, Miss., on June 6, 1865. During all this time he was not wounded, though narrowly escaping.

The 8th New Hampshire, which would fight as both infantry and cavalry, had formed in Manchester in 1861 and set sail from Boston for Mississippi early the next year. In nearly three years of war, the regiment, numbering fewer than a thousand men, would suffer casualties of one out of ten killed or wounded, at one point fighting fourteen engagements in two months, of which the most noted was the siege of Fort Hudson, Louisiana, where the faces of the dead slid from their skulls in the withering sun. Corporal—later Sergeant—Woods fought in that battle, but according to his contribution to the regimental history, it was another fight that left the most vivid impression:

> You ask how I used up, at Sabine Cross Roads, my eighty rounds
> of cartridges. Well, Captain Williamson had given orders that every
> other man might get off his horse and eat his dinner and I was fairly
> underway with mine when there was a rustle in the underbrush and a
> line of Confederate infantry dashed into the road and shouting "Sur-
> render, you Yankee cusses!" began to grab for the horses' bridles, so—
> emptying my carbine into the crowd—I made a dive for the saddle.

With pistol and sword, my great-grandfather's troop cut their way out of the ambush and formed up with Company D to turn the attack. "The rebel line wavered and partially broke, but their officers held their men, and as they returned the fire, our line was no more. Riderless horses ran in all directions. A few men got back; the most were captured or killed. But we held our section. Our company was the last to leave the field."

It was not Benjamin Woods's only close call. At Port Hudson, his file leader and the men on either side of him were killed in the first assault. Two weeks later, Woods was struck in the head, harmlessly, by a spent musket ball. And "late in the afternoon of the same day, while trying to procure water for some wounded comrades," the *History* tells us, "he ran the gauntlet of the rebel sharpshooters, a whole volley being fired at him alone, through which he escaped unhurt." Later, on the Red River, Sergeant Woods switched places with the soldier beside him; a moment afterward, the man fell dead.

The magic of his own story may have tempted my great-grandfather to believe in divine providence; his experience might equally have convinced him that war is the province of chance. I lean to the latter view, but a more credulous age could have seen Sergeant Woods's improbable good fortune as a talisman, making me wonder whether his cohort would have followed or fled him. Sometimes he might have seemed to point the way to their own survival; at others, it must have looked as though he drew death near himself only to warp it away toward them.

For me, the young soldier's story performed a signal service. It put a book-end to my account of fathers and sons, for now I knew I had defenders of the Union on both sides of my family.

I looked more closely at the photographs. The first shows the boy in uniform. He sits at ease, brass-buttoned jacket in stylish disarray, kepi straight and level across his close-cropped hair. A smudge of moustache seeks to exorcise his youth. His confident gaze engages the camera. In the second, he is a mature man with shaven cheeks and a heavy Van Dyke beard. He wears a formal three-piece suit. He is in three-quarter profile, his glance intense on a far horizon. His eyes are my father's. But neither in the smooth-cheeked boy nor in the stern bearded visage of the old New Hampshireman could I see presaged features of my own. No, I'd found my face in William Harvey Crawford's portrait—physically I'd been most strongly marked by the genetics of the maternal line. What I now could never know was whether either great grandsire had passed along any of the relentless valor the life of each embodied. They'd stood in the fire. I'd never been close enough to feel the flames.

WE ARE READING THE LIVES of three Americans of the last century, one born in the century before.

Each throughout his life evolved along the lines of an inner struggle with a real father and an imagined one, and each was inevitably in dialogue with his times. This second tension accounts for the high heroic faith that flashes through Louis Crawford's letters, the existential cool that shadows William Crawford's, and the postwar pragmatism that emerges from the pages of A. R. Woods. But the first issue is harder to define, precisely because in each case we're dealing with both a real parent and an imagined archetype. The father had known a life in time; the figure was necessarily a psychological construct of the son.

Each man's career carried a different weight, proceeded from a different imperative. For Louis, the army was a dream he now and then made real, combat an imagined good he rarely touched on. For his son, the army was a lifework; his death has the feel of a destiny. For my father, the army was a long interlude in a largely civilian career, but one that tested his capacities and courage in ways no civilian experience could match. All three were shadowed by strong fathers, but all three came into their own, less to please a parent than to achieve the project of becoming themselves.

It seems clear that Louis Crawford followed his father into active service because of the latter's legends of the Civil War, but clear as well that he could thrive in other trades; and it seems likely that William Crawford trooped off to West Point to honor his notion of duty to a dead sire, but even more likely that the romance of flying gripped him still more strongly than the profession of arms. But my uncle left no children, so there's no way of knowing whether they would have sustained the tradition or fled to civil pursuits.

Nor can my father make the case that blood speaks more strongly than history, although I think that in certain ways his is the most exemplary story. His father had been a battlefield surgeon, but he had entered the army an MD and left the same; medicine was his calling, the military a path down which he could pursue it. Granted, my father's father was also a combat veteran of the Civil War, and his ancestors had fought in America's wars since before the American Revolution. But they all pursued civilian trades as well, and neither my brother nor I embraced military careers, though Arthur R. Woods III, clung to the margins.

Of the three men I've taken as my subjects, only the first two were professional soldiers, and only one of them never touched on any other calling. Louis Crawford, as we've seen, looked for many harbors in which to moor his boat, and I've found indications that William's strongest drive was toward aviation. I think he might have been happy to wear wings even if they weren't a colonel's eagles.

Which leaves my father, whose story I in some ways know least. Finally, it draws me most. His army years were a career made by war. There's no chance he would have sought such service otherwise. A sedentary, bookish sort who had taught college English and was in the first years of establishing a successful legal practice, he went into the army in 1942 because it seemed to him that an able and honorable man could not do otherwise. I think he may have been surprised to discover there not only an aptitude but an appetite. I've explored the ways he trained for and embraced his duties, but I may not have made clear how ready he was to make them a life work. Like Louis Crawford, my father sought a regular commission in a postwar era where the army was shedding its soldiers at high speed. I think he would have been happy to remain in uniform for the remainder of his career, which he probably would have spent in military intelligence or civil affairs. And I think he would have retired with a colonel's eagles or a brigadier's star.

With that path closed, he returned contentedly to civilian life and a successful career as a lawyer, and in doing so now looks to me like a modern example of an ancient type, the citizen soldier, a squire of the old Roman republic who picks up a sword when war begins and returns to his vineyards when it's over. I see much to admire here, but if Arthur R. Woods MD felt the same, his son was not necessarily to know. "Your father's relationship with *his* father was chilly," my mother told me once. "I think he was always looking for ways to please Dr. Woods, but he never really knew what was expected."

These mirrored lives, real and imagined, suggest an emerging theme that posits the timeless persistence of warrior blood. But I'm not sure a taste for pageantry or a hunger for action glides through the generations on the wings of a gene, and even if the idea were sound I doubt my family would be the best ones to illustrate it. Their stories are richer than that. And while they speak to an author who appears to be entranced by war and in thrall to military lore, if the Hertford boxes had shown me a grandfather who was an early Imagist poet, an uncle who was a trained Method actor, and a father who was a minor abstract expressionist painter, I'd have been even more eager to explore their experiences, while if they had been successful businessmen, I would have taken no interest in them at all. The material drew me because of the force with which it spoke of its times, the complexity of character it revealed, the interwoven story of family and community it offered up—and perhaps most of all because of the sense it conveyed that I was enmeshed in a family a good deal more various and interesting than I, as a self-absorbed and indifferent youth, had been aware.

THERE IS A SENSE in which each of these men was not entirely suited to the military life, though one was born to it, one would die for it, and one willingly accepted it. Capt. Louis Crawford was eager to be a soldier, but he seems to have been eager for life as a whole, whatever form it took—as I've said, he came to remind me of Saul Bellow's Henderson, a man of fundamental decency beset by a passion for experience that often outruns his capacity for judgment. Lt. Col. William Crawford rose swiftly in a profession that mostly denied him his dream of flight. And Maj. Arthur Woods capably filled an army niche he was able to leave without apparent discontent. All three were good soldiers, but all three were marked by aspects of personality that may not have enlisted when they did.

Louis Crawford was a loose cannon. The ways he moved in and out of the service and in and out of the branches that composed it show in themselves a slightly anarchic character restless under discipline, however much he may have sought it. William Crawford was a far better fit, though as a lifelong professional officer he served a nation historically indifferent to its own standing army; an affable social being, he must have sometimes chafed against the narrowing of a potential self. And A. R. Woods lived lives outside the army that in the end fulfilled him as fully as the army did.

All this adds more color to their pictures. Like my grandfather's reckless approach to family life, my uncle's appalling youthful ideology, and my father's scholarly reserve, the sometimes loose fit of the uniforms they wore may have made them a challenge to serve with, but much more interesting to know.

TO HOLD THE LETTERS in my hand was to grasp not only history but its tactile dimension, scraps of paper with the smell of time: V-mail miniatures, crisp air mail flimsies, telegrams, yellowing onionskin stained by sweat and blood, neat pages of typing bearing school or regimental crests, scrawled handwritten sheets whose occasional illegibility may have concealed their most precious secrets. I employed these physical objects much as I did the patches, photos, art, artifacts, clippings, weapons. The pages not only carried information; they *were* information, and the days I spent touching them over and over were some of the best days I lived in the book.

As to their contents, the letters of all three men are discursive, and in much the same way. If Louis Crawford writes a page on flying, he may follow with a paragraph about household finance. If William takes us close to combat at one point, he may be chiding his mother for failing to fix her roof at the next. And if my father spends a paragraph in a disquisition on Chinese art, he may tag to it a brief note about a spy too slow to come in from the cold. This fitful progress is to be expected in private letters never intended for publication. I've chosen my quotes to minimize the discord.

Of course, there may be missing letters, ghosts of the unwritten ones. This feels especially true with Louis Crawford, whose files are now more than a century old. Their gaps mask significant moments in his story. With William Crawford, the record is so thorough, and the dedicated efforts of the recipients to order it so comprehensive, that loss seems unlikely. Yet between the last V-mail from New Guinea and the first from the Philippines there rests a silence. When Bill Crawford wrote the first, he had never—apart from the surreal San Juan fracas—heard a shot fired in anger. By the time he sent the second, he had come under enemy fire and had returned it. He had seen men wounded. He had looked upon the bodies of the dead. In the great idiom of the Civil War, he had been to see the elephant, and he had recorded the experience in prose that strives to be equal to the event.

For the most part, his letters are carefully cleansed of hints of danger. *Where I am now any chance of being wounded is practically nil.* As an officer, he would have ordinarily censored his own mail, and he did a thorough job of it. As a man of his time, he would have respected the convention that compelled combatants to convince their families of their relative safety. But the protective veil lifts on occasion, and when it does the effect is that of an ax breaching a smoldering wall to expose the fire raging behind it.

His father was less compelled by such caution—recall the joking about his death in a fiery crash—and his era was less reliant on secrecy, while my father's writing was governed by the same considerations of battlefield security that shaped Colonel Crawford's. Still, from the work of all three we derive a rich if unfinished picture, analogous perhaps—all proportions kept—to Gilbert Stuart's half-portrait of Washington or Mondrian's *Victory Boogie Woogie*.

THE 1903 JOURNAL is lamentably brief and Louis Crawford's few surviving manuscripts, aside from copies of his stories, are mostly sentimental notes to his wife, though they do include one long letter of revelatory power and a fictionalized autobiography of his youth, and they all afford glimpses into his antic disposition. Those describing his love of aviation are richly developed and detailed. He also typed up a few pages of family history—it is from those that I've drawn William Harvey Crawford's saga—for the instruction of his children, one of whom would tell his own wartime story in vivid notes and V-mails from the Pacific in 1944 and '45. To this can be added correspondence from my father from stateside camps, postwar Japan, and prewar Korea, outlining his training as an infantryman and experience as an intelligence officer.

Of course, the personal dimension of the stories gripped me. I was not a detached biographer. I was an embedded participant, fortified by the daily companionship of these men and their families, who were my family as well. I knew the deep felicity of mining their letters for the stories each page held, the frisson of holding in my hands the weapons they carried and the insignia of regiment and rank they wore. I hung their portraits on my workshop wall; I sorted through the boxes of the fading papers that had shaped their lives, lives directly antecedent to mine. That was the crux: their stories were in my bloodstream, I wanted to tell them slowly, reined in as I was by competing imperatives to share them with others and guard them as my own.

My family's tradition of military service goes back to the seventeenth century, but it may well end with me. I have no natural children and my brother's offspring have shown no interest in taking up arms. My brother himself served with a combat engineer battalion in Germany in the early 1950s and worked as a civilian executive for the Department of the Army for most of his life. My own army service was tranquil, and as I grow older the romance of battle steadily loses its appeal. But when I consider the lives of my forebears, I feel a degree of awe at their readiness to stand in the fire. And if any profile of a subject is also a portrait of its author, I see mirrored in these pages a self that stands in tenuous relationship to the tradition I've explored. Earlier generations of my family seemed able to resolve with easy grace the tension between duty and desire, in some instances by equating the two. Thus, my grandfather revered his father and emulated him. My uncle respected *his* father and walked the path he felt Louis had marked out. My own father had a more stilted relationship with the first A. R. Woods, but didn't hesitate to commit to the army, standing as he did in the shadow of not just one soldier but a whole parade.

But the world had changed for my brother and myself. Each of us was offered a war and neither of us refused it, yet our orders led us to a more sheltered form of service. In this outcome, an unspoken contract breaks down. It may be that the shift in family destiny is imagined by the son, not imposed by the father, but I must admit I felt an obscure sense of shame when I once heard the major refer to my Tokyo posting as a "good assignment for William." After all, there was a war on, even if it was one for which I never heard him express enthusiasm.

LOUIS CRAWFORD was the first figure whose profile I would undertake. I searched out many ways to tell his story. I polished his medals, hung his sword, reframed his photographs, and acquired an expensive handmade model of his plane even as I poured over his letters and journals and rebuilt in memory the stories I had heard in my childhood. He died long before I was born, more than thirty years younger than I am now. But I feel I've come to know him deeply, and that knowledge has bred a growing affection, and, perhaps oddly, a sense of relief at the outcome of his skirmish on that jungle trail.

Because if we accept that the wars of Bill Crawford and A. R. Woods had to be fought and won, their exploits stand as acts of civic duty. But the fin de siècle American adventure in the Philippines appears far from unambiguous—the white man's burden now looks more like the brown man's doom. Few historians today would be satisfied that the invasion of the Philippines in 1899 was wholly innocent of commercial ambition and imperial design, but I won't stand in judgment more than a century later on the actions of an unreflective teenager caught up in the passions of his time. Across the years, I can feel his chagrin at falling short in competence, though certainly not in courage, in his first encounter with the enemy. So I tend to think the boy sergeant's rue over a missed shot was a youthful failure to mark a passing mercy, for he had found a young man's world of hard service and high adventure, and he had gotten his first taste of combat without the trauma of his first experience of killing. Though he would certainly have seen the moment otherwise, perhaps my grandfather's was the better luck.

Louis Crawford, then, was the first link in what I thought might prove a chain of valor connecting the generations. It *was* that, but more than that it was the opening act of three original experiences whose strongest connection lay not down through the years but across them. If Louis was profoundly conscious of his role as William Harvey Crawford's son, William Crawford had barely known his father other than as a legend who could not have foreseen that the warrior dynasty he hoped to propagate would prove tragically short-lived. And Arthur hadn't known Louis at all. But Arthur and William, shaped by the same dark decades, had become—as the latter noted—not only brothers-in-law but brothers-in-arms. Theirs was a new, skeptical style of American soldiering that, in Normandy hedgerows and on Pacific beaches, proved to work pretty well. Though most ground troops preserved the tradition of fierce courage, that ad hoc style became corrupt in Vietnam, through the focus on body count and the reliance on air power against an enemy that had none. But in recent years modes of battle have again evolved.

SOMETIMES the men of my family seem to have wandered into the wrong war. Louis Crawford was avid for battle in France but found his action in the Philippines. Bill Crawford trained for the invasion of Germany but was posted to the Pacific. My father signed up for the Second World War but made his bones in Korea. The Korean War belonged to my brother's generation, but he didn't come under fire until he was mortared at a base camp in Vietnam while on an inspection tour. Vietnam should have been my war, but I finessed it. Gulf One was the obvious fallback, and—even though I had a tenured teaching job—I gave some thought to seeing if I could score a correspondent's gig. But I never pursued it. By then I was pushing fifty, and my bellicose fantasies were a shadow of their former selves.

My own army service had been brief, bloodless, and largely comic. My tour of active duty was curtailed because the army then had the humane policy of releasing soldiers early if they needed to make a fall opening date for school. It was bloodless because I was posted to Japan, where the greatest menace I faced would be Tokyo traffic. As to the comedy, to do it justice requires another book. I was stationed at Far East Network, Tokyo—you may imagine *Good Morning, Vietnam* without gunfire. We even had an Adrien Cronauer, though it wasn't me. The atmosphere was relaxed, to say the least. One morning, having just ripped some wire copy, I noticed the machine had made the paper physically warm. To the station commander, standing nearby, I observed, "Look, Captain, actual hot news." He groaned. "What am I to do with you, Woods?" "Love me, sir," I said piously, "just love me." Imagine saying that to a Marine. And we had a Marine, a gunnery sergeant to whom I gave apoplexy one morning by showing up for duty in a red T-shirt because it matched my medal. He sent me back to the barracks to change.

None of which was as bizarre as my recall to active duty the summer after separation. In the late 1960s, draftees contracted a six-year obligation—two years active duty, two in the ready reserve, and two on standby. During that second period, you could be dragooned for summer camp, but it was unheard of. Thus I was startled to find myself on a sun-scorched parade ground in Camp Pickett, Virginia, as a member of the 356th Psychological Operations Company out of the Bronx. I actually experienced the two weeks as agreeable, because this time out I knew what I was doing. I luxuriated on my bunk with my footlocker squared away and my laundry bag lashed to the foot of my cot and listened to the snores of my fellows. The duty day was entertaining. We bounced around the countryside in jeeps equipped with loudspeakers, demanding the surrender of an invisible enemy and promising fair treatment, while helicopters hovering above delivered the same message.

During those two weeks, men walked on the moon.

But when I was drafted in September 1966, it was fairly clear that much of my cohort would be tested in battle. I had no eagerness for that, but no great reluctance either, especially once it became apparent that my training was to be that of a war correspondent and not an infantryman. I felt ready enough to face fire behind a notebook's magic shield. But, as my ancestors had repeatedly learned before me, a soldier's wishes are nothing measured by the army's will. My orders took me to the comforts of Tokyo rather than the tensions of Saigon or the terrors of the jungle, and I spent my whole tour at FEN, ripping news and playing pop music for garrison troops.

Even so, the war wrapped a wing around me. I saw pyramids of silver coffins stacked outside the bowling alley at Tachikawa Air Base, and I shared the diversions of South Camp Drake—the PX, the NCO Club, the movie theater—with patients from the 249th General Hospital, battlefield casualties wounded badly enough to be triaged to Japan. They shuffled around the post in blue bathrobes, armless or blind or bullet-punched, sometimes with the famous thousand-yard stare. In their presence I didn't feel guilty—I'd gone where the army sent me, and in the eyes of those men it would have been utter folly to contest my good fortune. But I didn't feel comfortable, either.

My being among them provided memorable moments. One time a shattered Specialist Fifth Class thanked me profusely for providing the rock and roll other stations didn't program. A blind lieutenant praised FEN for offering uncensored news. My best night at the movies was spent watching *The Green Berets* with a crowd of wounded men convulsed with laughter or hurling imprecations at the hero for his clueless patriotism and war-worshipping stupidity.

The ambiguity of Vietnam afforded me a degree of protection against self-judgment. I had been given clear models to follow but I wasn't given an era that evoked them. As my friend Toby said, "I, for one, am glad we missed our generation's war."

In the end, so am I. In old age, I still have days when I wish my memories included episodes of combat, but for the most part I'm happy to have been spared the dark passages those memories would necessarily entail. I have friends who were not spared, and I honor their endurance. I know others who fled or fought against the war, and I respect their decisions, because my generation was denied a conflict that could claim our wholehearted allegiance. Subsequent American wars have by contrast presented the young with a different problem, which is one of the reasons American war stories are taking a different turn.

MY GRANDFATHER was a boy when he gave his eager heart to the army, my uncle scarcely older. My father was a man full grown, educated in law and the humanities, a husband and a parent, a head of household already beginning to fashion a life's career. He went to war not on a wave of enthusiasm but through stoic embrace of a fate the times had sent. Duty done, he dutifully returned to his civilian life. But not to paint too noble a portrait, it should be added that when he took up arms, he may also have been enacting one of the classic themes of American life and letters—men's flight from domesticity into war. He accepted years of separation from his family. He stayed in uniform longer than the emergency required. And he seriously considered a military career. These facts color his commitment to his wife and sons, which he honored faithfully. In any case, they complicate the picture.

But that picture had never been other than a puzzle. "I want very much to come back and be with the three of you, to be a family again," Woods wrote in 1949. "But I don't feel like I'd be altogether at home in my fat, happy country. There's something in Asian life, corrupt and filthy as it is, that seems more elemental than suburbia."

SOME BOOKS ask for a pilot. This felt like one. So I sorted out promising epigrams, finally settling on the verse from Emerson I began with, slightly misquoted from a book I cherished in childhood, an anthology of stories about the courage of children in the Second World War called *Youth Replies I Can*. Louis Crawford's chapter carries an old flag, the popular Harrigan and Hart song of 1874 "The Regular Army-O," and the "Irish saying" prefacing William Crawford's chapter perfectly illustrates his plight. Two lines from Snooks Eaglin flash like a yellow caution light for my father's story— Snooks Eaglin, the great New Orleans singer whose terse blues captures one of the tensions I hoped to explore.

Over the drafts and years, I had tried on others. *For in our youth, our hearts were touched with fire.* Too familiar. *Only the dead have seen the end of war.* Too obvious. *War is the health of the state.* Misleading. And there was a stack of poetry, from the *Iliad* to Afghanistan.

Any poem has its counterweight. F. Scott Fitzgerald and Louis Crawford, in their imagined meeting, are moved by Rupert Brooke's battle ode "Peace." They would also have been aware of Wilfred Owen's darker vision. *If you could hear, at every jolt, the blood / Come gargling forth from the froth-corrupted lungs. . . .* It was "Dulce et Decorum Est" that warned me away from some of the most elegant war prose ever written.

> Thus they determined at hazard of their lives to be honorably
> avenged, and to leave the rest; and on the battlefield, their feet stood
> fast, and in an instant, they passed away from the scene, not of their
> fear, but of their glory. Methinks that a death such as theirs gives the
> true measure of a man's worth; it may be the first revelation of his
> virtues, but it is at any rate their final seal.

Thucydides. Pericles's funeral oration on the Athenian dead. For thousands of years, these words have rightly honored heroes, and doubtless strengthened some soldiers' resolve. But I wasn't greatly surprised by the reaction of an army veteran of Iraq when I reminded him of them. He was a classics scholar who had learned the passage in the original. I told him I found the English version beautiful and suggested it might be even more so in ancient Greek.

"It is," he said, "but it's bullshit."

Still, such things are never simple. When this man went to war, his father wrote him, "The Combat Infantry Badge is the last honor I would ever have wanted you to receive, but it's the one I'm proudest of."

If Snooks Eaglin's epigram pointed toward one theme, it's still smaller than the book's subject, but it gestures toward a thesis too self-evident to ask for proof. Might not a father who flourished in military service inspire his offspring to seek the same profession? It was like proving that a ten-foot branch could span a nine-foot stream. No vast effort of argument seemed necessary. The point wasn't precedent but pattern, so I soon came to see that what joined these men was less the way they acted out a fantasy of paternal will than the ways they related to each other and the way each responded to his time.

Still, a poem by A. E. Housman crystallizes the initial notion, commemorating one colonial war as it ponders the advent of the next. "God save the Queen," chants the penultimate stanza before it yields to the last.

Oh, God will save her, fear you not:
Be you the men you've been,
Get you the sons your fathers got,
And God will save the Queen.

Get you the sons your fathers got. If this book were a movie, that would do for a log line. But I'm content to leave the lives I've been looking at without the yoke of a governing theme. Explanation isn't always a path to understanding. Often a figure is best illuminated by what we may see of his own inner light.

As to the poem, it's not necessary to endorse the politics to honor the sentiment.

From Pericles to Phil Klay, the rhetoric of combat changes. It would be productive to let the chorus give way to a single voice of our own day, that of Ernest Hemingway, who revised his attitudes from war to war.

Louis Crawford lived in a windy, sentimental time. The sight of Old Glory flowing from a flagpole moved him to the core. But William Crawford and Arthur Woods would have been indifferent to patriotic display. They disdained idle talk about honor and duty; if you possessed the first, you got on with the second. They would have scorned words like "fallen" and "sacrifice," and nodded in silent agreement with the most luminous passage in *A Farewell to Arms*.

> I was always embarrassed by the words sacred, glorious, and sacrifice. . . . I had seen nothing sacred, and the things that were glorious had no glory and the sacrifices were like the stockyards at Chicago if nothing was done with the meat except to bury it. . . . Abstract words such as glory, honor, courage, or hallow were obscene beside the concrete names of villages, the numbers of roads, the names of rivers, the numbers of regiments, and the dates.

That was the First World War. By the second war, Hemingway had gotten a bit windy and sentimental himself. In 1942, he solemnly intoned, "We will fight this war to enjoy the rights and privileges conveyed by the Declaration of Independence, the Constitution of the United States, and the Bill of Rights." In 1950 he returned to a more astringent view: "We are governed by what you find in the bottom of dead beer glasses that whores have dunked their cigarettes in." Which seems harsh as an assessment of the Truman administration; readers may judge whether the line is apposite in a later America. In any case, my father and my uncle never mixed their politics with their views on war.

ANOTHER CURIOUS LINK among the three was writing. Louis, ambitious to succeed as a journalist and writer of popular fiction, took correspondence courses in the short story and actually knew a measure of success. His style, while marked by the flowery romanticism of the women's magazine market of the period, could be simple and strong when he dealt with military themes. He had little formal education and left no evidence of any taste for modern literature, though he clearly admired Kipling and the English poetry of the 1914–1918 war.

Bill Crawford, who took an interest in journalism as a boy, created homemade newspapers and contributed short pieces to the local press, but he seems to have had no interest in "literature" and his own prose can be pedestrian. Occasionally, though, he wrote vivid accounts of his war, thoughtful critiques of its progress, and comic notes on family and friends. He also liked movies.

A. R. Woods benefited from a sound training in the best that had been thought and said in English, ancient, and modern languages. He was extremely well read. At Penn, with no more than a bachelor's degree, he taught a freshman composition class much in demand, widely known as "Woods on Words." As a lawyer, he added analytical powers to his established rhetorical skills and wrote briefs and arguments admired for their force and clarity by his peers. I don't know that he ever had an interest in writing fiction.

BECAUSE I WORK with the idea of family in these pages, I'm at risk of appearing to use the image of "blood" in a way that ratifies a worldview, *Blut und Boden*, which is racist to the core and thus plays no part in the links I'm seeking to establish. But it would be hard to deny that some wretched echo of this thinking disfigures my people's past. Certainly it's to be found in Bill Crawford's adoration of hearth and home and his "othering" of other people; and his father obviously cared about his ancestry. But I don't think my father gave much of a damn about his "blood" and I'm happy to say I've inherited that attitude, though my spouse never tires of reminding me that a lifetime of white privilege is what prompts my indifference as to its origins.

Still, I would insist that my three soldiers are better understood against the background of their times than through the tangle of the centuries—and perhaps best understood simply as lost voices asking to be heard, which is why I often had had the spooky feeling that the discovery of these letters and documents not only revealed an opportunity but imposed a task, that the dead were demanding I compose a threnody, that they were laying a charge on me like Hamlet's father's ghost, save that my challenge proposed celebration, not revenge. I was being asked, in Jonathan Lethem's beautiful phrase, to make a home in my heart for the dead. I would take on the assignment—I didn't want a ghost to grieve.

IN LIFE, these were men driven by multiple motives. But on the page, they become characters, and one could argue that the power of a character's dominant desire in the face of daunting obstacles is the key to his or her ability to compel our attention. It doesn't have to be a desire we share—who wants to be Ahab?—just one that we can believe prompts the hero to action. Thus we find Louis Crawford absolutely driven to be a soldier but destined to piece the dream together as best he can in the face of long odds—illness, dubious wars, no West Point ring, domestic tensions, scattered energies. His son William picks up the dream, though *his* hope of leading troops in battle is ironically undone by promotion and professional success. And A. R. Woods, willing to be a warrior, is unhappy to find himself used by the army in other capacities until he finally happens on the work he feels destined for.

Interesting conflicts open here. William Harvey Crawford may not have wanted his son to follow in his footsteps—1903 is not 1862—but the boy's own thirst for battle seems to have been unquenchable. Louis may have wanted his son to be a West Pointer, but how far were William's actions and choices authentic, and how far fashioned in response to an assumed obligation? And what was my father's deepest desire? (My mother once said she'd hoped she was marrying into the academic life.) How did his own family past shape his actions? There are no final answers to these questions, which necessarily haunt the narrative of these lives.

Other questions take the form of counterfactuals. Bill and Mary Crawford had no children, whether by chance or design it will always be impossible to know. But given one of my themes, I couldn't resist wondering what might have followed had William Crawford fathered a son? My third soldier would have been directly descended from the first two instead of joined to them through marriage. This warrior ghost by no means promised a better story, but he would have shaped a more symmetrical book: William Riddick Crawford, Jr., or William Harvey Crawford II, or the return of Louis, or some other name altogether, founded in family history or drawn from any other source the proud parents might choose. The range of possibilities was wide. My uncle was fond of both fliers and film stars, and his maternal grandmother had been named after a popular song. But I think I'll call the ghost Russell—a brother honoring a cherished sister by giving his son her middle name.

Russell Crawford would have been about my age. A double. The army would have been his destiny. As a boy he would have played with the lead soldiers that had long guarded the Hertford house. As a youth, he would have gone to West Point. As a man, he might have been an infantry officer with a long and distinguished career capped by high command, assuming he wasn't killed in Vietnam, a fairly large assumption in that he would have been a member of the class of 1966—some thirty of his classmates died. If Russell had left a written record as vivid as his father's, *Stand in the Fire* would have taken my family's military history deeper into the twentieth century and reflected a war closer to our own day.

But I was intrigued by a more radical possibility: that Bill Crawford's boy might have been a war resister, a principled patriotic youth as willing to be jailed or sent into exile as his father had been ready to fight. Then his story would have taken my account into a fertile new direction, complicating the picture of how fathers and sons might respond with equal honor in opposite ways to the call of duty in different times.

Strong stuff. But I didn't linger long with this fantasy, in part because the deeper I got into my father's story the more I could see its postwar Cold War tone offering a wider optic than another episode of battle could do, and in the end I was obliged to recognize that I was a part—a very modest part—of the overall story, with more authority to speak about a real father than I ever could have if my subject were an imaginary cousin. Leave it that an intriguing possibility must go forever unrealized.

THE RECORD, largely complete on military matters, is silent about other things. Lacking their private journals (Louis Crawford's 1903 diary apart, they didn't keep any), we have no direct account of the men's inner lives. Their politics may be inferred but are rarely made explicit. They tell us almost nothing about their views on religion. We learn of their pastimes only in passing. And they never write about sex. (As I've noted elsewhere, I'm not eager to know overmuch about the hours my mommy and daddy spent in the sack, but I do rather wish the epistolary conventions that rule the first half of the twentieth century had been a little less restrictive.)

I have a hunch that Louis Crawford was robustly erotic, if only because his general lust for life was so pronounced. I don't know anything about my grandmother Kate's sex life, but I do know she cautioned my mother about the sad necessity for a woman to submit to the bestial needs of men. "Hold onto the bedpost and plan meals," she advised Louise on her daughter's wedding day, the sort of Victorian counsel women of my mother's generation happily were sometimes able to ignore.

William Crawford's life holds similar mysteries. He was an impossibly beautiful West Point cadet and would certainly have attracted men and women alike. But apart from his platonic flirtation with Cy Caldwell, and Caldwell's angry obsession with him, there's no indication of homosexuality or homophobia, though sadly the culture of his times suggests the near inevitability of the second. He did once blurt out in a letter to his mother, "I know what semen is!" Scant context is provided. His letters to Mary from the Pacific never lack warmth, and on at least two occasions carry hints of the erotic, most charmingly when he reflects on the particular pair of high-heeled shoes he hopes she will be wearing when her warrior returns.

As to my father, I believe that Louise Woods's complaint that he lacked passion when they met on his first three-day pass is well explained by her brother's defense of his brother-in-law—basic training *does* exhaust a man, though I can't offer testimony from experience as I went off to the wars unpartnered. We know that she found his appetites restored on a subsequent occasion, and I know that they had a long and largely cheerful marriage. But what was most private in their private lives always remained so.

I PUT THE LAST LETTER back in its box and slowly closed the lid. The exploration of the paper trail left by these lives was done. But I returned to the pistol, feeling that it might prove the capstone to my interrogation of the past. A 1911 Colt .45 automatic: the iconic sidearm of uncounted wars.

In its narrow coffin the weapon lay coiled on an oily rag. I lifted it reverently and weighed it in my hand, heavy as a heavy stone. I slipped the clip and studied the bullet—fat, gold, greasy—crouched at the summit of the magazine. Then I worked the slide to be sure there was no round in the chamber. The ammunition might be over a century old, but that gave no assurance it wasn't still deadly. I found I wanted to fire the pistol and saw in my mind a thicket out in the countryside where I could safely pull the trigger. But wisdom cautioned otherwise. There was every chance the sleeping bullets would explode, turning the gun into a bridge of torn metal, linking the horizon of memory to the undiscovered country of accidental death.

Whose weapon was it? If the .45 had been stored in one of the three boxes, I would have had a provenance. But it dwelled alone.

The army had not adopted the Colt until 1911, so Louis Crawford couldn't have carried it in the Philippines. But he could have worn it on the

Mexican border. Captain A. R. Woods, MD, might have brought it home from France. It certainly could have been part of Bill Crawford's gear on Luzon, or perhaps A. R. Woods, Jr., strapped it to his leg in a canvas holster as he jolted around in his jeep hunting spies or saboteurs in the backcountry of Korea. If there seemed no path to a certain answer, I could at least narrow the field. I traced the serial number. The pistol had been manufactured by Ithaca Arms in 1944. My uncle's or my father's, then. The former had relied mostly on his M1A1 folding stock carbine, the latter on his snub-nosed .38. But both soldiers would have been fully qualified on the .45 and either could have possessed it. I suspected it was Bill Crawford's, but there was no way to know for sure.

The heavy handgun held other mysteries. It might have been fired in battle, or never fired at all. It might have been brought home as a memento, or thought of as a tool for self-defense, though to my knowledge there was never a weapon in my parents' house. In any case, it had been resting largely undisturbed for over sixty years, in its flannel shroud, in its wooden box, on an attic shelf in the old house in North Carolina.

I put the pistol back where I'd found it. Ghostmaker. I had no further questions for it. *Res ipsa loquitor.* Let another generation sound the mystery of the haunted object if it chose.

But simply to hold the pistol compelled the recognition of how deeply the work of my forebears was grounded in killing. Their accounts of that aspect are circumspect and the few comments I've read by those who knew them best underplay the reality or even deny it.

I have a photograph of my grandfather on bivouac in the Philippines taken at the time he went through his first firefight. On the back, his daughter has written, "I don't think for one moment Daddy was actually aiming at that little brown brother." Given what I'd learned of Louis Crawford's cordial temperament, I was long inclined to take her at her word. Similarly, when my uncle speaks of being "amused" under machine-gun fire, or relieved when he jumps into an empty dugout expecting to come face to face with a Japanese soldier, I was puzzled by the first response and gratified by the second. I suspect that's because my own capacity for violence, never tested, has allowed the pacifist in me to hold sway.

But there's really no reason to think these men didn't take seriously their obligation to kill if they had to, or to condemn them if they took a momentary joy in it. Warriors who have written with full candor about combat certainly speak of the fear they felt at the time and the grief and shame they felt thereafter. But they also speak of the exhilaration.

My grandfather was a teenaged rifleman facing an armed enemy. I think when he missed his man, he missed his moment. I think when he wrote in his diary that night "Riley had better luck," he meant it. And I think when he had other opportunities to engage, he took them. If in doing so he also saved some of his fellows, I think that increased the present joy and lessened the later sadness.

My uncle was a professional infantry officer who in his staff position was instrumental in the deaths of thousands. It may have given him pause. It did not cause him to pause in his work. It did not stop him from writing calmly, *We will be killing here for years to come*. It did not stop my mother, while mourning his loss, from honoring the memory of "the many blows he struck."

Certainly there is proof in his letters that he had face-to-face encounters with his enemy. He may have felt the joy. He didn't live long enough to feel the sorrow. But before he shipped out for the Pacific he prepared himself for what he knew he would be facing by having a talk with the Rev. Edmund Jillson, the minister at Holy Trinity in Hertford, seeking absolution, or perhaps divine authority, for what he was about to do. Jillson, a good man I remember from my childhood, was a pipe-smoking Episcopal priest fashioned in the mode of the aristocratic Southern ecclesiastic. He offered the usual comforting shibboleths about the domain of Caesar and the mercy of God. I have no idea whether this increased Bill Crawford's poise on the battlefield. I do know one young soldier on Leyte prayed: "God help us. Come yourself. Don't send Jesus. This is no place for a child."

As to my father, of all three he may make the best case for the capacity for principled violence built into the characters of many good men. If he surprised my mother by turning in a short time from a corpulent lawyer into a hardened soldier, he may have surprised himself more. Certainly he sought service in the war he had trained for. *My gang here is ready to take our chances—but we want to get going*. And when disappointed in that goal he was quick to volunteer for one of the postwar jobs that still carried the promise of danger, and to find himself posted in a part of the world that remained a war zone. His letters recount the risks he took and the violence he encountered, and they make clear his wish to remain employed in a task that would call for physical courage as well as intelligence.

This perspective comprises a welcome challenge to my blithe conviction that I've always understood my characters. In them, I hope I've shown my reader much to admire: Louis Crawford's lust for life, his son's faithfulness to duty, my father's quickness to rise to the demand history placed upon his generation. All of them lived as husbands and sons, some as fathers and brothers. They were hunters and fishermen, travelers and adventurers, gardeners, artists, technicians, citizens, soldiers, scholars, sportsmen, and spies.

And killers when they had to be.

THE LETTERS and the rest of the material had given me much to work with, but there were only a few hundred documents all told. Now and then I found the sparse landscape frustrating: if only each man had kept a sustained daily journal, written a hundred trenchant letters, and supplied the thirsty historian with a huge trove of other documents, my task would have been simpler and my book perhaps more sound. Yet in the end I took pleasure in the space left open for responsible conjecture. Like an archaeologist who seeks to rebuild a city from the remnants of a wall, I knew the excitement of penetrating a psyche using the tools of imagination, though there was a certain cost: I could never be certain whether my portrait was a painting or a photograph, and strangely this was the more true as I moved closer to my own era. I came to feel I knew my grandfather, who died decades before my birth, with congenial intimacy. My uncle, of whom I knew much more, remained the more elusive. And my father, whom in ways I knew quite well, retained a still greater degree of mystery. But perhaps that was only because he had always wished to do so.

Except for the handful of my uncle's carbons clearly meant for a larger audience, each of the letters has been directed at one recipient, and that's a problem: they tend to make only one sound. They can give a rich picture of half a relationship, and at best will offer the facts and moods from which we may assemble a convincing portrait of their authors. Still, I can't help regretting that—to choose only a few examples—I have so few letters between fathers and sons. I have nothing from my grandfather to his father, whose stirring example had formed him; nothing between my father and my uncle, who shared a war; crucially, very little from the women who saved the letters I've drawn on to the men who wrote them. And since the letters are almost entirely to women, they confine themselves to the protective male perspective of their times. I'm eager for voices I can never hear—my father's orders to his agents, my uncle's commands to his troops, my grandfather's instructions to the sergeants who saddled his horses or caged the carrier pigeons in his plane.

Other voices are silent as well. These men-at-arms, exchanging correspondence with friends and fellow soldiers, might where possible have spoken more freely about the details of their lives and work than they would have to wives or sisters. I can imagine a looser, coarser language, a more candid account of violence, and at least an echo of ordinary vice.

But the same limitations can work as strengths. Given constancy of character, a voice may develop over time that illustrates the growth of the personality behind it, and we will see this best when the voice speaks to only one listener. This is especially true in William Crawford's letters. We encounter him first as a cocky, self-important boy, and take leave of him as a hardened, self-reflective man. The tone is more even in A. R. Woods's letters, but he is an adult when we meet him, with voice and personality fully formed. As for Louis Crawford, his heart is always on his sleeve, and his correspondence is the happier for it.

What I'd found in these diaries and letters, fragments and photographs, was only a glimpse into long passages of larger lives. The army was only a part of their stories. But it's the part my family chose most fully to remember, through the agency of the women who faithfully packed those memories away.

Even so, the sum total of their experiences is threaded through every piece of correspondence, and as I worked with the letters, I found myself held as much by the ordinary moments as by the martial drama, the fire fights, the fatal missions. I looked to the legends of the everyday, so like our own. *Saw Tom Nixon last week for drinks and dinner, he was in rare form. Mary still has the flu, but she's better. If you can get a three-day pass next week, let's stay at the Plaza. Saw* Fantasia, *we both loved it.* Sometimes this quotidian stuff seems more vivid than the violence. It's our own lives, set several paces back in time, that's all. Like a page discolored by a teardrop, these average efforts tell us who our company is—gallant doomed companions, whom, like ourselves, it won't always need a war to kill.

WHILE I'D DRAWN almost all the material I needed from the Hertford house and my scant research, the book seemed to call for boots on the ground. I knew the look of a typical stateside army installation from my own service, so the tedium of traveling to my father's southern posts, and I'd seen some of the Japan that he lived in. I flew to Texas to inspect the remnants of Kelly Field, where a small museum housed in a derelict Quonset hut preserves a faint memory of the fliers of the First World War—a wall of sepia photographs and a few tattered uniforms. It was enough to evoke my grandfather's ghost, as were some days in the Southwest traveling along the Mexican border. And I went to West Point, where I stood on the plain where my uncle had paraded, paused in the cadet chapel where he had obediently trooped to prayers, and spent time on the bluffs above the Hudson where he had courted Mary Shelburne in his scant free time. I even managed to get to Puerto Rico, to stroll the streets of the old city of San Juan, where Lieutenant Crawford had begun to feel the burden of his provincialism lift. But trips to the Philippines and Korea were beyond my resources.

Then there were the graves: my father's (1976) and mother's (2000) in the churchyard behind Holy Trinity in Hertford, where there is also a small memorial to Bill Crawford, though he is buried at Fort McKinley in Manila. Mary Crawford McLaurin's grave—she died in 2014 at the age of ninety-nine—is in Bath, North Carolina, where she spent most of her long life, an admired master gardener. My brother died in 2007. His ashes are in a veterans cemetery in west Texas.

And in the end, there was Arlington, with its hills and fields of shining stones, its hushed ceremonials, its flags and guards and crypts and cenotaphs. There all four of my grandparents are interred. I paid my respects at each site, though the grail was my mother's father's grave, which I found on a steep hillside, the small white marble stone bathed in spring sunlight.

LOUIS R CRAWFORD
1ST LT
CAVALRY
DEC 3 1883
APR 10 1921

He had held other ranks and served in other branches, but whether this inscription was the army's decision or his, it felt right to me. He'd ended as he began—a horse soldier.

In my pocket I carried one of the lead soldiers my grandfather had molded and played with as a boy, then passed down to his son, whose sister passed them down first to my brother, and then to me. I fished it out and placed it gently in the grass beside the marble stone.

I took one step back from the grave, came to attention, and gave the slow salute.

Good-by, my father—good-by, all my fathers.
—F. Scott Fitzgerald, *Tender Is the Night*

NOTES AND ACKNOWLEDGMENTS

A little on method.

Stand in the Fire contains elements of fiction and fact that flow into each other. I'll give three instances. The conversation between Louis Crawford and his father in Philadelphia in 1900 is an obvious invention, but I enter the room where it takes place through an old photograph. The scene is imagined, the setting is real. I could hardly have been present at my uncle's encounter with a senior cadet on Bill Crawford's first night at West Point, but the plebe's quick wit was celebrated in my family's stories. Again, while the tale of General Swing's quest for a three-hundred-watt bulb sounds like an implausible comic flourish, its genesis may be found in E. M. Flanagan's *The Angels*. So too with my other protagonists, whose real lives are from time to time illustrated by imagined episodes, though only when the facts justify their creation.

In using this technique I'm in good company, notably that of Norman Mailer, who has asserted, "I would go so far as to say that any history that gets built entirely upon fact is going to be full of error and will be misleading. Something can be true and still be fiction." Mailer is here describing the practice of what has been called "creative nonfiction," a label I dislike since the first word is either self-evident or self-important and the second defines vast tracts of writing by what they are not. Still, the category is useful. It contends clearly that a given work is grounded in history more firmly than in imagination while admitting in all modesty that the defining facts can never be completely known.

Given this freedom, I'm obliged to note some limitations. Writing fiction, I can take a character where the logic of the story leads. Writing history, I'm constrained by the evidence at hand. In a happy reverie, I imagine finding in the silver trunk letters or journals showing that Bill Crawford disdained the racial arrangements prevalent in his childhood, that he was skeptical of the rabid anti-Semitism broadcast by his society, that he identified fascism as a fatal virus early on, perhaps most of all that he had reached out a hand in friendship to Benjamin O. Davis and stood side by side with the black cadet against all odds. But no such letters or journals were to be found because none was ever written. I had to live with the facts.

Stand in the Fire is based largely on primary sources—the letters, journals, diaries, and miscellaneous documents that I inherited from the men and women who are its subjects. The book makes no claim to reshaping the history it reviews, though it necessarily adds a number of new details to that history—perhaps no other account of the Roosevelt administration includes the image of Eleanor taking a tumble at a White House ball. But my concern has been more with the adventures of my heroes than with the larger story of their times.

That said, I have taken seriously the responsibility of squaring the known facts with my account, both to authenticate its claims and to ground the reader in a rapidly receding past. Accordingly, I've drawn on a handful of secondary sources. They are few—the book is a story, not a work of scholarship—but imperative in their effect.

Inevitably we begin with the internet, where my main sources were the websites maintained by the Department of the Army and the US Army Center of Military History, which yielded an overview of the various campaigns in which my soldiers served. But it's not so much for the big picture that this oceanic resource, with all its strengths and shortcomings, has earned my gratitude, as for its swift providing of myriad small details. When my grandfather mentioned the ship that took him to the Philippines, I entered her name and got the vessel's whole history. When I wanted to know the service ceiling of a Curtiss JN-4, the answer lay a few clicks away. Curious about the Colt .45 I'd turned from a weapon into a paperweight, I typed in the serial number and promptly found its provenance. So, too, for telling details on all my other characters and their times. The point is not that I used many of these bits and pieces in the book, but that they gathered in the wings to add depth to the story, and I can't swear I would have had the resolve to chase them down had they not been ready to hand. To historians, this ease of access is old news, but to me it was an unfamiliar pleasure.

Several books served me well. Stanley Karnow's comprehensive history

In Our Image: America's Empire in the Philippines (New York: Random House, 1989) provided a detailed background to Louis Crawford's service in the islands in 1903, as well as to William Crawford's battles there some forty years later. Karnow's description of the appalling terrain gave me a vivid picture of the perils, even in the absence of an enemy, both men faced. *Fire and Blood: A History of Mexico* (New York: Macmillan, 1973), by T. R. Fehrenbach, provided a background to the Madero revolution that furnished the setting for Lieutenant Crawford's novella and created the contested border he patrolled.

The historian who placed F. Scott Fitzgerald at Fort Oglethorpe the year my grandfather was stationed there is M. F. Holland in his portrait *Eisenhower between the Wars* (New York: Praeger, 2001). For pertinent facts of Fitzgerald's life and quotations from his letters, I am indebted to Arthur Mizener's seminal biography *The Far Side of Paradise* (New York: Vintage, 1960).

In researching my uncle's career, I found a real treasure in E. M. Flanagan's *The Angels: A History of the 11th Airborne Division* (Novato, CA: Presidio, 1989). Flanagan, a retired lieutenant general who served with the division as a young artillery officer, composed his exhaustive account when many veterans still survived to be interviewed, giving him access to compelling anecdotes as well as to official records. Several stories about my uncle are among these, stories I would never have known without General Flanagan's book. I must acknowledge as well Gordon Rottman's monograph *US Airborne Units in the Pacific Theater 1942–45* (Oxford: Osprey, 2007) for its technical analysis of weapons, tactics, and the operational planning and outcomes of various campaigns; and the historians Richard Connaughton, John Pimlott, and Duncan Anderson for their account of *The Battle for Manila* (Novato, CA: Presidio, 2002). Continuing attention to the troubled majesty of West Point, special note must be taken of the work of James Salter, whose *Burning the Days* (New York: Random House, 1997) provided a proving ground for my evolving understanding of William Crawford's character.

When I reached Japan and Korea, three books informed me. Duval Edwards's *Spycatchers of the US Army in the War with Japan* (Gig Harbor, WA: Red Apple, 1994) was the source of much information about the CIC's work, whose details my father was not free to disclose. Horace Bristol's volume of photographs, *Korea* (Tokyo: Toppan, 1948), found among my father's papers, enabled me to attempt the description of the cityscape through which A. R. Woods travels in the opening scene of his section of the book. And my ignorance of the exceptional complexity of diplomatic, military, and political conditions in the postwar Korean peninsula was reduced by Allan R. Millett's *The War for Korea, 1945–1950: A House Burning* (Lawrence: University Press of Kansas, 2005), without which I would have been at a loss to provide adequate context for my father's experience. The quotations by Ernest Hemingway are drawn from *A Farewell to Arms* (New York: Scribner's, 1929), *Men at War* (New York: Crown, 1942), and *Across the River and into the Trees* (New York: Scribner's, 1950). Two books that made no direct contribution to this one will deepen any noncombatant's understanding of their subject—Karl Marlantes's *What It Is Like to Go to War* (New York: Grove, 2011) and Chris Hedges's *War Is a Force That Gives Us Meaning* (New York: Public Affairs, 2002).

I am grateful to all the above. But my chief debt is to two women, Kate Crawford and Louise Woods, who preserved the materials on which this book is built. I doubt that, in doing so, they had any notion of serving something larger than a family history. They may not even have seen themselves as providing their descendants with a window to the family's past. Devotion to these men—a devotion never free of informed reserve—would have been enough to prompt their actions, which, after all, were unceremonious and even a bit offhand. They simply, in their different times and generations, gathered the letters, diaries, photographs, and military memorabilia and tossed them into boxes to be stored in a dusty attic until such time as they might be sent for. Apart from the few uninformed forays I made in my childhood, that time lay more than a century off from the day my grandmother began the collection by gently putting her young husband's boyhood battle diary away.

The women's care was not reciprocated, but I don't fault men in war zones for failing to make the preservation of their mail from home a top priority. In some instances, to do so might have been explicitly forbidden as a security risk. But the fact that they didn't robs my work of possible voices.

Reliance on domestic sources can also leave the impression that Louise and Kate confined themselves to domestic roles. They did not. Each in her time conceived a larger life than her society necessarily approved. My grandmother, born to plantation graces, in widowhood filled out her small survivor's benefits by becoming a capable businesswoman, an agent of the

New York Life insurance company who was often the most successful sales-woman in her region. My mother was not only an artist and art teacher, but one of the founders of a Washington, DC-area preparatory school, which today boasts a formal garden that bears her name. These were not women ready to limit their lives to a family archivist's role, but as both writer and descendant, I can never be sufficiently grateful that was one of the things they did.

There are other obligations—I've no doubt forgotten some, due to the erosion of time. But some, I will always remember: Joyce Harrison, editor in chief of the University Press of Kansas, without whom this book might still be in search of a publisher, and her assistant, Andrea Laws. Then Christopher Hamner and Steven Trout, the book's external readers, whose imprimatur paved the way.

I am profoundly grateful to Ann Adelman for her elegant, scrupulous line editing, and to Corinne Browne for introducing me to Ann. Corinne is the author of *Casualty*, one of the finest books to come out of the Vietnam war.

Closer to home, I especially thank Donald and Linda Mooring for listening patiently and responding thoughtfully to many readings from this book while it was a work in progress. Don retired many years ago from the Air Force and built a sterling second career as a musician; Linda somehow survived us both. Other family and friends—William Walker Woods, Walter Johnson, Toby Thompson, Peter Rand, Michael Stephens, Thomas Beach, Wally Andrews, and Tim O'Brien—added their encouragement and support. William, my nephew, serves as a dean at Schreiner College in Texas and writes compelling fiction in the little spare time he has. Walter, an engineer at Boeing and weapons advisor on this book, hunts big game on his Texas preserve. I have no closer friend than Toby, author of one of the first and finest biographies of Bob Dylan, which launched his career as a leading Dylanologist, though his range as a writer is hardly limited to one subject. Peter, author of many elegant books, is perhaps best known for *China Hands*, which explores the career of his father, the *New Yorker* reporter Christopher Rand. Thomas, who trained helicopter door gunners for service in Vietnam, is a craftsman and Zen Buddhist long resident in Vermont at work on his own memoir. Michael—poet, playwright, novelist, essayist—has, for more than fifty years, put out distinguished work in presses large and small. Wally is a world traveler non pareil, whose unpublished journals fill volumes that would make his name should he ever choose to release them. To Tim O'Brien, primus inter pares of American writers on Vietnam, I owe a lifetime's friendship. Tim is the National Book Award–winning author of *The Things They Carried*—and no mean magician.

My title I peeled off the label of a Warren Zevon album.

What more? As a writer who still works primarily with paper and pen, I am grateful to Marian Kidd for prompt and expert typing, and to Christopher Howard-Woods for his meticulous review and precise formatting of the typescript. Finally, I'm grateful to Bob Anderson, for wise counsel on the wars within; and to my beloved Joan for . . . well, *everything*.

~

IN MEMORIAM

Stand in the Fire is the last published work of William Crawford Woods, whose literary career spanned six decades. Fittingly, this book is about his family (three men in particular)—a labor of love and obligation inspired by the boxes of letters saved by the women in his family from the men in their lives who heeded the call of duty, well before his own military service. All four now rest in peace. William lived long enough to hear the positive affirmation of prepublication reviewers who were moved by his writing and to approve final page proofs. If only he could have held the book itself in his hands.